Microsoft®
WINDOWS® 10

INTERMEDIATE

Microsoft® WINDOWS® 10

INTERMEDIATE

STEVEN M. FREUND

CENGAGE
Learning·

SHELLY CASHMAN SERIES®

Australia • Brazil • Japan • Korea • Mexico • Singapore • Spain • United Kingdom • United States

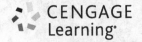

Microsoft Windows 10: Intermediate
Steven M. Freund

SVP, GM Skills & Global Product Management: Dawn Gerrain

Product Director: Kathleen McMahon

Senior Product Team Manager: Lauren Murphy

Associate Product Manager: William Guiliani

Senior Director, Development: Marah Bellegarde

Product Development Manager: Leigh Hefferon

Managing Content Developer: Emma F. Newsom

Developmental Editor: Lyn Markowicz

Product Assistant: Erica Chapman

Manuscript Quality Assurance: Jeffrey Schwartz, John Freitas, Serge Palladino, Susan Pedicini, Danielle Shaw, Susan Whalen

Senior Production Director: Wendy Troeger

Production Director: Patty Stephan

Senior Content Project Manager: Matthew Hutchinson

Manufacturing Planner: Julio Esperas

Designer: Diana Graham

Text Designer: Joel Sadagursky

Cover Template Designer: Diana Graham

Vice President, Marketing: Brian Joyner

Marketing Director: Michele McTighe

Marketing Manager: Stephanie Albracht

Compositor: Lumina Datamatics, Inc.

Cover image(s): Mario7/Shutterstock.com; Mrs. Opossum/Shutterstock.com

Mac users: If you're working through this product using a Mac, some of the steps may vary. Additional information for Mac users is included with the data files for this product.

The material in this book was written using Microsoft Windows 10 and Office 2016 and was Quality Assurance tested before the publication date. As Microsoft continually updates, your experience may vary slightly from what is seen in the printed text.

For product information and technology assistance, contact us at
Cengage Learning Customer & Sales Support, 1-800-354-9706
For permission to use material from this text or product, submit all requests online at **www.cengage.com/permissions.**
Further permissions questions can be e-mailed to
permissionrequest@cengage.com

Library of Congress Control Number: 2015953091

ISBN: 978-1-305-65675-8

Cengage Learning
20 Channel Center Street
Boston, MA 02210
USA

Cengage Learning is a leading provider of customized learning solutions with employees residing in nearly 40 different countries and sales in more than 125 countries around the world. Find your local representative at **www.cengage.com.**

Cengage Learning products are represented in Canada by Nelson Education, Ltd.

To learn more about Cengage Learning, visit **www.cengage.com**
Purchase any of our products at your local college store or at our preferred online store **www.cengagebrain.com**

Printed at EPAC Mexico, 07-16

Microsoft
WINDOWS® 10

INTERMEDIATE

Contents

1 Introduction to Windows 10

Objectives

You will have mastered the material in this module when you can:

- Describe Windows 10
- Explain the following terms: app, operating system, workstation, and server
- Differentiate among the various editions of Windows 10
- Use a touch screen and perform basic mouse operations
- Run Windows 10 and sign in to an account
- Identify the objects on the Windows 10 desktop

- Run an app
- Navigate within an app
- Run the File Explorer
- Switch between apps
- Customize the Start menu
- Search for an app or a file
- Install an app
- Use the search box
- Add reminders
- Sign out of an account and shut down the computer

What Is Windows 10?

An **operating system** is a computer program (set of instructions) that coordinates all the activities of computer hardware, such as memory, storage devices, and printers, and provides the capability for you to communicate with the computer.

Windows 10 is the newest version of Microsoft Windows, which is a popular and widely used operating system. The Windows operating system simplifies the process of working with documents and apps by organizing the manner in which you interact with the computer. Windows is used to run apps. An **app** (short for application) consists of programs that are designed to make users more productive and/or assist them with personal tasks, such as word processing or browsing the web.

Windows commonly is used on desktops, laptops and other mobile devices, and workstations. A **workstation** is a computer connected to a server. A **server** is a computer that controls access to the hardware and software on a network and provides a centralized storage area for programs, data, and information. Figure 1–1 illustrates a simple computer network consisting of a server, three workstations, and a printer connected to the server.

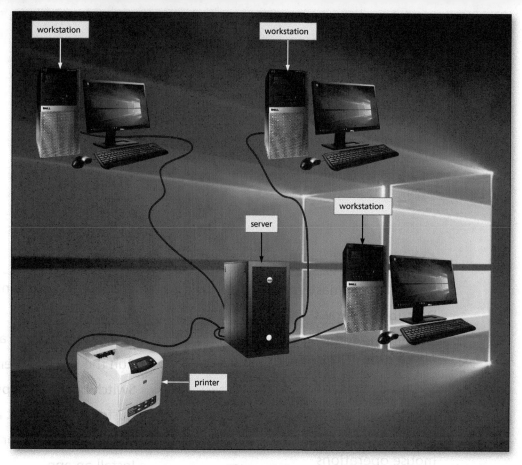

Figure 1–1

Windows is easy to use and can be customized to fit individual needs. The operating system simplifies working with documents and programs, transferring data between documents, interacting with the different components of the computer, and using the computer to access information on the Internet or an intranet. The **Internet** is a worldwide group of connected computer networks that allows public access to information about tens of thousands of subjects and gives users the ability to use this information, send messages, and obtain products and services. An **intranet** is an internal network that uses Internet technologies.

Windows 10 is designed to provide a similar user interface across multiple devices such as desktops, laptops, tablets, and smartphones. The Windows 10 interface combines some of the most successful features of previous versions of Windows such as the Start menu, an optimal interface for touch input, and enhanced search functionality. Several other improvements over previous versions of Windows make Windows 10 a suitable choice for all users.

This book demonstrates how to use Windows 10 to control the computer and communicate with other computers, both on a network and the Internet. In Module 1, you will learn about Windows and how to use some of its basic features.

Multiple Editions of Windows 10

Windows 10 is available in multiple editions. The first, **Windows 10 Home**, is simplified and designed primarily for home and small office users. **Windows 10 Pro** is designed for businesses and technical professionals. **Windows 10 Enterprise** has the same features as Windows 10 Pro, but is designed for large enterprises where IT professionals need to manage and secure computers and mobile devices easily. **Windows 10 Education** contains many of the same features as Windows 10 Enterprise, but is designed for faculty, staff, and students. **Windows 10 Mobile** and **Windows 10 Mobile Enterprise** are editions optimized for mobile devices, such as smartphones and tablets. Windows 10 Mobile Enterprise includes functionality for large businesses to manage mobile devices.

For a computer, minimum system requirements specify that the processor is 1 GHz or faster, random access memory (RAM) is at least 1 GB (for 32-bit systems) or 2 GB (for 64-bit systems), the hard drive has at least 16 GB available space for a 32-bit system and 20 GB for 64-bit systems, and the video card supports DirectX 9 graphics with WDDM (Windows Display Driver Model) 1.0 or higher driver.

Windows can be customized using a Microsoft account. When you add a Microsoft account, you can sign in to the account and then sync (synchronize) your information with all of your Windows devices. This allows you to set your desktop background and color settings, for example, and then sync those settings with your other devices. When you sign in to your Microsoft account with another Windows device, your settings will appear the same as they do on your other Windows 10 devices.

Navigating Using Touch or a Mouse

Windows 10 provides touch support. With touch, you can use your fingers to control how Windows functions. For example, you can swipe your finger from the right to display the Action Center. (The Action Center is discussed in greater detail later in this book.) Touch also allows Windows 10 to more easily work on touch-enabled devices, such as laptops, tablets, and smartphones.

Using a Touch Screen

Windows users who have computers or devices with touch screen capability can interact with the screen using gestures. A **gesture** is a motion you make on a touch screen with the tip of one or more fingers or your hand. Touch screens are convenient because they do not require a separate device for input. Table 1–1 presents common ways to interact with a touch screen.

Table 1–1 Touch Screen Gestures			
Motion	**Description**	**Common Uses**	**Equivalent Mouse Operation**
Tap	Quickly touch and release one finger one time.	Activate a link (built-in connection). Press a button. Run a program or an app.	Click
Double-tap	Quickly touch and release one finger two times.	Run a program or an app. Zoom in (show a smaller area on the screen, so that contents appear larger) at the location of the double-tap.	Double-click

Table 1.1 *continued*

Motion	Description	Common Uses	Equivalent Mouse Operation
Press and hold 	Press and hold one finger to cause an action to occur, or until an action occurs.	Display a shortcut menu (immediate access to allowable actions). Activate a mode enabling you to move an item with one finger to a new location.	Right-click
Drag or slide	Press and hold one finger on an object and then move the finger to the new location.	Move an item around the screen. Scroll.	Drag
Swipe	Press and hold one finger and then move the finger horizontally or vertically on the screen.	Select an object. Swipe from edge to display the Action Center.	Drag
Stretch	Move two fingers apart.	Zoom in (show a smaller area on the screen, so that contents appear larger).	None
Pinch	Move two fingers together.	Zoom out (show a larger area on the screen, so that contents appear smaller).	None

© 2015 Cengage Learning

Using an On-Screen Keyboard

When using touch, you can access an on-screen keyboard that allows you to enter data using your fingers. To display the on-screen keyboard, click the Touch keyboard button on the taskbar. You tap a key on the keyboard to enter data or manipulate what you see on the screen. Figure 1–2 displays the on-screen keyboard.

on-screen keyboard

Figure 1–2

Using a Mouse

Windows users who do not have touch screen capabilities typically work with a mouse that has at least two buttons. For a right-handed user, the left button usually is the primary mouse button, and the right mouse button is the secondary mouse button. Left-handed people, however, can reverse the function of these buttons.

Table 1–2 explains how to perform a variety of mouse operations. Some apps also use keys in combination with the mouse to perform certain actions. For example, when you hold down the CTRL key while rolling the mouse wheel, text on the screen may become larger or smaller based on the direction you roll the wheel. The function of the mouse buttons and the wheel varies depending on the app.

Table 1–2 Mouse Operations			
Operation	**Mouse Action**	**Example***	**Equivalent Touch Gesture**
Point	Move the mouse until the pointer on the desktop is positioned on the item of choice.	Position the pointer on the screen.	None
Click	Press and release the primary mouse button, which usually is the left mouse button.	Select or deselect items on the screen or run an app or app feature.	Tap
Right-click	Press and release the secondary mouse button, which usually is the right mouse button.	Display a shortcut menu.	Press and hold
Double-click	Quickly press and release the primary mouse button twice without moving the mouse.	Run an app or app feature.	Double-tap
Triple-click	Quickly press and release the primary mouse button three times without moving the mouse.	Select a paragraph.	Triple-tap
Drag	Point to an item, hold down the primary mouse button, move the item to the desired location on the screen, and then release the mouse button.	Move an object from one location to another or draw pictures.	Drag or slide
Right-drag	Point to an item, hold down the right mouse button, move the item to the desired location on the screen, and then release the right mouse button.	Display a shortcut menu after moving an object from one location to another.	Press and hold, then drag
Rotate wheel	Roll the wheel forward or backward.	Scroll vertically (up and down).	Swipe
Free-spin wheel	Whirl the wheel forward or backward so that it spins freely on its own.	Scroll through many pages in seconds.	Swipe
Press wheel	Press the wheel button while moving the mouse.	Scroll continuously.	None
Tilt wheel	Press the wheel toward the right or left.	Scroll horizontally (left and right).	None
Press thumb button	Press the button on the side of the mouse with your thumb.	Move forward or backward through webpages and/or control media, games, etc.	None

*Note: The examples presented in this column are discussed as they are demonstrated in this chapter.

Scrolling

A **scroll bar** is a horizontal or vertical bar that appears when the contents of an area may not be visible completely on the screen (Figure 1–3). A scroll bar contains **scroll arrows** and a **scroll box** that enable you to view areas that currently cannot be seen on the screen. Clicking the up and down scroll arrows moves the screen content up or down one line. You also can click above or below the scroll box to move up or down a section, or drag the scroll box up or down to move to a specific location.

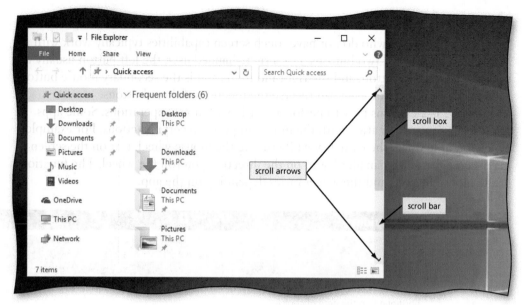

Figure 1–3

Using Keyboard Shortcuts

In many cases, you can use the keyboard instead of the mouse to accomplish a task. To perform tasks using the keyboard, you press one or more keys on the keyboard, sometimes identified as a **keyboard shortcut**. Some keyboard shortcuts consist of a single key, such as the F3 key. For example, to display the Start menu, you can press the F3 key while viewing the desktop. Other keyboard shortcuts consist of multiple keys, in which case a plus sign separates the key names, such as CTRL+ESC. This notation means to press and hold down the first key listed, press one or more additional keys, and then release all keys. For example, another way to display the Start menu is by pressing CTRL+ESC; that is, hold down the CTRL key, press the ESC key, and then release both keys.

Starting Windows 10

It is not unusual for multiple people to use the same computer in a work, educational, recreational, or home setting. Windows enables each user to establish a **user account**, which identifies to Windows the resources, such as apps and storage locations, a user can access when working with the computer.

Each user account has a user name and may have a password and an icon, as well. A **user name** is a unique combination of letters or numbers that identifies a specific user to Windows. A **password** is a private combination of letters, numbers, and special characters associated with the user name that allows access to a user's account resources. A **picture password** also can be used to control access to a user's account resources. A picture password requires that the user perform mouse or touch gestures on specific areas of the picture to sign in to Windows. An icon is a small image that represents an object; thus, a **user icon** is a picture associated with a user name.

When you turn on a computer, Windows starts and displays **a lock screen** (shown in Figure 1–5) consisting of the time and date. After tapping, sliding, or clicking anywhere on the lock screen, depending on your computer's settings, Windows may or may not display a sign-in screen that shows the user names and user icons for users who have accounts on the computer (Figure 1–4). This **sign-in screen** enables you to sign in to your user account and makes the computer available for use. Clicking the user icon begins the process of signing in to, also called logging on to, your user account.

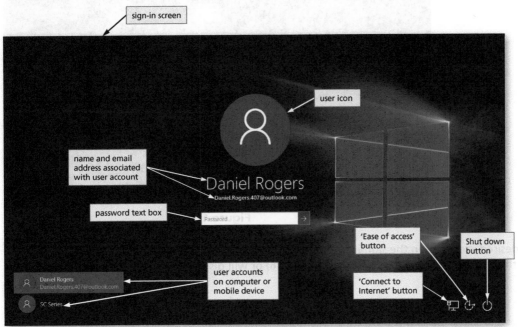

Figure 1–4

BTW
Strong Passwords
You should consider using a strong password with your Windows user account. A strong password is more secure because it is more difficult to guess. Strong passwords have at least eight characters and contain a combination of uppercase and lowercase letters, numbers, and special characters.

At the bottom of the sign-in screen are the 'Connect to Internet' button, the 'Ease of access' button, and a Shut down button. The 'Connect to Internet' button shows the current status of the network connection. Your 'Connect to Internet' button may look different, depending on the type of network connection you are using (wired or wireless). Clicking the 'Ease of access' button displays the Ease of access menu, which provides tools to optimize a computer to accommodate the needs of users with mobility, hearing, and vision impairments.

Clicking the Shut down button displays a menu containing commands related to restarting the computer, putting it in a low-power state, and shutting down the computer. The commands available on your computer may differ.

BTW
Shut Down Options
If you are walking away from your computer for only a brief period, you should put the computer in Sleep mode instead of turning it off completely. Keeping the computer in Sleep mode for this short period often uses less power than powering on the computer.

- The **Sleep command** saves your work, turns off the computer fans and hard drive, and places the computer in a lower-power state. To wake the computer from sleep mode, press the power button or lift a laptop's cover, and sign in to the computer.

- The **Shut down command** exits currently running apps, shuts down Windows, and then turns off the computer.

- The **Restart command** exits currently running apps, shuts down Windows, restarts the computer, and then restarts Windows.

To Sign In to an Account

The following steps, which use the user account for Daniel Rogers, sign in to an account based on a typical Windows installation. *Why? After starting Windows, you might be required to sign in to access the computer's resources.* You may need to ask your instructor how to sign in to your account.

1

- Click the lock screen (Figure 1–5) to display a sign-in screen.

lock screen

Figure 1–5

2

- If necessary, click the desired user icon on the sign-in screen, which, depending on settings, either will display a second sign-in screen that contains a password text box (Figure 1–6) or will display the Windows desktop.

Q&A

Why do I not see a user icon?
Your computer may require you to type a user name instead of clicking an icon.

How can I get past the lock screen if I do not have a mouse?
Swipe up on the lock screen to display the sign-in screen.

What is a text box?
A text box is a rectangular box in which you type text.

Why does my screen not show a password text box?
Your account does not require a password.

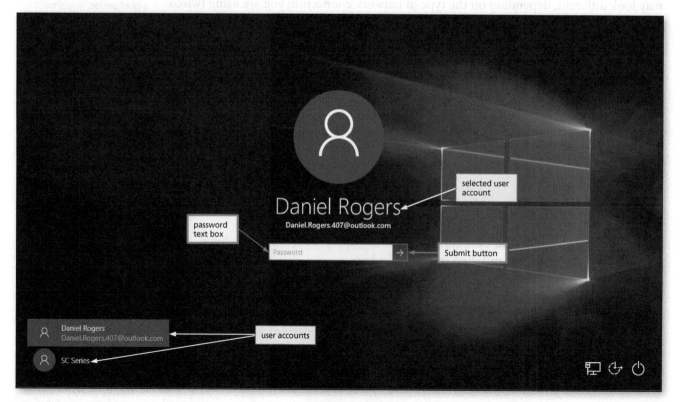

selected user account

password text box

Submit button

user accounts

Figure 1–6

❸

- If Windows 10 displays a password text box, type your password in the text box and then click the Submit button to sign in to your account and display the Windows desktop (Figure 1–7).

Q&A Why does my desktop look different from the one shown in Figure 1–7?
The Windows 10 desktop is customizable, and your school or employer may have modified the screen to meet its needs. Also, your screen resolution, which affects the size of the elements on the screen, may differ from the screen resolution used in this book.

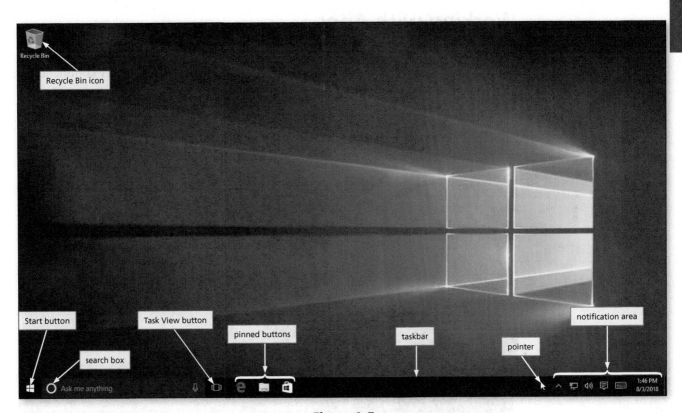

Figure 1–7

The Windows 10 Desktop

Think of the Windows desktop as an electronic version of the top of your desk. You can perform tasks such as placing objects on the desktop, moving the objects around the desktop, and removing items from the desktop.

When you run an app in Windows, it appears on the desktop. Some icons also may be displayed on the desktop. For instance, the icon for the **Recycle Bin**, the location of files that have been deleted, appears on the desktop by default. You can customize your desktop so that icons representing apps and files you use often appear on your desktop. When you run an app, that app's button appears on the taskbar. By default, the **taskbar** appears at the bottom of the Windows desktop and displays the Task View button, the Microsoft Edge app button, the File Explorer button, the Store app button, and app buttons representing apps that currently are running. The Microsoft Edge, File Explorer, and Store app buttons are pinned to the taskbar. Pinned app buttons always are displayed on the taskbar, regardless of whether the app is running or not. The right side of the taskbar contains the notification area, date, and

BTW

Pinned Buttons
If you use an app frequently, you should consider pinning that app button to the taskbar so that you can access it easily. Pinning and unpinning app buttons is discussed later in this module.

time. The **notification area** contains icons designed to provide information about the current state of the computer. For example, the notification area can tell you if your virus protection is out of date, how much battery life you have remaining (if you are using a mobile device), and whether you are connected to a network. The taskbar also displays the **search box** to the left of the app buttons, which allows you to search help, files and folders, and information on the Internet.

Working with Apps

Apps in Windows 10 run on the desktop and work smoothly with touch and other input devices. Windows 10 apps use the **Split View menu** as the primary command interface for the app (Figure 1–8).

Figure 1–8

One way to run an app is by using the Start menu. The **Start menu** provides commands to display a list of apps, run apps, sign out of a user account, switch to a different user account, display computer or mobile device settings, put the computer in a low power state, restart the computer or mobile device, and shut down the computer or mobile device. The Start menu also may contain one or more tiles. A **tile** is a square or rectangular graphical element on the Start menu that you can click to run an app (Figure 1–9).

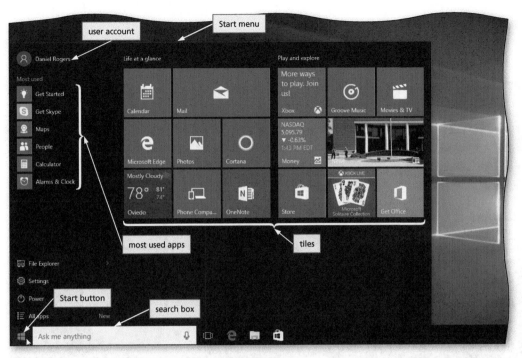

Figure 1–9

To Run an App Using the Start Menu

Why? *When you install an app, one or more commands or tiles are added to the Start menu so that you easily can run the app.* The following steps, which assume Windows is running, use the Start menu to run the Weather app based on a typical installation. Although the steps illustrate running the Weather app, the steps to run any app are similar.

1
- Click the Start button to display the Start menu (Figure 1–10).

Figure 1–10

②

- Click All apps (shown in Figure 1–10) to display a list of all apps installed on the computer or mobile device (Figure 1–11).

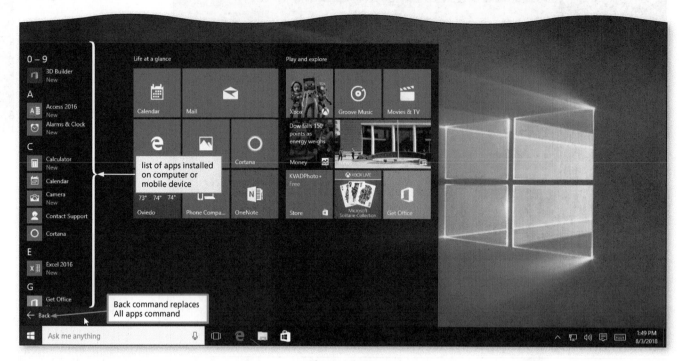

Figure 1–11

③

- Scroll to display the Weather app (Figure 1–12).

Q&A | What do the folders and arrows indicate?
Folders on the Start menu contain additional commands. To view the commands, click the folder name.

Figure 1–12

4

- Click Weather in the All apps list to run the Weather app (Figure 1–13).

Q&A What happens when you run an app?

The Weather app runs in the desktop using a window. A **window** is a rectangular area that displays data and information. The top of a window has a **title bar**, which is a horizontal space that contains the window's name.

Figure 1–13

5

- Type your current city in the 'City or ZIP Code' text box and then click your city in the list that appears (Figure 1–14).

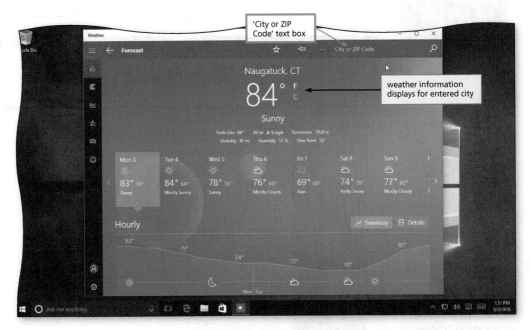

Figure 1–14

Other Ways

1. Type **Weather** in search box, click Weather

2. Display Start menu, click Weather tile

3. Click microphone button in search box, say "open weather"

To Navigate within an App

To navigate within an app, you can use the scroll bar or touch gestures to see more of the app, or you can display the Split View menu for an app. In the Weather app, the Split View menu lets you move from the Home screen to other places, and even display maps, historical weather, and news. *Why? You may intend to travel and see weather information in addition to the current temperature and forecast.* The following steps display the current world weather information.

1

- Click the Maps button to display the radar imagery for the current location (Figure 1–15).

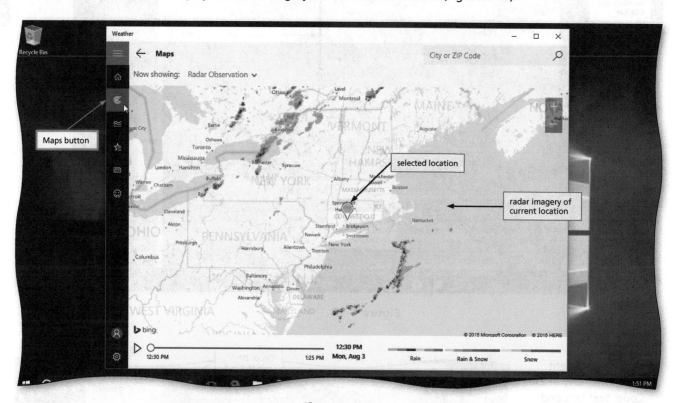

Figure 1–15

2

- Click the Settings button to display the settings for the Weather app (Figure 1–16).

3

- Click the Home button to return to the Home screen displaying the temperature and forecast for the selected location (shown in Figure 1–14).

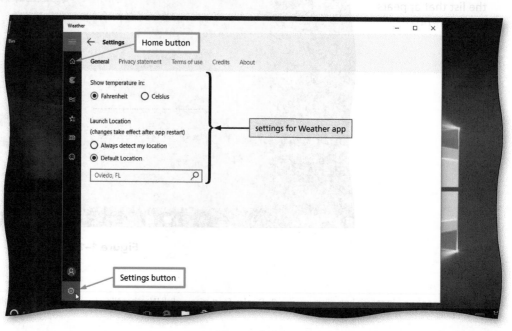

Figure 1–16

To Open and Maximize the File Explorer Window

In Windows, you can use the File Explorer to view your files and organize them into folders, as well as access these files and folders. *Why? If you want to move files and folders around on your hard drive, or copy or move files to or from a removable drive, such as a USB flash drive, the File Explorer can help you perform these operations.* The following steps open and maximize the File Explorer window.

- Click the File Explorer button on the taskbar to run the File Explorer (Figure 1–17).

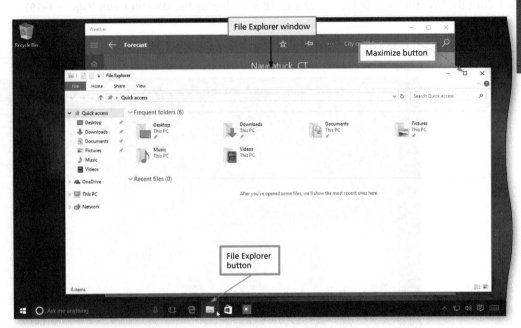

Figure 1–17

- Click the Maximize button (shown in Figure 1–17) on the title bar to maximize the File Explorer window (Figure 1–18).

Q&A

What happens to the Maximize button after I click it?
When the window is maximized, the Maximize button turns into the Restore Down button. Clicking the Restore Down button will return the window to the size and position it was before you maximized it.

Figure 1–18

Other Ways

1. Drag title bar to top of screen

2. Right-click title bar, click Maximize on shortcut menu

To Switch between Apps

In Windows, you can switch between apps easily. *Why? You may have several apps running and want to work with a different app than the one you currently are using.* The following step switches from the File Explorer to the Weather app.

- Click the Weather app button on the taskbar to display the Weather app (Figure 1–19).

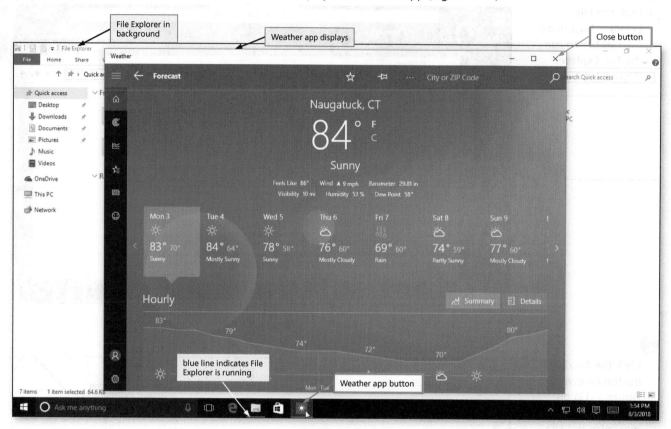

Figure 1–19

Other Ways	
1. Press ALT+TAB to switch between open apps	2. Click Task View button on taskbar, click desired app

To Exit an App

When you have finished using an app, you should exit the app. *Why? When you exit an app, the system resources Windows requires to run the app can be released and made available to other apps running on your computer or mobile device.* The following step exits the Weather app because you have finished using it.

1

- Click the Close button on the title bar (shown in Figure 1–19) to exit the Weather app and remove the Weather app button from the taskbar (Figure 1–20).

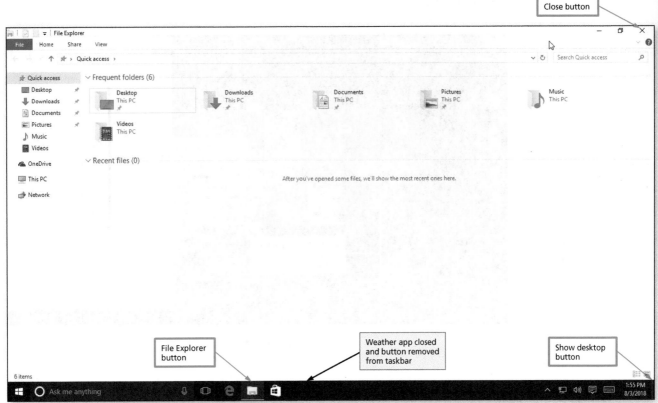

Figure 1–20

Other Ways

1. Right-click app button on taskbar, click Close window on shortcut menu

2. Press ALT+F4

To Display the Windows Desktop

The Show desktop button to the right of the notification area on the taskbar will minimize all open windows and display the desktop. *Why? The desktop provides many useful functions, and you may need to quickly minimize (or hide) all open windows.* The following steps display the Windows desktop.

1

- Click the Show desktop button (shown in Figure 1–20) on the taskbar to minimize all open windows and show the desktop.

2

- Click the File Explorer button on the taskbar to redisplay the File Explorer window (shown in Figure 1–20).
- Click the Close button on the File Explorer window (shown in Figure 1–20) to close the File Explorer window.

Jump Lists

Some commands on the Windows 10 Start menu may include an arrow that you can click to display a jump list. A **jump list** is a list that appears next to some items on the Start menu and contains commands to access related features or locations quickly (Figure 1–21).

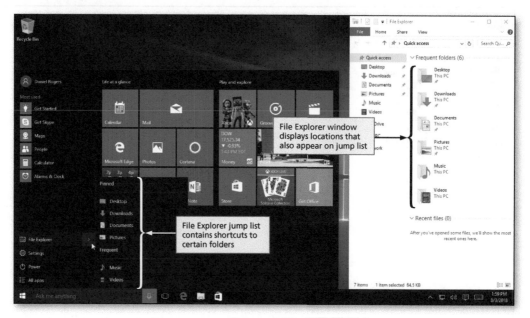

Figure 1–21

To Display a Jump List

As shown in Figure 1–21, the File Explorer command on the Start menu contains a jump list that allows you to access quickly different locations in the File Explorer window. For example, if you click the Documents command on the File Explorer jump list, the File Explorer window will open with the Documents folder displayed. *Why? Using a jump list makes it easier to access related locations or features corresponding to an app.* The following steps use a jump list to display the Documents folder in the File Explorer.

- Click the Start button to display the Start menu (Figure 1–22).

Figure 1–22

2

- Click the 'Show jump list' button next to the File Explorer command to display the jump list for the File Explorer (Figure 1–23).

Figure 1–23

3

- Click Documents on the jump list (shown in Figure 1–23) to display the contents of the Documents folder in the File Explorer window (Figure 1–24). The contents of your Documents folder may differ.

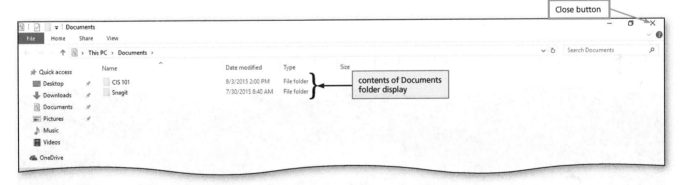

Figure 1–24

4

- Click the Close button on the File Explorer window title bar to close the window.

To Pin an App to the Start Menu

As mentioned previously, the Start menu contains commands and tiles that you can click to perform an action, such as displaying a folder or running an app. Clicking a tile on the Start menu is one of the fastest ways to run an app because you do not have to navigate the All apps list to locate the name of the app you want to run. *Why? Pinning an app to the Start menu will add a tile for that app to the Start menu so that you easily can run the app.* The following steps pin the Sports app to the Start menu.

1

- Click the Start button on the taskbar to display the Start menu.
- Click All apps to display the All apps list.
- Scroll to display the Sports app in the All apps list (Figure 1–25).

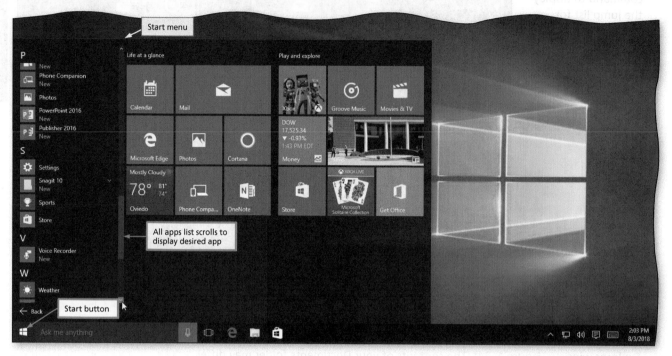

Figure 1–25

2

- Right-click the Sports app to display a shortcut menu (Figure 1–26).

Figure 1–26

3

- Click 'Pin to Start' on the shortcut menu to pin the app to the Start menu (Figure 1–27).

Q&A Why did the 'Unpin from Start' command display on the shortcut menu instead of the 'Pin to Start' command?
If the Sports app already is pinned to the Start menu, Windows will instead display commands for unpinning the app.

Figure 1–27

Live Tiles

Several tiles in Windows 10 are examples of live tiles. In Figure 1–27, the Sports, Weather, Money, and News tiles are examples of live tiles. A **live tile** displays content from certain apps directly on the tile. For example, the Sports app's tile shows current sports information. Other apps – such as the Weather app, Money app, and News app – also feature live tiles. The Weather app displays weather information for your current location, the Money app displays financial news, and the News app displays general news.

To Turn Off a Live Tile

Why? *If you do not like the appearance of live tiles or never look at the information presented on the tile, you might want to turn off the live tile.* The following steps turn off the live tile for the Sports app.

1

- If necessary, display the Start menu.
- Right-click the Sports tile to display a shortcut menu (Figure 1–28).

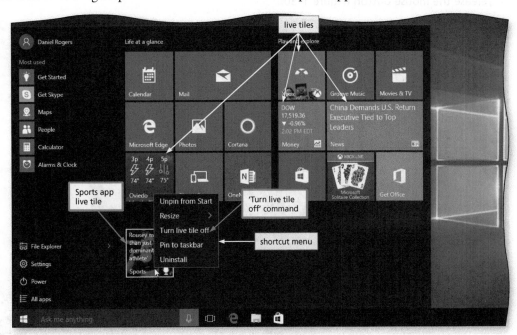

Figure 1–28

2

- Click 'Turn live tile off' on the shortcut menu to turn off the live tile for the Sports app (Figure 1–29).

Figure 1–29

To Move a Tile on the Start Menu

Why? You might choose to move a tile to a different location on the Start menu so that you can keep similar tiles together. The following steps move the Sports tile so that it appears near the Money tile.

1

- Drag the Sports tile to the desired location (in this case, under the money tile). Watch the tiles reposition as you drag, so that you can see a preview of where the tile will display when you release the mouse button. Do not release the mouse button (Figure 1–30).

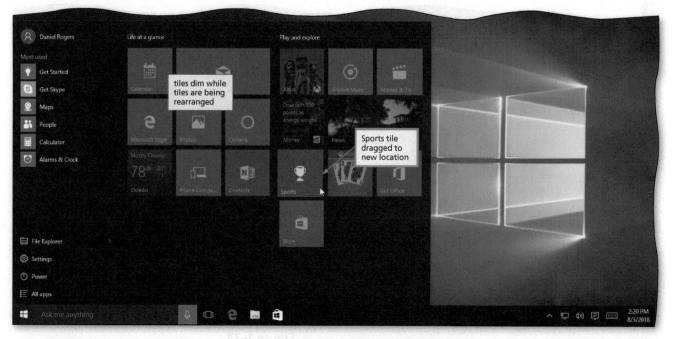

Figure 1–30

2

- Release the mouse button to move the tile to its new location (Figure 1–31).

Q&A What if the tiles on my Start menu do not match Figures 1–30 and 1–31?
Drag the Sports tile to a location of your choosing on the Start menu and then release the mouse button.

Figure 1–31

To Resize a Tile on the Start Menu

Tiles on the Start menu can display in four different sizes: small, medium, wide, and large. Medium tiles, which are the most common size, are two times the width and height of small tiles. Wide tiles are twice the width of medium tiles, and large tiles are twice the height of wide tiles. *Why? Resizing tiles on the Start menu will help you organize them in a way that makes the most sense for how you work.* The following steps resize the Sports tile.

1

- If necessary, display the Start menu.
- Right-click the Sports tile to display the shortcut menu.
- Point to Resize on the shortcut menu to display the Resize submenu, which lists the resizing options (Figure 1–32).

Q&A Can I resize any tile to be one of the four mentioned sizes?
No. Some tiles have only certain sizes available. For example, if you install an app on your computer, the app's tile may support fewer than four sizes.

Figure 1–32

• Click Wide on the Resize submenu to change the size of the Sports tile (Figure 1–33).

Figure 1–33

To Remove a Pinned App from the Start Menu

When you first buy a computer or mobile device or after using it for a while, you might notice tiles on the Start menu that you use infrequently. If you do not use these tiles, you might want to remove them from the Start menu. *Why? Removing unused tiles from the Start menu will help you keep the Start menu organized so that you easily can locate tiles you use the most.* The following steps remove the Sports tile from the Start menu.

• If necessary, display the Start menu.
• Right-click the Sports tile to display a shortcut menu (Figure 1–34).

Figure 1–34

②

- Click 'Unpin from Start' on the shortcut menu to remove the pinned app from the Start menu and reorganize the remaining tiles (Figure 1–35).

Figure 1–35

To Pin an App to the Taskbar

In addition to pinning apps to the Start menu, you also can pin frequently used apps to the Windows taskbar. As mentioned previously, the Task View, Microsoft Edge, File Explorer, and Store buttons are pinned to the taskbar by default. ***Why?*** *Pinning an app to the taskbar allows you to run the app by clicking only one button. If an app is pinned to the Start menu instead, you would have to click two times (one time to display the Start menu and one time when selecting the app to run).* The following steps pin the Mail app to the taskbar.

①

- If necessary, display the Start menu.

- Right-click the Mail tile to display a shortcut menu (Figure 1–36).

Figure 1–36

- Click 'Pin to taskbar' on the shortcut menu to pin the Mail app button to the taskbar.

- Click the Start button to close the Start menu (Figure 1–37).

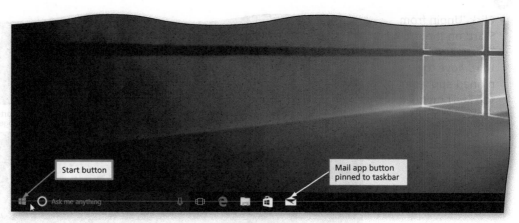

Start button

Mail app button pinned to taskbar

Figure 1–37

To Remove a Pinned App from the Taskbar

If an app button that you seldom use appears on the taskbar, you can remove the app button so that it no longer displays. **Why?** *The space on the taskbar is limited; consider pinning the buttons for the apps that you use most frequently.* The following steps remove the pinned Mail app button from the taskbar.

- Right-click the Mail app button on the taskbar to display a shortcut menu (Figure 1–38).

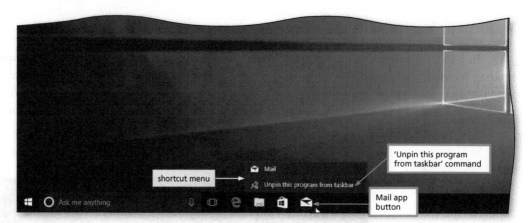

shortcut menu

Mail

Unpin this program from taskbar

'Unpin this program from taskbar' command

Mail app button

Figure 1–38

- Click 'Unpin this program from taskbar' on the shortcut menu to remove the pinned Mail app button from the taskbar (Figure 1–39).

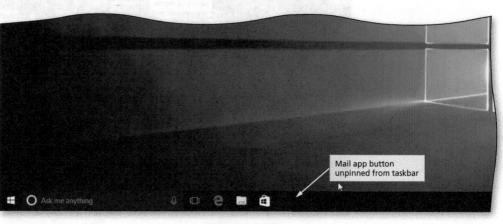

Mail app button unpinned from taskbar

Figure 1–39

To Run an App Using the Search Box

In addition to running apps using tiles or commands on the Start menu or by using buttons on the taskbar, you also can run an app using the search box. ***Why?*** *If you want to run an app that is not pinned to the Start menu or taskbar, it might be faster to use the search box to locate and run the app than by navigating the All apps list on the Start menu.* The following steps use the search box to run the WordPad app.

1

- Click the search box on the taskbar.

- Type **WordPad** to display the search results (Figure 1–40). Your search results might differ.

Q&A Does capitalization matter when you enter the search text?
No. Similar search results would appear if you type wordpad, WORDPAD, or WoRdPaD.

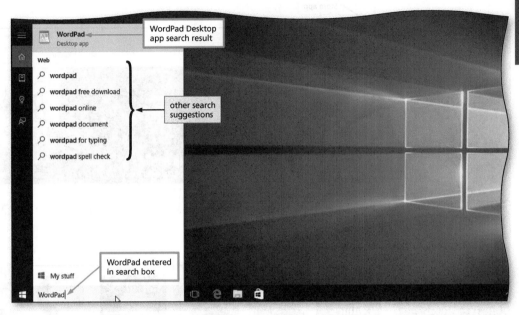

Figure 1–40

2

- Click WordPad at the top of the search results to run the WordPad app, display the WordPad app button on the title bar, hide the search results, and clear the search text from the search box (Figure 1–41).

3

- Click the Close button on the WordPad title bar to exit WordPad.

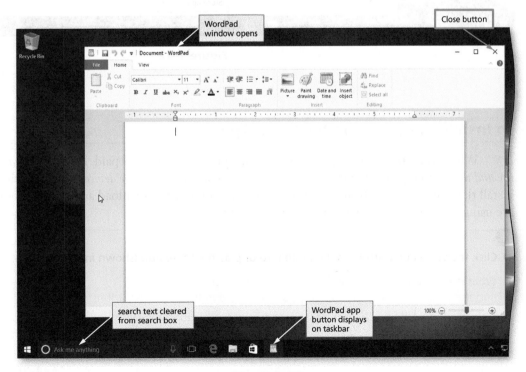

Figure 1–41

Free and Paid Apps

Many apps are available for Windows, which you can find using the Store app (Figure 1–42). Some apps are free, allowing you to download them without making a payment. Other apps require payment, so you will need to pay the fee before you can download them.

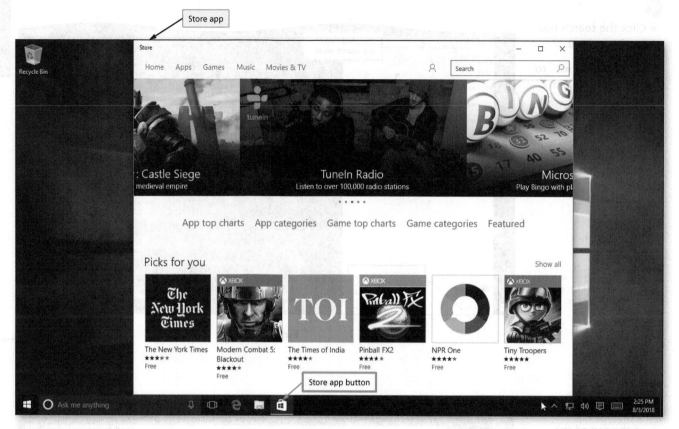

Figure 1–42

To Install an App Using the Store App

When using the Store app, you can install apps that are free or paid. *Why? You find an app that you want to use and then download and install it so that it is on your computer or mobile device.* The following steps download and install the Wikipedia app from the Store. If you are not able to download and install apps on the computer you are using, read these steps without performing them.

1
- Click the Store app button on the taskbar to display the Store app (shown in Figure 1–42).

Q&A What if the Store app does not appear on my taskbar?
Run the Store app using another method presented in this module: click its name on the Start menu's All apps list, click the Store tile on the Start menu, or search for the Store app using the search box.

2

- Type **Wikipedia** in the Search box in the Store window to display search results corresponding to the search text (Figure 1–43).

Q&A What if I do not know the exact name of the app I want to install?
You can scroll the Store window to display various apps or click the category names to display apps in that category.

Figure 1–43

3

- Click the Wikipedia search result to display information about the Wikipedia app (Figure 1–44).

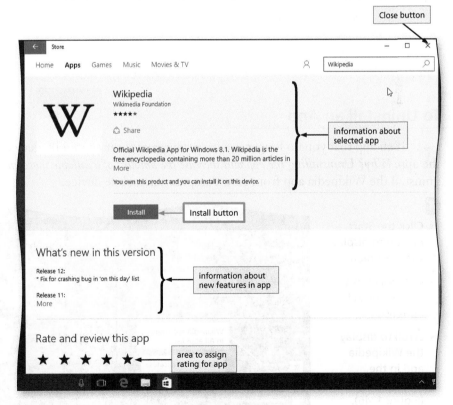

Figure 1–44

4

- Click the Free or Install button to download and install the Wikipedia app. When the app has finished downloading and installing, click the Open button to open the Wikipedia app (Figure 1–45).

Q&A | Where is the Open button?
The Open button replaces the Install button after the app has been installed and is ready to use.

Figure 1–45

5

- Click the Close button to close the Wikipedia window.
- Click the Close button (shown in Figure 1–44) to close the Store window.

Q&A | How can I run the Wikipedia app?
Apps you download from the Store will appear in the All apps list on the Start menu. Use the skills presented in this module if you want to pin the app on the Start menu or taskbar for easier access.

To Uninstall an App

If an app that you no longer use is on your computer or mobile device, you should consider uninstalling the app. *Why? Uninstalling the app will increase the amount of available space on your hard drive.* The following steps uninstall the Wikipedia app from your computer or mobile device.

1

- Click the Start button to display the Start menu.

- Click All apps to display the All apps list.

- Scroll to display the Wikipedia app in the All apps list (Figure 1–46).

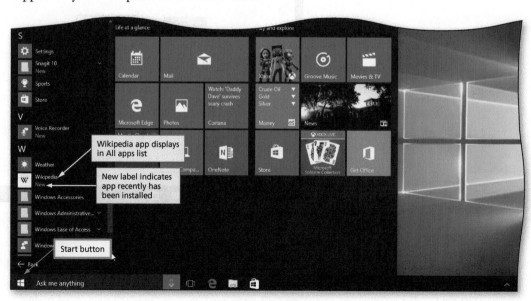

Figure 1–46

2

- Right-click the Wikipedia app to display a shortcut menu (Figure 1–47).

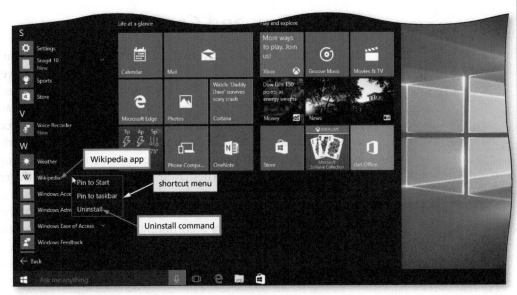

Figure 1–47

3

- Click Uninstall on the shortcut menu to display a confirmation message (Figure 1–48).

Figure 1–48

4

- Click the Uninstall button on the shortcut menu to uninstall the Wikipedia app from your computer or mobile device (Figure 1–49).

- Click the Start button to hide the Start menu.

Figure 1–49

Search Box and Cortana

The search box is a new feature in Windows 10 that allows you to search for files and folders in Windows, as well as search for information on the web. The search box also enables you to interact with Cortana. **Cortana** is a personal assistant that you can speak to using your computer or mobile device's microphone and ask questions or give instructions (Figure 1–50). For example, you can ask Cortana to add a meeting with your boss to your calendar, and it will automatically add the event. You also can have Cortana remind you to perform certain actions. For example, you can request that Cortana remind you Tuesday at 7:00 p.m. to take out the trash. Cortana also can help track packages, gather flight information, or locate other factual information on the Internet. Cortana is intuitive; the more you use it, the more it learns about you and forms its search results accordingly. Before you can use Cortana for the first time, you must follow a brief setup process. To use Cortana and take advantage of its full functionality, you must be signed in to Windows with a Microsoft account, and you must enable Cortana.

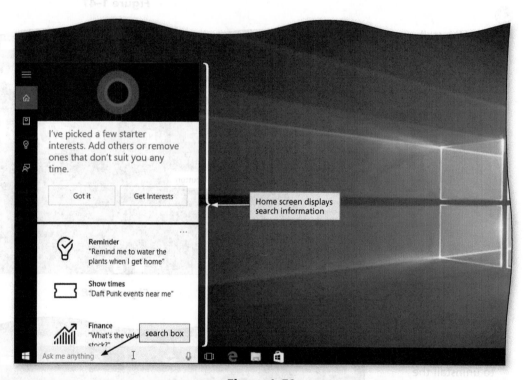

Figure 1–50

TO ENABLE CORTANA

If you need to enable Cortana, you would perform the following steps.

1. Click the search box to display information about Cortana.
2. Click the Next button.
3. Read the information about Cortana, as well as the privacy statement. If you agree and wish to continue, click the I agree button.
4. Enter your name or nickname and then click the Next button.

To Search the Web Using the Search Box

In addition to searching for files and folders on your computer or mobile device, Windows also will search the Internet for the search text. *Why? It may be faster to use the search box to locate information on the Internet instead of running a browser and using a search engine to locate information.* The following steps search the web using the search box.

● Click the search box to activate it (Figure 1–51).

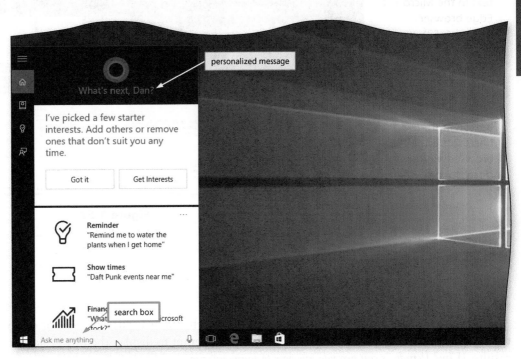

Figure 1–51

● Type **national parks** in the search box to display search results and additional recommended search text (Figure 1–52).

Q&A Why do the search results and suggested search text differ from Figure 1–52? Windows 10 uses the web and your previous search history to provide the most relevant search results. For this reason, your results might vary.

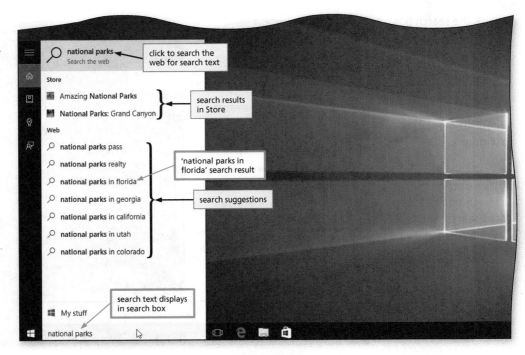

Figure 1–52

- Click 'national parks in florida' to display the search results for the 'national parks in florida' search text in the Microsoft Edge browser (Figure 1–53). Your search results might vary.

- Click the Close button in the Microsoft Edge browser window to close the browser.

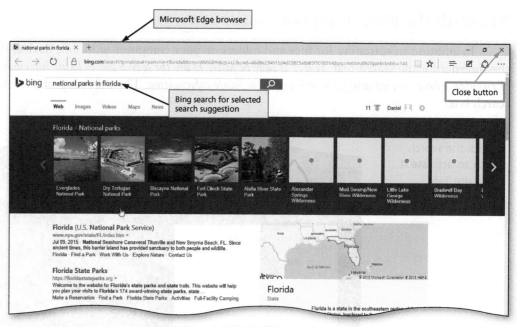

Figure 1–53

To Ask a Question Using the Search Box

In addition to entering search text to locate search results in files, folders, or on the Internet, you also can type questions in the search box, and Windows will attempt to display the most relevant answer in the search results. *Why? Windows can provide answers to many questions so that you do not have to search content on websites for the specific answer.* The following steps ask a question using the search box.

- Click the search box to activate it.

- Type **How many ounces are in a pound?** in the search box to enter the question (Figure 1–54).

- Click outside the search box to hide the search results.

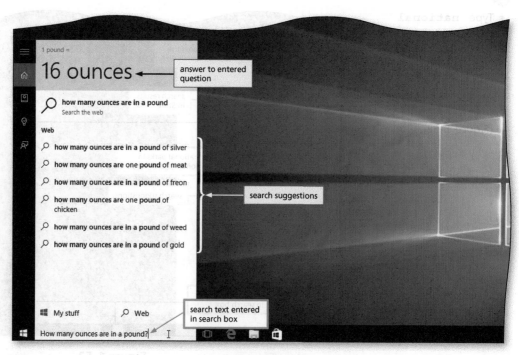

Figure 1–54

To View the Notebook

The Notebook provides a location where you can specify settings for information and suggestions that appear when you click the search box. For example, if you want to display information about your favorite sports team, you can specify that sports team in the Notebook to indicate that you want to see information about that team. **Why?** *Specifying your preferences in the Notebook will help Windows display the information that is most meaningful to you.* The following steps specify your favorite sports team so that information about the team will display.

1
- Click the search box to activate it.

- Click the Notebook button to display the Notebook menu (Figure 1–55).

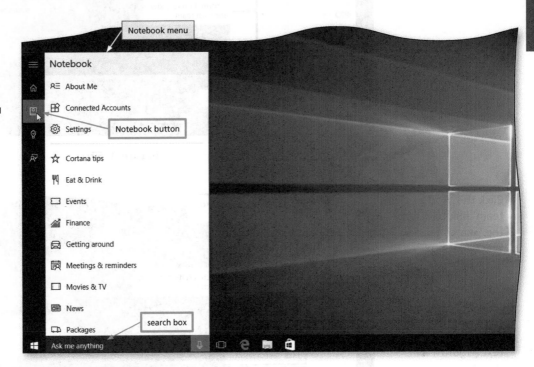

Figure 1–55

2
- If necessary, scroll to display the Sports category (Figure 1–56).

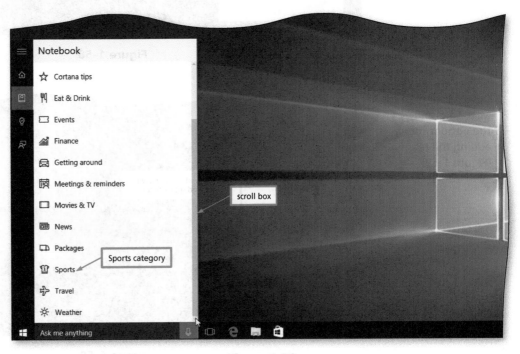

Figure 1–56

- Click Sports
  to display the
  Sports options
  (Figure 1–57).

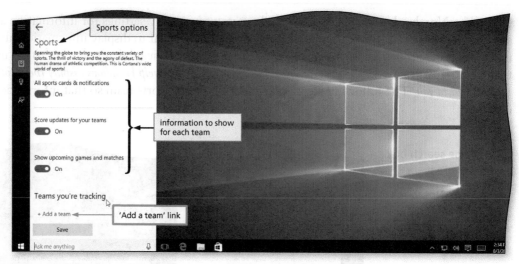

Figure 1–57

- Click the 'Add a
  team' link to display
  the 'Search for a
  team' text box.

- Type **Miami** in
  the 'Search for a
  team' text box to
  display the results
  matching the search
  text (Figure 1–58).

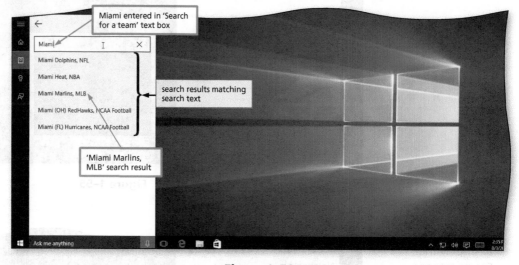

Figure 1–58

- Click 'Miami Marlins,
  MLB' to display
  the options for
  adding the team
  (Figure 1–59).

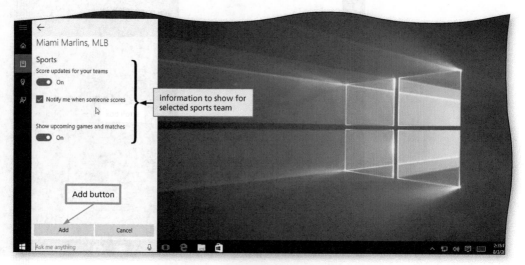

Figure 1–59

6

- Click the Add button (shown in Figure 1–59) to add the Miami Marlins to the list of teams you want to track (Figure 1–60).

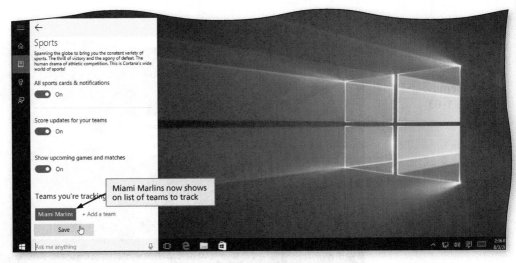

Figure 1–60

7

- Click the Home button to display information relevant to your interests and your current location.
- If necessary, scroll the information to display the information about the Miami Marlins (Figure 1–61).

Q&A Why can I not find information about the Miami Marlins when I scroll?
You might not find information about the sports team you added if they have not played a game recently or if there is no news about the team to share.

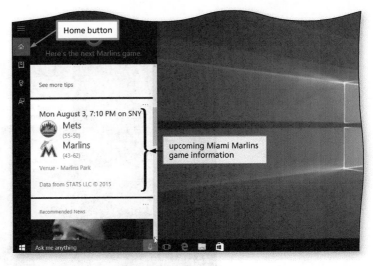

Figure 1–61

To Set a Reminder Using the Search Box

Another feature available in the search box is the ability to set reminders. *Why? If you use your computer or mobile device frequently and need to be reminded of an event at a future date and time, you can set a reminder to display at the desired time.* The following steps set a reminder using the search box.

1

- If necessary, click the search box to activate it.
- Click the Reminders button to view current reminders (Figure 1–62).

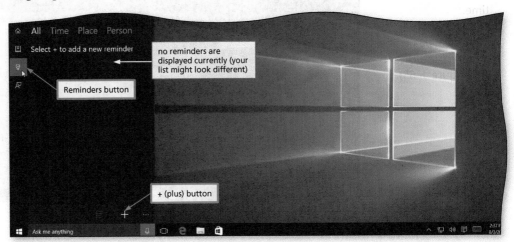

Figure 1–62

- Click the + (plus) button (shown in Figure 1–62) to add a reminder (Figure 1–63).

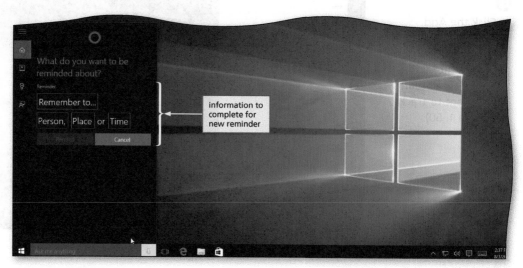

Figure 1–63

- Type **Submit Assignment 4** in the Remember to . . . text box (Figure 1–64).

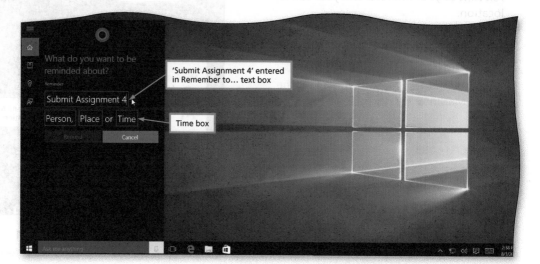

Figure 1–64

- Click the Time box to display the options to set the reminder time.
- Click 12 for the hour, click 00 for the minutes, and click PM (Figure 1–65).

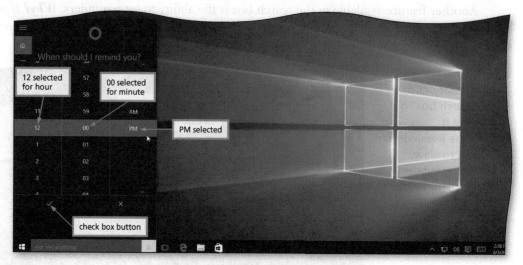

Figure 1–65

5
- Click the check box button to display information about the reminder (Figure 1–66).

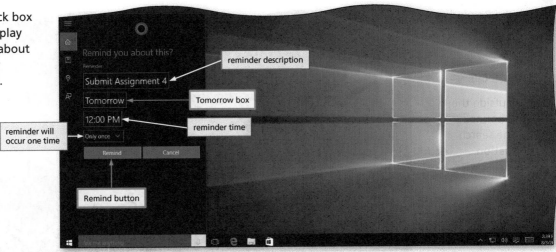

Figure 1–66

6
- Click the Tomorrow box to set a different date for the reminder (Figure 1–67).

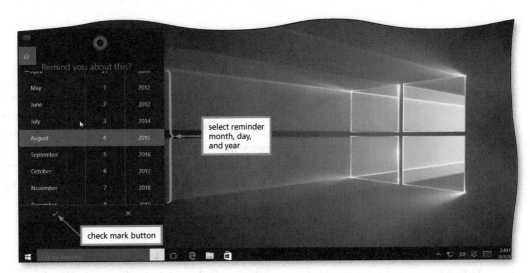

Figure 1–67

7
- Choose a month, day, and year in the future, and then click the check box button to return to the reminder options (Figure 1–68).

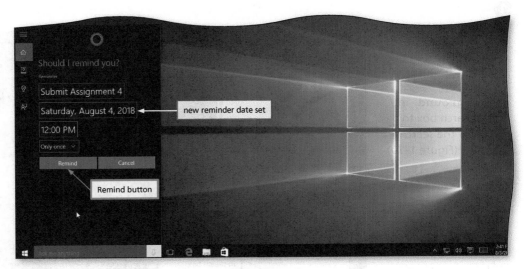

Figure 1–68

• Click the Remind
button to set the
reminder and display
the Reminder list
(Figure 1–69).

• Click outside the
search box to
hide the search
information.

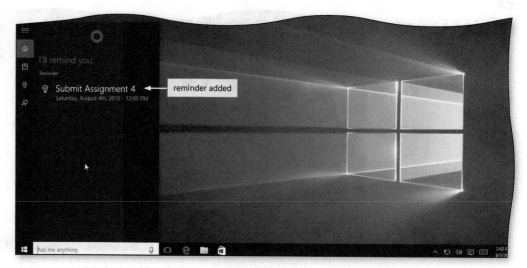

Figure 1–69

Getting Help

In previous versions of Windows, you would use Windows Help and Support to locate
help information. Windows 10 has simplified the help functionality by allowing you
to search for help using the search box. If you need help performing a task, type a
description of the task in the search box, and Windows will provide search results
linking to the proper window and setting that will help you accomplish that task. For
example, if you type "change the background" in the search box, the search results
will include a link to the Settings app, which includes the settings to change the
background image.

To Get Help Using the Search Box

Why? *If you are having trouble locating where to find a particular feature in Windows, you can use the search box to
locate that feature.* The following steps use the search box to locate where to change the desktop background.

1

• Click the search box
to activate it.

• Type **change
desktop
background** in
the search box to
display the search
results (Figure 1–70).

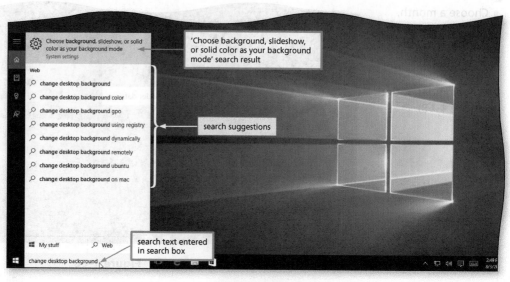

Figure 1–70

2

- Click 'Choose background, slideshow, or solid color as your background mode' in the search results to display the personalization settings where you can adjust the desktop background (Figure 1–71).

- Click the Close button to close the Personalization window.

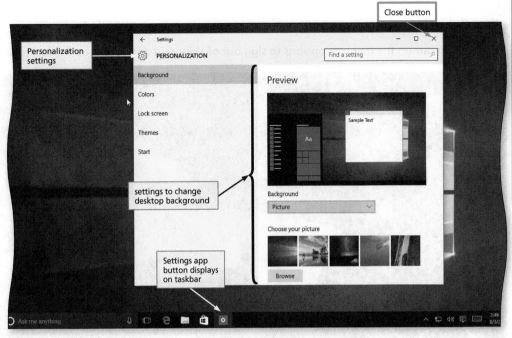

Figure 1–71

Shutting Down Windows

After completing your work with Windows, you should end your session by signing out of your account. In addition to signing out, several options are available for ending your Windows session. You can choose to sign out only, to lock the computer until you come back, to put the computer in sleep mode that saves power, or to shut down the computer as well as sign out of your account.

To Sign Out of an Account

If you are leaving the computer but do not want to turn it off, you can choose to sign out of your account. *Why?* *You might be using a computer in the school lab and need to leave the class. The computer does not need to be shut down because a student in the following class will need to use the computer.* The following steps sign out of an account.

1

- Click the Start button to display the Start menu.

- Click the name associated with your user account to display a menu of options (Figure 1–72).

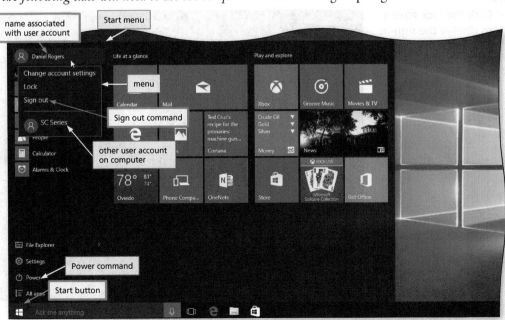

Figure 1–72

● Click Sign out on the menu of options to sign out of Windows and return to the lock screen (Figure 1–73).

lock screen

2:52

Monday, August 3

Figure 1–73

To Shut Down the Computer

When you have finished using the computer, you should shut it down. ***Why?*** *You are finished using the computer and want to shut it down to conserve power.* The following steps shut down the computer.

● Click the lock screen to display the sign-in screen (Figure 1–74).

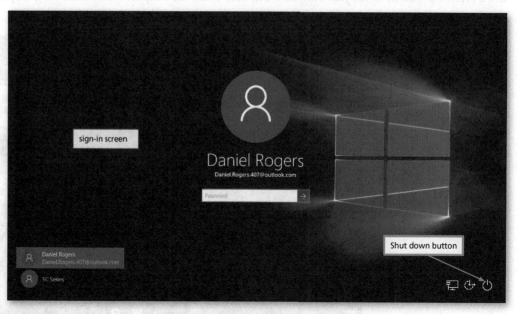

sign-in screen

Daniel Rogers
Daniel.Rogers.407@outlook.com

Password

Daniel Rogers
Daniel.Rogers.407@outlook.com

SC Series

Shut down button

Figure 1–74

- Click the Shut down button on the sign-in screen to display the Shut down menu (Figure 1–75).

Figure 1–75

- Click Shut down on the Shut down menu to shut down the computer (Figure 1–76).

Q&A Can I just shut down the computer without first signing out?
Yes. Click Power on the Start menu (shown in Figure 1–72). Next, click Shut down on the Power menu to shut down the computer.

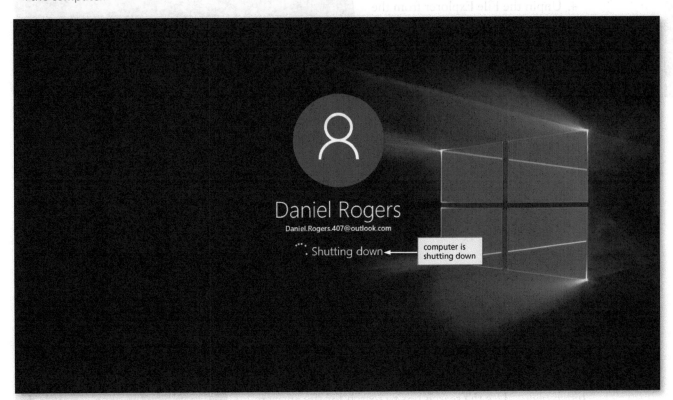

Figure 1–76

Summary

In this module, you have learned how to work with the Windows 10 interface and some of its basic features. Topics covered included describing Windows 10 and elements of the Windows 10 interface, differentiating among the various editions of Windows 10, using a touch screen and performing basic mouse operations, running Windows 10 and signing in to an account, running an app and navigating within an app, running the File Explorer, switching between apps, customizing the Start menu, searching for an app or file, installing an app, using the search box, and adding reminders. Finally, you learned to sign out of an account and shut down the computer.

Apply Your Knowledge

Reinforce the skills and apply the concepts you learned in this module.

Exploring Windows 10

Instructions: You will use Windows 10 to perform the following tasks. For each task, record the exact steps you take and submit them in the format required by your instructor.

Perform the following tasks:

1. Pin the Photos app to the taskbar.

2. Unpin the Photos app from the taskbar.

3. Pin the File Explorer to Start menu.

4. Unpin the File Explorer from the Start menu.

5. Change the size of a tile on the Start menu (choose from any available size).

6. Turn on a live tile.

7. Turn off a live tile.

8. Move a tile to a different area on the Start menu.

9. Search for an app.

10. Run the Store app.

11. Exit the Store app.

Figure 1–77

Extend Your Knowledge

Extend the skills you learned in this module and experiment with new skills. You will use the search box to complete the assignment.

Obtaining Help

Instructions: Use the search box to search for the answers to the following questions.

1. Find information about Windows shortcuts by entering **Windows shortcuts** in the search box. Browse the search results to locate websites that can help you answer the following questions:

   a. What keyboard shortcut is used to copy a file?

   b. What keyboard shortcut is used to paste a file?

   c. How do you display a shortcut menu?

2. Determine the appropriate search text to use in the search box and then use the search box to locate information to answer the following questions:

   a. What is Windows Defender?

Figure 1–78

   b. What is Windows Firewall?

   c. What settings can you control for kids who use your computer?

   d. What are five ways to protect your computer from viruses and other threats?

   e. What is a user account?

   f. What is the difference between a local user account and a Microsoft account?

3. Use the search box or other available method in Windows to obtain answers to the following questions:

   a. How do you turn on Windows Firewall?

   b. How do you perform a full scan of your computer or mobile device using Windows Defender?

   c. How do you add a printer?

   d. How do you display the Control Panel?

   e. How do you change the screen saver?

   f. How do you change the date and time?

   g. How do you connect to a wireless network?

Expand Your World

Using Microsoft Edge

Create a solution that uses cloud or web technologies by learning and investigating on your own from general guidance.

Part 1 Instructions: Running Microsoft Edge

1. If necessary, connect to the Internet.

2. If necessary, display the desktop and then run Microsoft Edge.

Figure 1–79

Continued >

Expand Your World *continued*

Part 2 Instructions: Exploring the Cengage Website

1. Type `cengage.com` in the 'Search or enter web address' text box and then press the ENTER key.

2. Answer the following questions:

   a. What web address is displayed on the address bar?

   b. What window title appears on the browser tab?

3. If necessary, scroll to view the contents of the webpage. List three links shown on this webpage.

4. Click any link on the webpage. Which link did you click?

5. Describe the webpage that was displayed when you clicked the link.

6. If requested by your instructor, click the More actions button and then click the Print button to print the webpage.

Part 3 Instructions: Exploring the National Park Service Website

1. Click the web address in the address bar to select it.

2. Type `nps.gov` in the address bar and then press the ENTER key.

3. What title is displayed on the browser tab?

4. Scroll the webpage to view its contents. Do any graphic images appear on the webpage?

5. Does the webpage include an image that is a link? (Pointing to an image on a webpage and having the pointer change to a hand indicates the image is a link.) If so, describe the image.

6. Click the image to display another webpage. What title is displayed on the browser tab?

7. If requested by your instructor, print the webpage.

Part 4 Instructions: Displaying Previously Displayed Webpages

1. Click the Back button. What webpage is displayed?

2. Click the Back button two times. What webpage is displayed?

3. If requested by your instructor, print the webpage.

4. Click the Close button on the Microsoft Edge title bar to exit Microsoft Edge.

In the Lab

Design, create, modify, and/or use files following the guidelines, concepts, and skills presented in this module. Labs 1 and 2, which increase in difficulty, require you to create solutions based on what you learned in the module; Lab 3 requires you to apply your creative thinking and problem-solving skills to design and implement a solution.

Lab 1: Setting Reminders in Windows 10

Problem: You have just started a new job and want to be sure that you meet all project deadlines and attend required meetings. You have added these events to your calendar, but also want to set reminders for these events in Windows 10 (Figure 1–80).

Perform the following steps:

1. Click the search box to activate it.

2. Click the + (plus) button to add a new reminder.

3. Type `Weekly meeting with supervisor` in the Remember to... box.

4. Click the Time box and then select 2:00 PM for the reminder time.

5. Set the meeting to occur every Wednesday.

6. Click the Remind button.

7. Set the following additional reminders. Choose descriptive text to identify each reminder:

   a. Accounting report due every Tuesday at 3:00 PM.

   b. Meeting with IT Department on March 19, 2018, at 9:00 AM.

   c. Complete system backup every Wednesday at 4:00 PM.

   d. Attend team lunch every Friday at 12:00 PM.

   e. Financial system training on April 12, 2018, at 11:00 AM.

8. Record the steps you took to perform these actions, and submit them in a format required by your instructor.

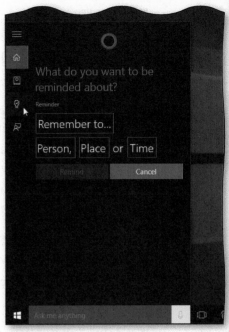

Figure 1–80

Lab 2: **Working with Multiple Apps**

Problem: You have learned that Windows supports multitasking, which is the ability to have multiple apps open at once and switch between them (Figure 1–81). You would like to experiment with the different methods by which you can switch between apps.

Perform the following steps:

Part 1: Running Microsoft Edge, the File Explorer, and WordPad

1. Display the desktop and then click the Microsoft Edge app button on the taskbar to run Microsoft Edge.

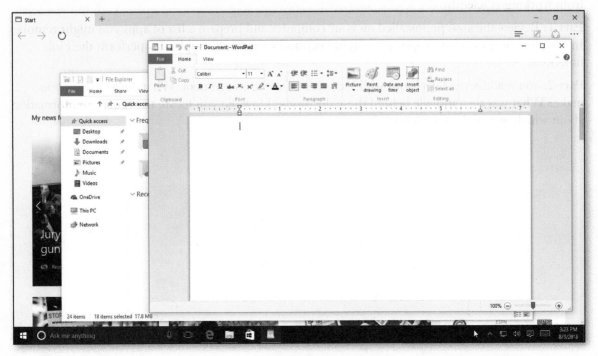

Figure 1–81

Continued >

In the Lab *continued*

2. Click the File Explorer button to open the File Explorer window.

3. Type `WordPad` in the search box and then click the WordPad Desktop app search result to run the WordPad app.

Part 2: Switching among the Windows

1. Press ALT+TAB to switch to the next open window.

2. Press CTRL+ALT+TAB to view the programs that are running. Press the TAB key. Click the WordPad live preview to switch to the WordPad app.

3. Click the Task View button on the taskbar to view the programs that are running. Click the Microsoft Edge live preview to switch to Microsoft Edge.

Part 3: Reporting Your Findings

1. What happens when you press ALT+TAB?

2. What is the difference between pressing ALT+TAB and CTRL+ALT+TAB?

3. What happens when you click the Task View button?

Part 4: Close All Open Windows

1. Click the Close button for each of the three open windows to close the windows. If a dialog box is displayed that prompts you to save changes to the WordPad document, click the Don't Save button.

Lab 3: **Consider This: Your Turn**

Reviewing Installed Apps

Problem: You have been hired at a local accounting company to oversee the delivery, installation, and configuration of new computers for each of the company's 20 employees. The company's president has asked you to remove apps that might be a distraction to the employees and prevent them from working efficiently.

Part 1: Review the apps preinstalled on your computer and prepare a list of apps you might remove. In addition, prepare a list of apps you might keep and would help employees perform their job functions.

Part 2: You made several decisions while searching for this assignment. What decisions did you make? What was the rationale behind these decisions? How did you locate the required information about which apps to keep or remove?

2 | Working with the Windows 10 Desktop

Objectives

You will have mastered the material in this module when you can:

- Create, name, and save a document directly in the Documents folder
- Use WordPad to print and edit a document
- Change the view and arrange objects in groups in the Documents folder
- Create and name a folder in the Documents folder
- Move documents into a folder

- Add and remove a shortcut on the Start menu
- Open a document using a shortcut on the Start menu
- Open a folder using a desktop shortcut
- Open, modify, and print multiple documents in a folder
- Delete multiple files and folders
- Work with the Recycle Bin

Introduction

In Module 2, you will learn about the Windows 10 desktop. With thousands of hardware devices and software products available for computers and mobile devices, users need to manage these resources quickly and easily. One of Windows 10's impressive features is the ease with which users can create and access documents and files.

Mastering the desktop will help you take advantage of user-interface enhancements and innovations that make computing faster, easier, and more reliable and that offer seamless integration with the Internet. Working with the Windows 10 desktop in this module, you will find out how these features can save time, organize files and folders, and ultimately help you work more efficiently.

Creating a Document in WordPad

As introduced in Module 1, an app is a set of computer instructions that carries out a task on the computer. An app sometimes is referred to as a program. For example, you create written documents with a word-processing app, spreadsheets and charts with a spreadsheet app, and presentations with a presentation app.

To learn how to work with the Windows 10 desktop, you will create two daily reminders lists, one for Mr. Raymond and one for Ms. Estes. Because they will be reviewing their lists throughout the day, you will need to update the lists with new reminders as necessary. You decide to use WordPad, a popular word processing program available with Windows 10, to create the daily reminders lists. The finished documents are shown in Figure 2–1.

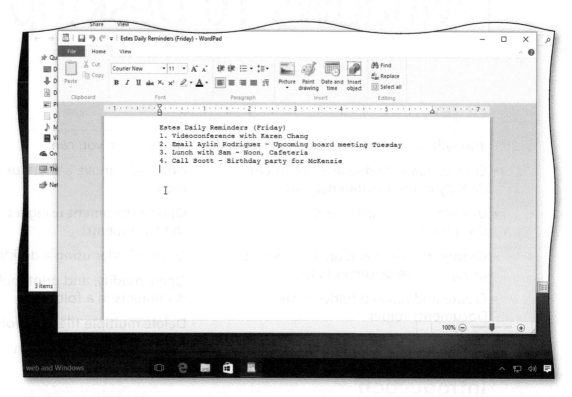

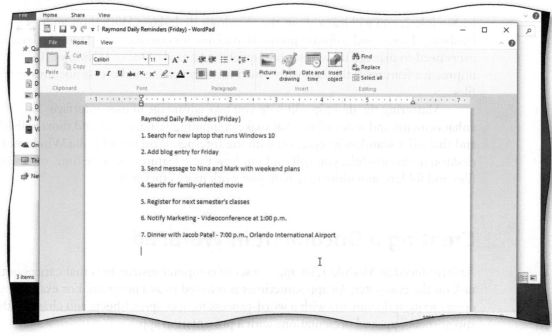

Figure 2–1

To Run an App and Create a Document

Why? *You first will create the daily reminders document for Mr. Raymond using WordPad by running the WordPad app, typing the reminders, and then saving the document in the Documents folder.* The following steps run WordPad and create a daily reminders document for Mr. Raymond.

- Type **wordpad** in the search box to prompt Windows 10 to search for the WordPad app.

- Click the WordPad desktop app search result to run WordPad and open the Document - WordPad window (Figure 2–2).

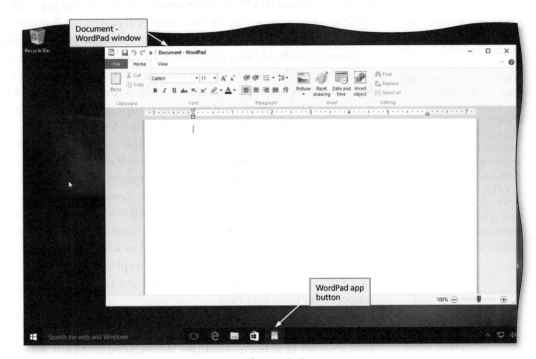

Figure 2–2

- Type **Raymond Daily Reminders (Friday)** and then press the ENTER key two times.

- Type **1. Search for new laptop that runs Windows 10** and then press the ENTER key.

- Type **2. Add blog entry for Friday** and then press the ENTER key.

- Type **3. Send message to Nina and Mark with weekend plans** and then press the ENTER key.

- Type **4. Search for family-oriented movie** and then press the ENTER key (Figure 2–3).

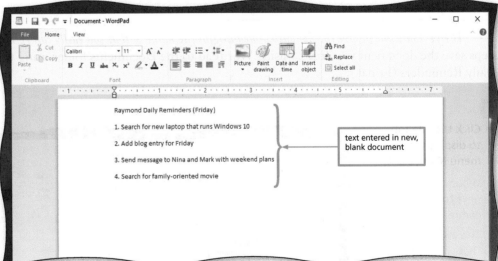

Figure 2–3

Other Ways

1. Display Start menu, click All apps, click Windows Accessories, click WordPad

Saving Documents

When you create a document using an app, such as WordPad, the document is stored in the main memory (RAM) of the computer. If you exit the app without saving the document or if the computer accidentally loses electrical power, the document will be lost. To protect against the accidental loss of a document and to allow you to modify the document easily in the future, you should save the document. Although you can save a file on the desktop, it is recommended that you save the document in a different location to keep the desktop free from clutter. For example, you can save files to the Documents folder.

The **Documents folder** contains a specific user's documents and folders. When you save a document, you are creating a file. A **file** refers to a group of meaningful data that is identified by a file name. For example, a WordPad document is a file, an Excel spreadsheet is a file, a picture created using Paint is a file, and a saved email message is a file. When you create a file, you must assign a file name to the file. All files are identified by a file name, which should be descriptive of the saved file.

To associate a file with an app, Windows 10 assigns an extension to the file name, consisting of a period followed by three or more characters. Most documents created using the WordPad app are saved as Rich Text Format documents with the .rtf extension, but they also can be saved as plain text with the .txt extension. A Rich Text Format document allows for formatting text and inserting graphics, which is not supported in plain text files.

Many computer users can tell at least one horror story of working on their computers for a long period of time and then losing all of their work because of a power failure or software problem. To ensure you do not lose files, save often to protect your work.

To Save a Document in the Documents Folder

Why? You want to save the file with a meaningful file name so that you easily can retrieve it later. The following steps save the document you created using WordPad to the Documents folder using the file name, Raymond Daily Reminders (Friday).

- Click the File tab to display the File menu (Figure 2–4).

Q&A What is the arrow next to the Save as command?

The arrow indicates that several preset ways to save the file are available, which can be accessed by clicking the arrow.

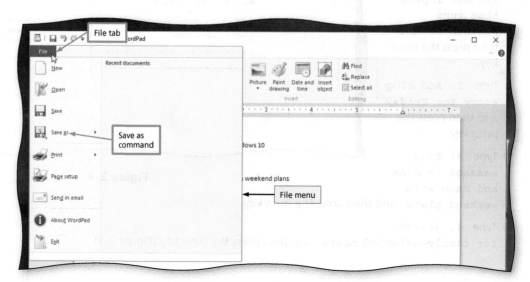

Figure 2–4

2

- Click the Save as command on the File menu to display the Save As dialog box.

- Type **Raymond Daily Reminders (Friday)** in the File name box (Figure 2–5).

Figure 2–5

3

- Click Documents in the Navigation pane to specify that you want to save to the Documents folder (Figure 2–6).

Q&A Why do the contents of my Documents folder look different?

Depending on the files and folders you have saved on your computer, your Documents folder's contents may differ.

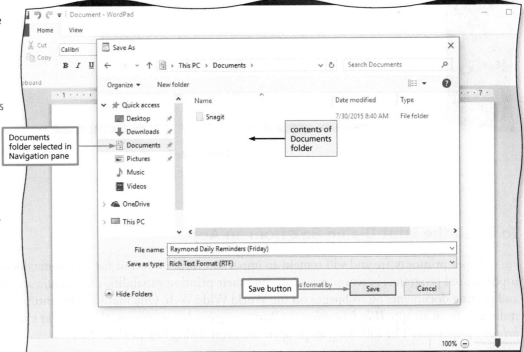

Figure 2–6

4

- Click the Save button (Save As dialog box) to save the document and close the Save As dialog box (Figure 2–7).

Q&A

Why did the WordPad title bar change?

Now that you have saved the document with a file name, the file name will appear on the title bar. To display a preview of the Raymond Daily Reminders (Friday) - WordPad window, point to the WordPad app button on the taskbar.

Will I have to use the Save as command every time I want to save a document?

Now that you have saved the document, you can use the Save command to save changes to the document without having to type a new file name or select a new storage location. If you want to save the file with a different file name or in a different location, you would use the Save as command. By changing the location using the address bar, you can save a file in a different folder or drive.

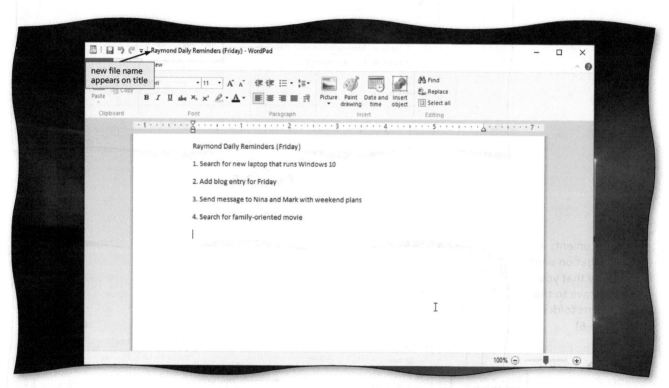

Figure 2–7

To Open the Print Dialog Box from an App

Paper printouts are and will remain an important form of output for electronic documents. Many sophisticated programs, however, are expanding their printing capabilities to include sending email messages and posting documents on webpages on the World Wide Web. One method of printing a document is to print it directly from an app. *Why? Opening the Print dialog box before printing the document will allow you to specify your printing preferences.* The following steps open the Print dialog box in WordPad.

1

- Click the File tab to display the File menu (Figure 2–8).

Figure 2–8

2

- Click Print on the File menu to display the Print dialog box (Figure 2–9).

Q&A What do the four options in the Page Range area represent?

The option buttons give you the choice of printing all pages of a document (All), selected parts of a document (Selection), current page (Current Page), or selected pages of a document (Pages). The selected All option button indicates all pages of a document will print.

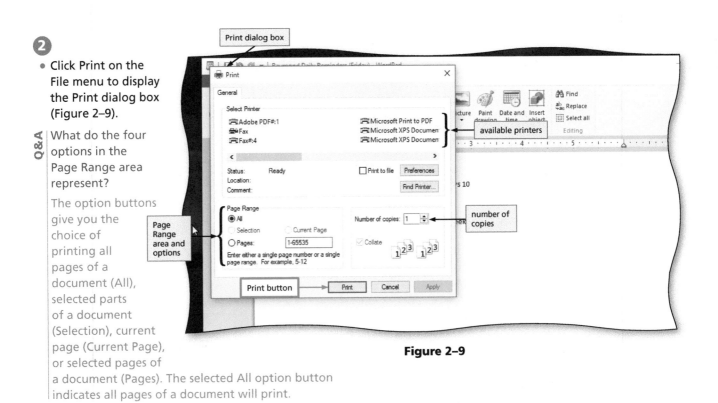

Figure 2–9

Other Ways

1. Press ALT+F, press P

To Print a Document

    Why? *It sometimes is important to have a printout of a document in case you need to reference the information when you do not have access to a computer.* The following step prints the Raymond Daily Reminders (Friday) document.

- Ready the printer according to the printer's instructions.

- If necessary, click the appropriate printer name to select your printer.

- Click the Print button (Print dialog box) (shown in Figure 2–9) to print the document and return to the Raymond Daily Reminders (Friday) - WordPad window (Figure 2–10).

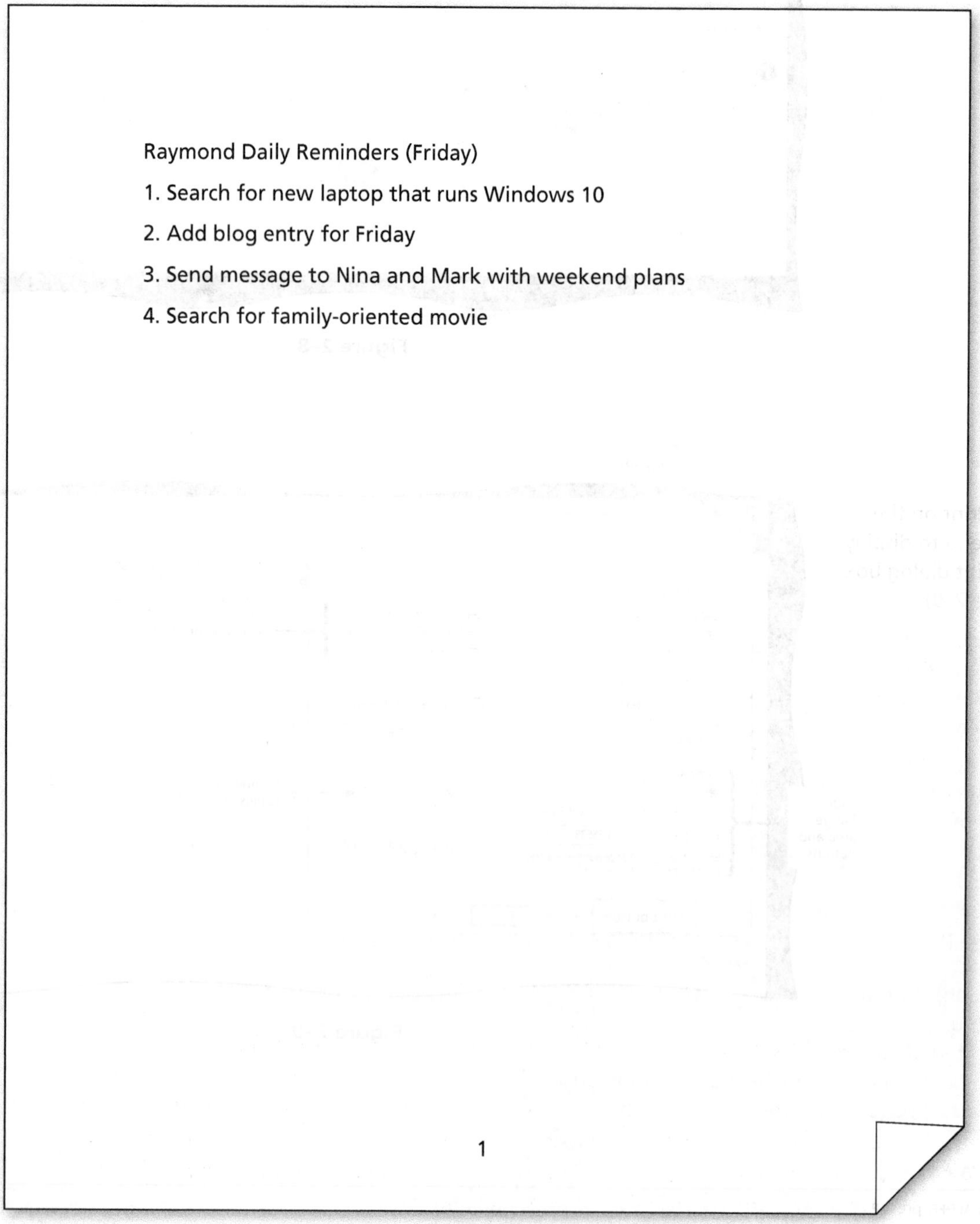

Raymond Daily Reminders (Friday)

1. Search for new laptop that runs Windows 10

2. Add blog entry for Friday

3. Send message to Nina and Mark with weekend plans

4. Search for family-oriented movie

1

Figure 2–10

To Edit a Document

For any document, edits can be as simple as correcting a spelling mistake or as complex as rewriting the entire document. *Why? Undoubtedly, you will want to make changes to a document after you have created it and saved it.* The following step edits the Raymond Daily Reminders (Friday) document by adding a new reminder.

- Click the blank line following the fourth daily reminder.

- Type `5. Register for next semester's classes` and then press the ENTER key (Figure 2–11).

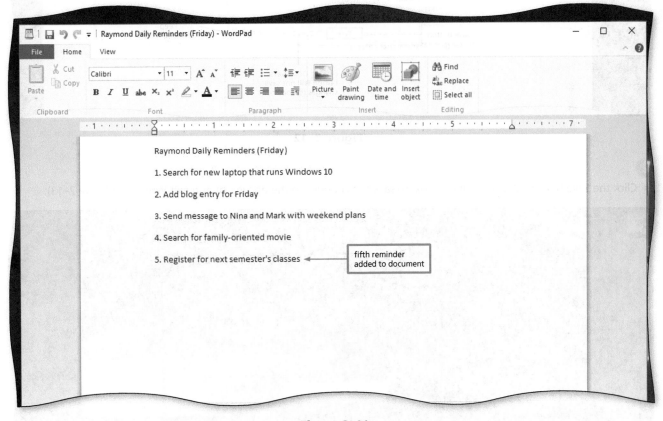

Figure 2–11

To Save and Close a Document

If you forget to save a document after you have edited it, a dialog box will be displayed asking if you want to save the changes. This is how many programs help protect you from losing your work. If you choose to not save the changes, then all edits you made since the last time you saved will be lost. If you click the Cancel button, the changes are not saved, but the document remains open and you can continue working. *Why? You have made several changes to the document since the last time you have saved it, so you want to save it again.* The following steps close and save the Raymond Daily Reminders (Friday) document.

1

- Click the Close button on the title bar to display the WordPad dialog box (Figure 2–12).

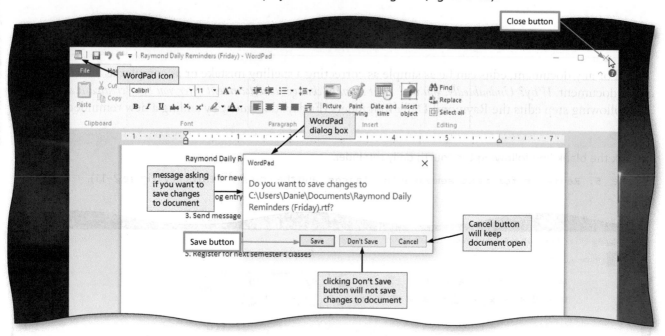

Figure 2–12

2

- Click the Save button (WordPad dialog box) to save the changes to the document and exit WordPad (Figure 2–13).

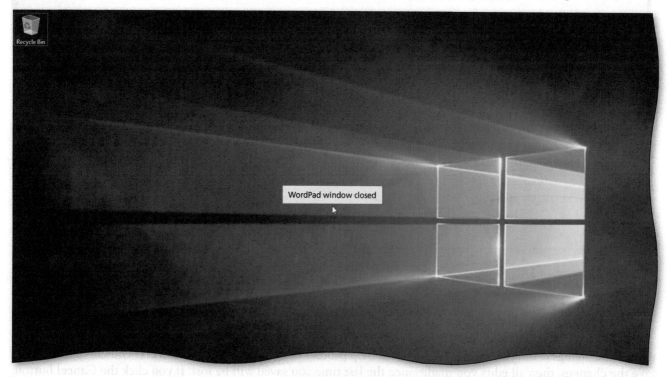

Figure 2–13

Other Ways

1. On title bar, double-click WordPad icon, click Save

2. On title bar, click WordPad icon, click Close, click Save

3. On File menu, click Exit, click Save (WordPad dialog box)

4. Press CTRL+S, press ALT+F, press X; or press ALT+F4, press ENTER

Creating a Document in the Documents Folder

After completing the reminders list for Mr. Raymond, the next step is to create a similar list for Ms. Estes. Running an app and then creating a document (the application-centric approach) was the method used to create the first document. Although the same method could be used to create the document for Ms. Estes, another method is to create the new document in the Documents folder without first running an app. Instead of running a program to create and modify a document, you first create a blank document directly in the Documents folder and then use the WordPad app to enter data into the document. This method, called the **document-centric approach**, will be used to create the document that contains the reminders for Ms. Estes.

To Open the Documents Folder

Why? *You first must open the Documents folder so that you can create a new file in that location.* The following step opens the Documents folder.

1

- Click the File Explorer button on the taskbar.
- If necessary, click Documents in the Quick access list in the Navigation pane (Figure 2–14).

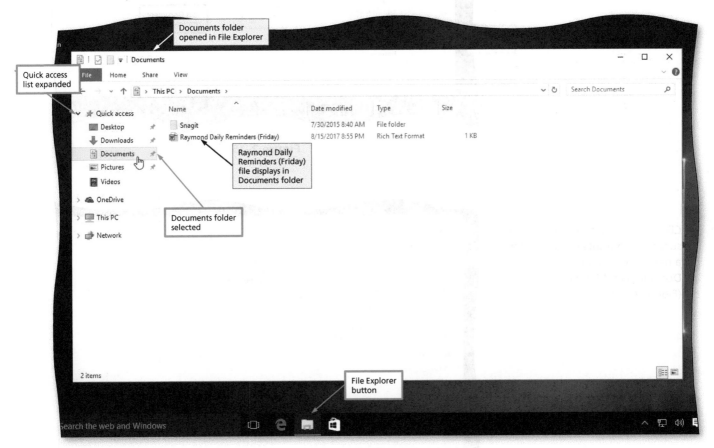

Figure 2–14

Other Ways

1. Right-click File Explorer button on taskbar, click Documents on shortcut menu

To Create a Blank Document in the Documents Folder

The phrase, creating a document in the Documents folder, might be confusing. The document you actually create contains no data; it is blank. You can think of it as placing a blank piece of paper with a name inside the Documents folder. The document has little value until you add text or other data to it. *Why? You need to instruct Windows to create the document so that you can prepare to enter content in the document.* The following steps create a blank document in the Documents folder to contain the daily reminders for Ms. Estes.

1

- Right-click an open area of the Documents folder to display the shortcut menu.

- Point to New on the shortcut menu to display the New submenu (Figure 2–15).

Q&A   Why does my shortcut menu look different?

Depending on the apps you have installed on your computer, the list of commands on the shortcut menu might differ.

Figure 2–15

2

- Click Text Document on the New submenu to display an entry for a new text document in the Documents folder window (Figure 2–16).

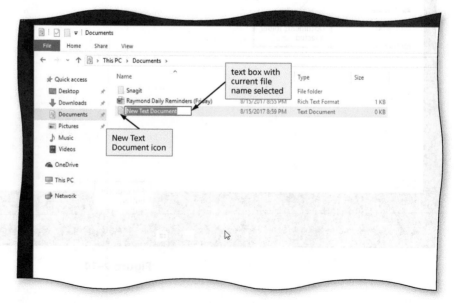

Figure 2–16

To Name a Document in the Documents Folder

In Figure 2–16, the default file name (New Text Document) is highlighted and the insertion point is blinking, indicating that you can type a new file name. ***Why?*** *After you create a blank document, you need to name the document so that it is easily identifiable.* The following step assigns the file name, Estes Daily Reminders (Friday), to the blank document you just created.

• Type **Estes Daily Reminders (Friday)** in the icon title text box and then press the ENTER key to assign a name to the new file in the Documents folder (Figure 2–17).

Figure 2–17

Other Ways

1. Right-click icon, click Rename on shortcut menu, type file name, press ENTER
2. Click icon to select icon, press F2, type file name, press ENTER
3. Click file name, pause, click file name, type new file name, press ENTER

To Open a Document with WordPad

Although you have created the Estes Daily Reminders (Friday) document, the document contains no text. To add text to the blank document, you must open the document. ***Why?*** *Because text files open with Notepad by default, you need to use the shortcut menu to open the file using WordPad.* The following steps open a document in WordPad.

• Right-click the Estes Daily Reminders (Friday) document icon to display the shortcut menu.

• Point to Open with on the shortcut menu to display the Open with submenu (Figure 2–18).

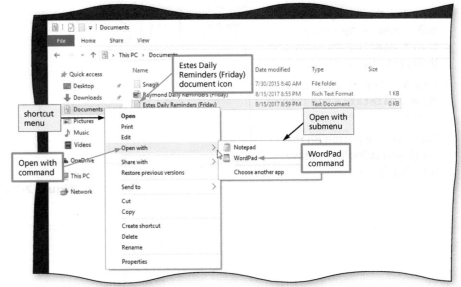

Figure 2–18

2

- Click WordPad on the Open with submenu to open the Estes Daily Reminders (Friday) document in WordPad (Figure 2–19).

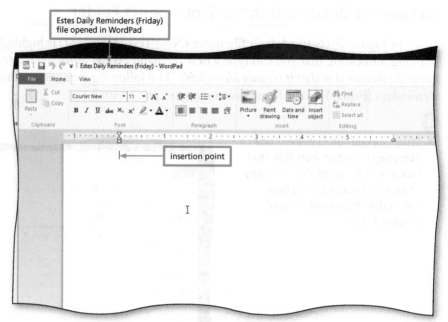

Figure 2–19

To Add Text to a Blank Document

Why? *After the document is open, you can add text by typing in the document.* The following step adds text to the Estes Daily Reminders (Friday) document and then saves the document.

1

- Type **Estes Daily Reminders (Friday)** and then press the ENTER key twice.

- Type **1. Videoconference with Karen Chang** and then press the ENTER key.

- Type **2. Email Aylin Rodriguez - Upcoming board meeting Tuesday** and then press the ENTER key.

- Type **3. Lunch with Sam – Noon, Cafeteria** and then press the ENTER key.

- Click the Save button on the Quick Access Toolbar to save the file (Figure 2–20).

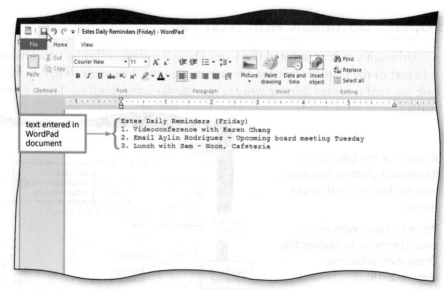

Figure 2–20

Why does the Estes Daily Reminders (Friday) document look different than the Raymond Daily Reminders (Friday) document?

The Estes Daily Reminders (Friday) file was first created and saved as a text file, which is different in appearance than the Raymond Daily Reminders (Friday) file, which first was saved in Rich Text Format (.rtf).

To Save a Text Document in Rich Text Format (.rtf)

Typing text in the Estes Daily Reminders (Friday) document modifies the document, which results in the need to save the document. If you make many changes to a document, you should save the document as you work. ***Why?*** *When you created the blank text document, Windows 10 assigned it the .txt file name extension, so you will need to use the Save as command to save it in Rich Text Format, which is WordPad's default format.* Using the Rich Text Format will allow you to use all of WordPad's features, including formatting options. The following steps save the document in Rich Text Format.

- Click the File tab to display the File menu.
- Point to the Save as arrow to display a list of available file types (Figure 2–21).

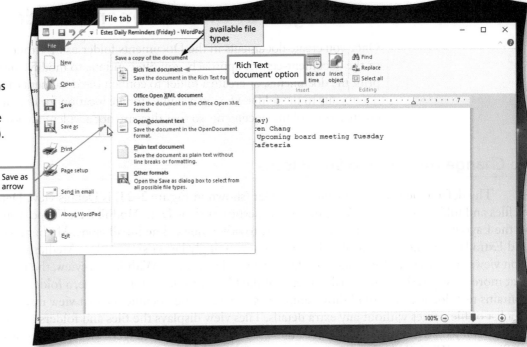

Figure 2–21

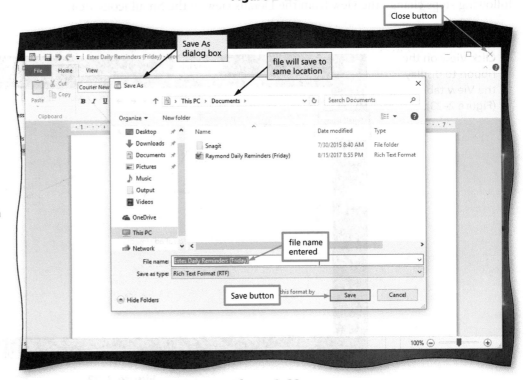

❷

- Click 'Rich Text document' to display the Save As dialog box.
- If necessary, type **Estes Daily Reminders (Friday)** in the File name box to change the file name (Figure 2–22).
- Click the Save button (Save As dialog box) to save the document in Rich Text Format.

Figure 2–22

To Close the Document

You have saved your changes to Estes Daily Reminders (Friday), and now you can close the document. The following step closes the Estes Daily Reminders (Friday) document.

1 Click the Close button on the WordPad title bar to close the document and exit WordPad.

Working with the Documents Folder

Once you create documents in the Documents folder using either the application-centric or the document-centric approach, you can continue to modify and save the documents, print the documents, or create a folder to contain the documents and then move the documents to the folder. Having a single storage location for documents makes it easy to create a copy of the documents so that they are not accidentally lost or damaged.

To Change the View to Small Icons

The default view in the Documents folder (shown in Figure 2–23) is Details view. Details view shows a list of files and folders, in addition to common properties, such as Date Modified and Type. You can use the buttons in the Layout group on the View tab to change to other views. The Small icons, Medium icons, Large icons, and Extra large icons views display the icons in increasingly larger sizes. When Medium, Large, or Extra large icon views are selected, Windows provides a live preview option. With live preview, the icons display images that more closely reflect the actual contents of the files or folders. For example, a folder icon for a folder that contains text documents would show sample pages from those documents. List view displays the files and folders as a list of file names without any extra details. Tiles view displays the files and folders as tiles, which consist of an icon and icon description. With all of these views, the default arrangement for the icons is to be alphabetical by file name. *Why? You want to change the layout of the icons in the Documents folder to one that suits your desires.* The following steps change the view from the Details view to the Small icons view.

1

• Click View on the ribbon to display the View tab (Figure 2–23).

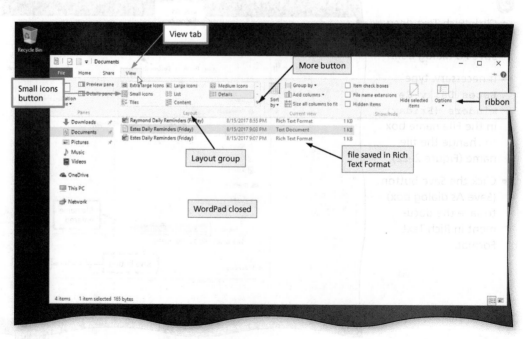

Figure 2–23

2

● Click the Small icons button (View tab | Layout group) to change the view to display small icons (Figure 2–24).

🔎 **Experiment**

● Click each of the buttons in the Layout group to see the various ways that Windows can display folder contents. After you have finished, be sure to select the Small icons view.

◁ | What if I do not see the Small icons button?
Q&A | If you do not believe all the views are displaying in the Layout group, your screen resolution might be too low. To
display the remaining views, click the More button (View tab | Layout group) (shown in Figure 2–23) to display a
gallery with all the options.

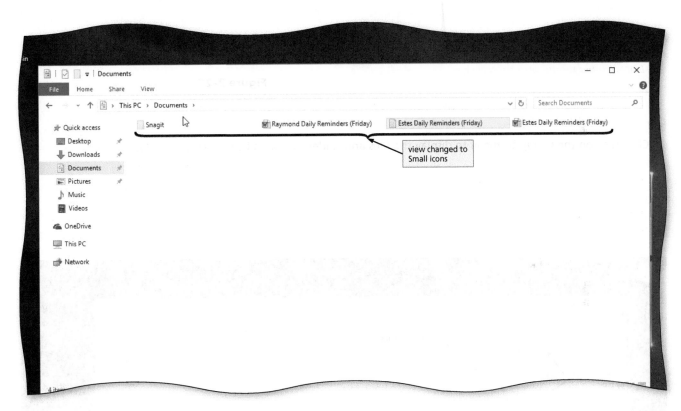

Figure 2–24

Other Ways

1. Right-click open space in Documents folder, point to View on shortcut menu, click Small icons on View submenu

To Arrange Items in Groups by File Type

Other methods are available for arranging the icons in the Documents folder. One practical arrangement is to display the icons in groups based on file type. This arrangement places files of the same type (File Folder, Text Documents, Microsoft Word Documents, Microsoft PowerPoint Presentations, and so on) in separate groups. *Why? When a window contains many files and folders, this layout makes it easier to find a particular file or folder quickly.* The following steps group the icons in the Documents folder by file type.

1

- Click View on the ribbon to display the View tab.

- Click the Group by button (View tab | Current view group) on the Group by menu (Figure 2–25).

Q&A What if the Group by button does not appear on the ribbon?

If your computer's screen resolution is low or the window is not large enough, the commands on the ribbon might be displayed differently. If you see a Current view button instead on the View tab, click the Current view button, click the Group by button on the Current view menu, and then click Type on the Group by submenu.

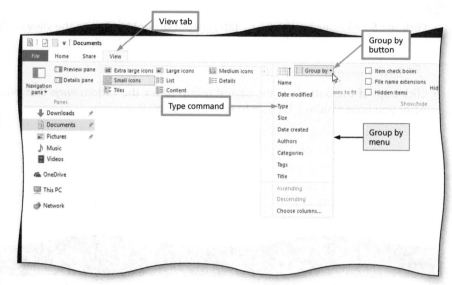

Figure 2–25

2

- Click Type on the Group by menu to display the files and folders grouped by type (Figure 2–26).

Q&A Can I group the files and folders in other ways?

You can group the files by any of the options on the Group by menu. This includes options such as Name, Date modified, Type, and Size. To remove the groupings, select (None) on the Group by menu. The Ascending and Descending options change the order of the groups from alphabetical order to reverse alphabetical order.

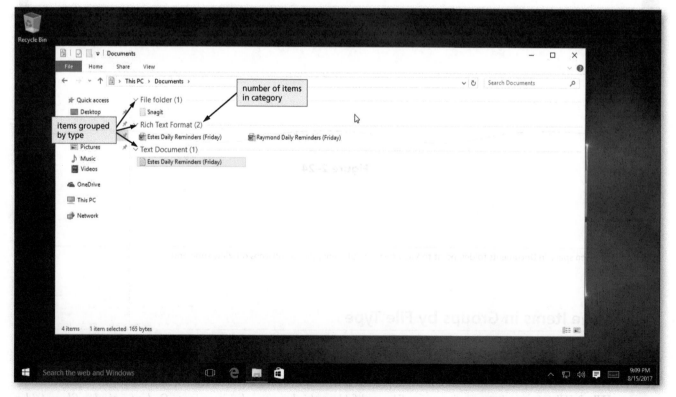

Figure 2–26

Other Ways

1. Right-click empty area of Documents folder, point to Group by on shortcut menu, click Type on Group by submenu

To Change to Medium Icons View

The following steps change the view to Medium icons.

1 Click View on the ribbon to display the View tab.

2 Click Medium icons (View tab | Layout group) to change the view to Medium icons view (Figure 2–27).

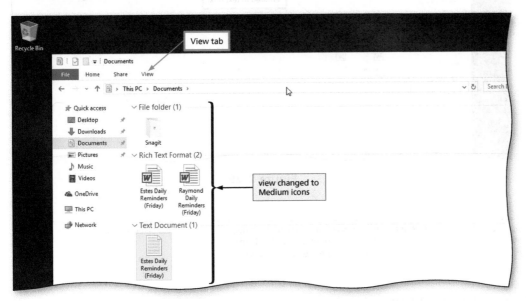

Figure 2–27

To Create and Name a Folder in the Documents Folder

Windows 10 allows you to place one or more documents into a folder in much the same manner as you might take a document written on a piece of paper and place it in a file folder. You want to keep the Raymond and Estes documents together so that you can find and easily distinguish them from other documents stored in the Documents folder. *Why?* *To keep multiple documents together in one place, you first must create a folder in which to store them.* The following steps create and name a folder titled Daily Reminders in the Documents folder to store the Raymond Daily Reminders (Friday) and Estes Daily Reminders (Friday) documents.

1

• Click the New folder button on the Quick Access Toolbar to create a new folder (Figure 2–28).

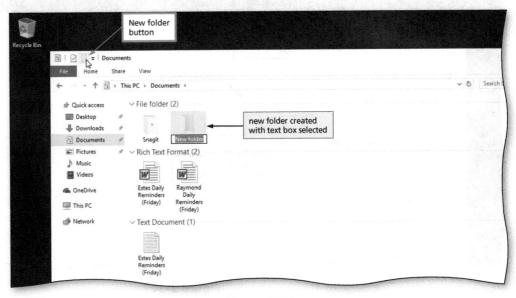

Figure 2–28

2

- Type **Daily Reminders** in the icon title text box and then press the ENTER key to name the folder and store the folder in the Documents folder (Figure 2–29).

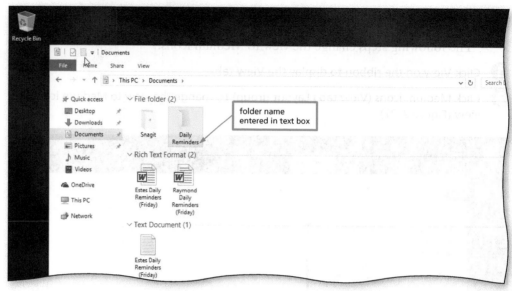

Figure 2–29

Other Ways

| 1. Click New folder button (Home tab | New group), type file name, press ENTER | 2. Right-click open space in Documents folder, point to New on shortcut menu, click Folder on New submenu, type file name, press ENTER | 3. Press CTRL+SHIFT+N |

To Move a Document into a Folder

The ability to organize documents and files within folders allows you to keep the Documents folder organized when using Windows 10. **Why?** *After you create a folder in the Documents folder, the next step is to move documents into the folder.* The following steps move the Raymond Daily Reminders (Friday) and the Estes Daily Reminders (Friday) documents into the Daily Reminders folder.

1

- Right-click and drag (also known as right-drag) the Raymond Daily Reminders (Friday) icon to the Daily Reminders folder icon to display the shortcut menu (Figure 2–30).

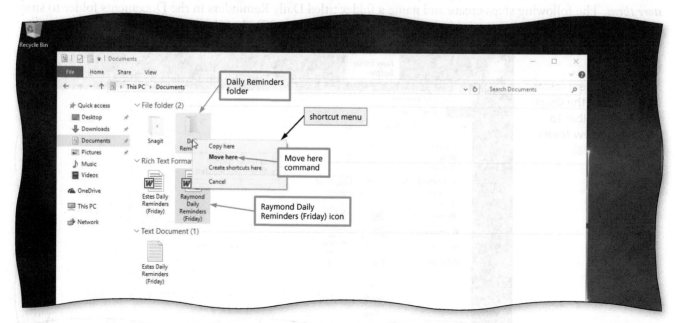

Figure 2–30

2

- Click the Move here command on the shortcut menu to move the Raymond Daily Reminders (Friday) icon to the Daily Reminders folder (Figure 2–31).

Q&A What are the other options on the shortcut menu?

When you right-drag, a shortcut menu is displayed that lists the available options. In this case, the options include Copy here, Move here, Create shortcuts here, and Cancel. Selecting Copy here creates a copy of the Raymond document in the Daily Reminders folder, Create shortcuts here puts a link to the Raymond document (not the file or a copy of the file) in the Daily Reminders folder, and Cancel terminates the right-drag process. The options on the shortcut menu might change, depending on the type of file and where you are dragging it.

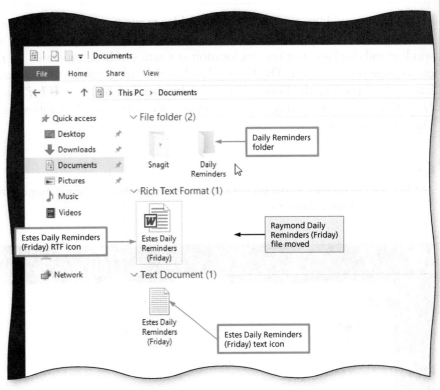

Figure 2–31

3

- Right-drag the Estes Daily Reminders (Friday) RTF icon to the Daily Reminders icon and move it to the Daily Reminders folder.

- Right-drag the Estes Daily Reminders (Friday) text icon to the Daily Reminders icon and move it to the Daily Reminders folder (Figure 2–32).

Q&A What happened to the Rich Text Document and Text Document groups?

The documents have been moved to the Daily Reminders folder, so the groups no longer were needed. Only if other RTF and text documents were contained in the Documents folder would the groupings remain.

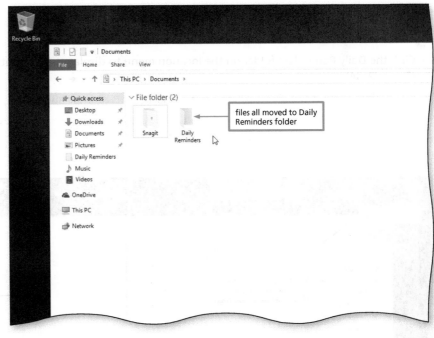

Figure 2–32

Other Ways

1. Drag document icon to folder icon

2. Right-click document icon, click Cut on shortcut menu, right-click folder icon, click Paste on shortcut menu

To Change Location Using the Address Bar

If you would like to navigate to the folder to see if your files are there, you have several ways to do this. One way in Windows 10 is to use the address bar. The address bar appears at the top of the Documents folder window and displays your current location as a series of links separated by arrows. By clicking the arrows, you can change your location. The Forward and Back buttons can be used to navigate through the locations you have visited, just like the Forward and Back buttons in a browser. *Why? You would like to view the contents of the Daily Reminders folder by changing the location in the address bar.* The following steps change your location to the Daily Reminders folder.

1

- Click the Documents arrow on the address bar to display a location menu that contains a list of folders in the Documents folder (Figure 2–33).

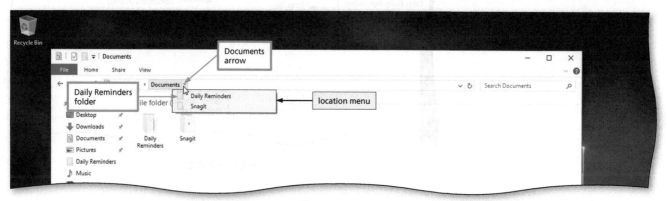

Figure 2–33

2

- Click the Daily Reminders folder on the location menu to display the contents of the Daily Reminders folder (Figure 2–34).

Q&A
What should I do if the arrow to the right of Documents did not appear?

If the arrow did not appear, double-click the Daily Reminders folder in the Documents folder to display the contents of the Daily Reminders folder.

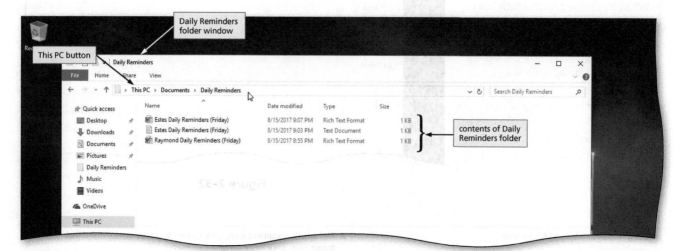

Figure 2–34

3

- Click the This PC button (shown in Figure 2–34) on the address bar to switch to the This PC window (Figure 2–35).

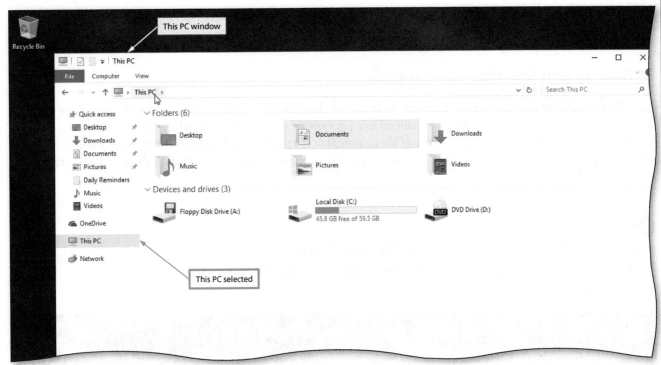

Figure 2–35

4

- Click the arrow to the right of This PC on the address bar to display a location menu (Figure 2–36).

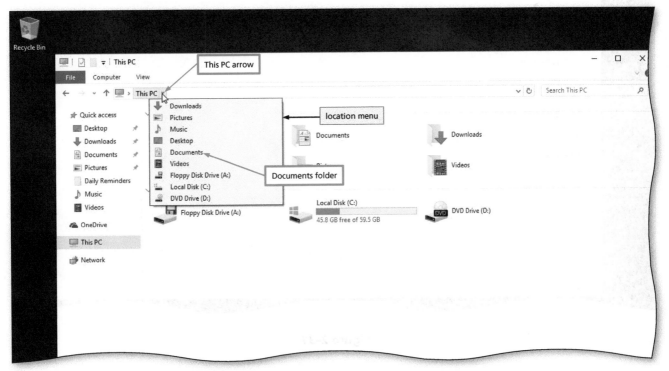

Figure 2–36

- Click Documents on the location menu to move to the Documents folder.
- Click the Documents arrow to display a location menu.
- Click the Daily Reminders folder on the location menu to move to the Daily Reminders folder.

To Display and Use the Preview Pane

Now that you are viewing the contents of the Daily Reminders folder, you can add a Preview pane to the layout, which will provide you with an enhanced live preview of your documents. *Why? When you select a document, the Preview pane displays a live preview of the document to the right of the list of files in the folder window.* The following steps add the Preview pane to the layout of the Daily Reminders folder and then display a live preview of the Raymond document.

- Click View on the ribbon to display the View tab (Figure 2–37).
- Click the Preview pane button (View tab | Panes group) to display the Preview pane.

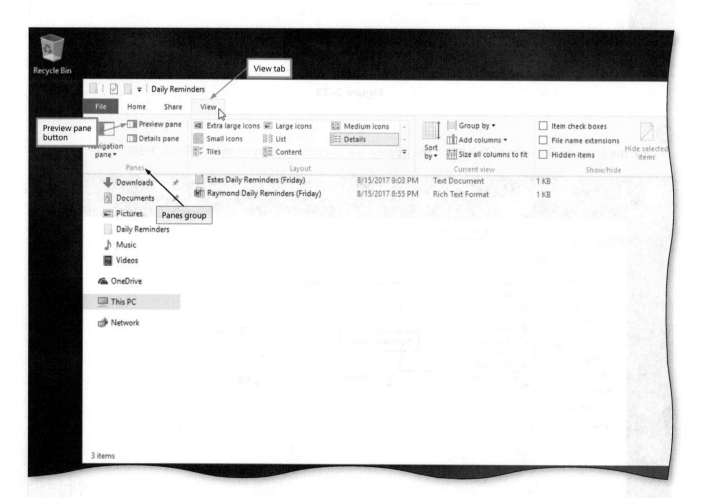

Figure 2–37

2

- Click the Raymond Daily Reminders (Friday) document icon on the right to display a preview of the document in the Preview pane (Figure 2–38).

🔍 **Experiment**

- Select different documents to display their preview in the Preview pane. When you have finished, select the Raymond Daily Reminders (Friday) document.

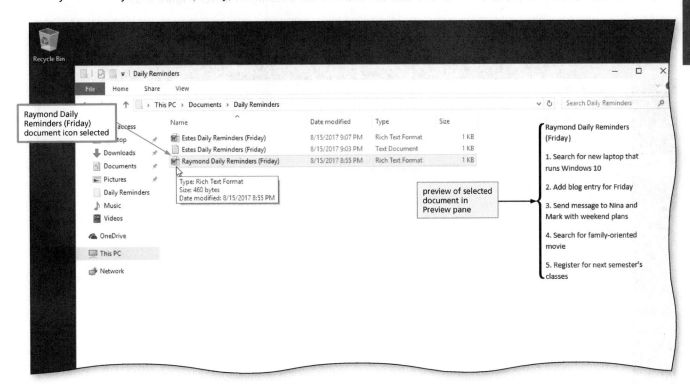

Figure 2–38

Other Ways

1. Press ALT+V, press P   2. Press ALT+P

To Close the Preview Pane

After verifying that your files are in the Daily Reminders folder, you can close the Preview pane and then use the address bar to return to the Documents folder. The following steps close the Preview pane.

1 Click View on the ribbon to display the View tab.

2 Click the Preview pane button (View tab | Panes group) to close the Preview pane.

Other Ways

1. Press ALT+V, press P

To Change Location Using the Back Button on the Address Bar

In addition to clicking the arrows in the address bar, you also can change locations by using the Back and Forward buttons. *Why? Clicking the Back button allows you to return to a location that you previously have visited.* The following step changes your location to the Documents folder.

• Click the Back button on the address bar one time to return to the Documents folder (Figure 2–39).

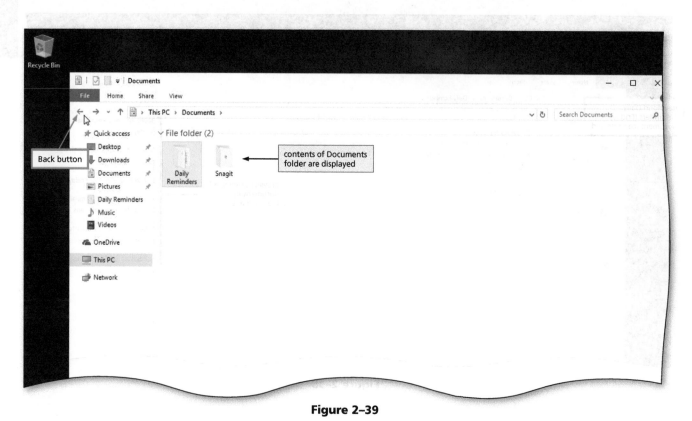

Figure 2–39

Creating Folder Shortcuts

One way to customize Windows 10 is to use shortcuts to run apps and open files or folders. A shortcut is a link to any object on the computer or on a network, such as an app, a file, a folder, a webpage, a printer, or another computer or mobile device. Placing a shortcut to a folder on the Start menu or on the desktop can make it easier to locate and open the folder.

A shortcut icon is not the actual document or app. You do not actually place the folder on the menu; instead, you place a shortcut icon that links to the folder on the menu. When you delete a shortcut, you delete the shortcut icon but do not delete the actual folder, document, or app; they remain on the hard drive.

To Pin a Folder to the Start Menu

Why? Pinning the Daily Reminders folder to the Start menu will enable easier access to the folder, instead of having to open the File Explorer window and navigate to the folder each time. The following steps pin the Daily Reminders folder to the Start menu.

1

- Right-click the Daily Reminders folder to display a shortcut menu (Figure 2–40).

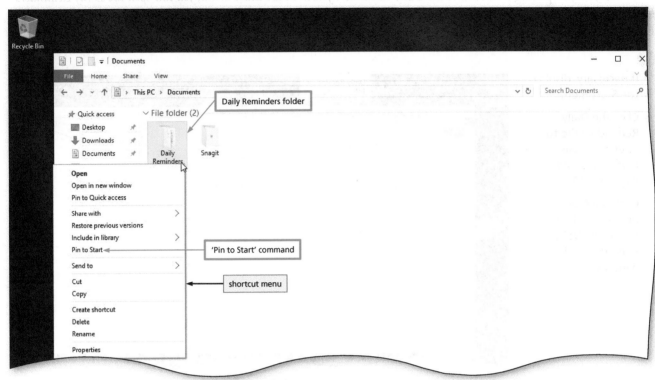

Figure 2–40

2

- Click 'Pin to Start' on the shortcut menu to pin the Daily Reminders folder to the Start menu.
- Click the Start button to display the Start menu so that you can see the Daily Reminders folder icon pinned to the Start menu. You might have to scroll to see the pinned folder (Figure 2–41).

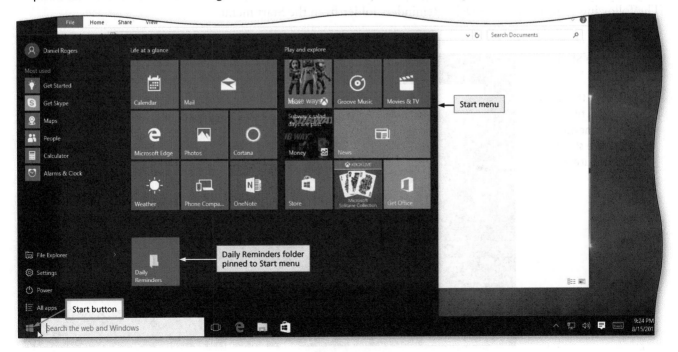

Figure 2–41

To Open a Folder Using a Pinned Icon on the Start Menu

Why? After placing a shortcut to the Daily Reminders folder on the Start menu, you can open the Daily Reminders folder by clicking the Start button and then clicking the Daily Reminders tile. The following step opens the Daily Reminders folder window from the Start menu and then closes the window.

- If necessary, display the Start menu.
- Click the Daily Reminders tile to open the Daily Reminders folder (Figure 2–42).
- Click the Close button on the title bar of the Daily Reminders folder window.

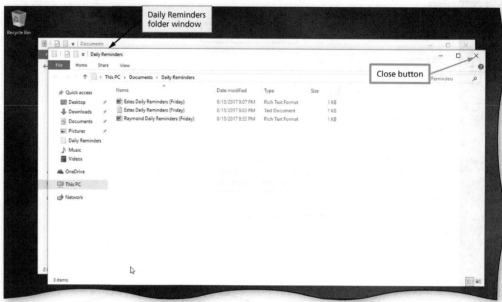

Figure 2–42

To Remove a Pinned Folder Icon from the Start Menu

The capability of adding shortcuts to and removing them from the Start menu provides great flexibility when customizing Windows 10. Just as you can add shortcuts to the Start menu, you also can remove them. *Why? If you find that you are no longer using a pinned icon on the Start menu, you should remove it to minimize clutter.* The following steps remove the Daily Reminders folder from the Start menu.

- Display the Start menu.
- Right-click the Daily Reminders tile on the Start menu to display the shortcut menu (Figure 2–43).

Figure 2–43

2

- Click 'Unpin from Start' on the shortcut menu to remove the Daily Reminders shortcut from the Start menu (Figure 2–44).

- Click somewhere on the desktop to close the Start menu.

Figure 2–44

To Create a Shortcut on the Desktop

You also can create shortcuts directly on the desktop. It is best that only shortcuts be placed on the desktop rather than actual folders and files. *Why? This is to maximize the efficiency of file and folder searching, which will be covered in a later module.* The following steps create a shortcut for the Daily Reminders folder on the desktop.

1

- Right-click the Daily Reminders folder to display the shortcut menu.

- Point to Send to on the shortcut menu to display the Send to submenu (Figure 2–45).

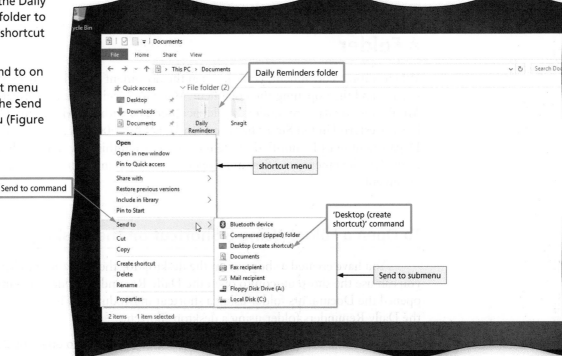

Figure 2–45

2

- Click 'Desktop (create shortcut)' on the Send to submenu to create a shortcut on the desktop.
- Close the Documents folder window (Figure 2–46).

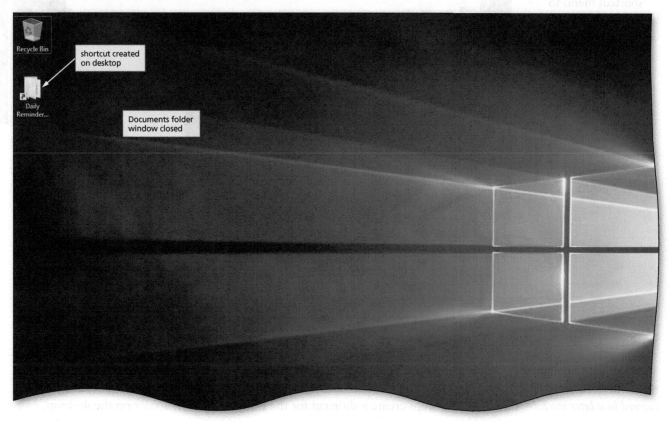

Figure 2–46

Opening and Modifying Documents within a Folder

When editing a document, you can open the document directly instead of first running the app and then opening the document. You have received new information to add to Mr. Raymond's daily reminders. A videoconference with the Marketing Department in the western United States has been scheduled for 1:00 p.m., and the Marketing Department must be notified of the meeting. To add this new item to the daily reminders document, you first must open the Daily Reminders folder that contains the document.

To Open a Folder Using a Shortcut on the Desktop

You have created a shortcut on the desktop for the Daily Reminders folder, so you can use the shortcut icon to open the Daily Reminders folder the same way you opened the Documents folder using a shortcut in Module 1. The following step opens the Daily Reminders folder using a desktop shortcut.

1 Double-click the Daily Reminders shortcut on the desktop to open the Daily Reminders folder.

To Open and Modify a Document in a Folder

Why? *You want to perform additional modifications to the Raymond Daily Reminders (Friday) file.* The following steps open the Raymond Daily Reminders (Friday) document and add new text about the videoconference.

1

- Open the Raymond Daily Reminders (Friday) document in WordPad.

2

- Move the insertion point to the blank line below item 5 in the document.

- Type `6. Notify Marketing - Videoconference at 1:00 p.m.` and then press the ENTER key to modify the Raymond Daily Reminders (Friday) document (Figure 2–47).

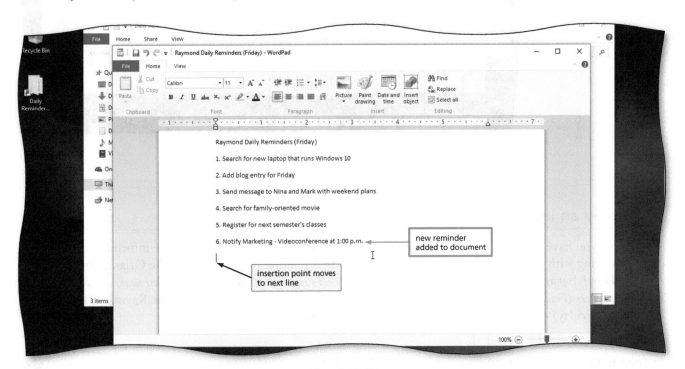

Figure 2–47

To Open and Modify Multiple Documents

Windows 10 allows you to have more than one document open and one app running at the same time so that you can work on multiple documents. The concept of multiple apps running at the same time is called **multitasking.** To illustrate how you can work with multiple windows open at the same time, you now will edit the Estes Daily Reminders (Friday) document to include a reminder to talk to Scott about McKenzie's birthday party. You will not have to close the Raymond Daily Reminders (Friday) document. The following steps open the Estes Daily Reminders (Friday) document and add the new reminder.

1

- Open the Estes Daily Reminders (Friday) document in WordPad.

Q&A Why did the WordPad icon on the taskbar change?

When only one document is open in WordPad, the WordPad icon appears like a single button. If multiple documents are open, the icon changes to appear as a stacked button to indicate more than one document is open.

- Move the insertion point to the end of the document in the WordPad window.

- Type **4. Call Scott – Birthday party for McKenzie** and then press the ENTER key (Figure 2–48).

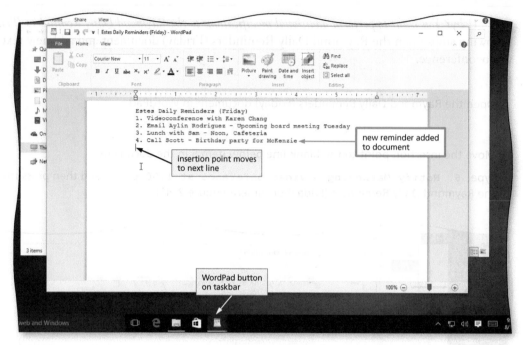

Figure 2–48

To Display an Inactive Window

After you have modified the Estes Daily Reminders (Friday) document, you receive information that a dinner meeting with Jacob Patel has been scheduled for Mr. Raymond for 7:00 p.m. in the Orlando International Airport. ***Why?*** *You are directed to add this entry to Mr. Raymond's reminders. To do this, you must make the Raymond Daily Reminders (Friday) - WordPad window the active window.* The following steps make the Raymond Daily Reminders (Friday) - WordPad window active and enter the new reminder.

- Point to the WordPad app button on the taskbar to display a live preview of the two documents (Figure 2–49).

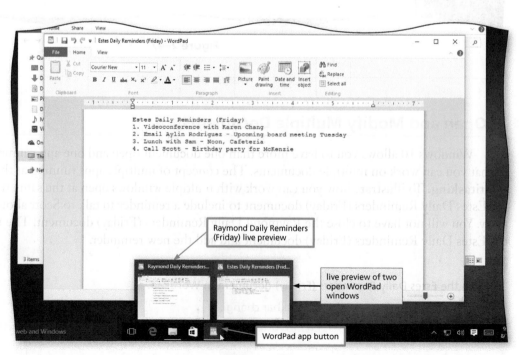

Figure 2–49

2

- Click the Raymond Daily Reminders (Friday) live preview to make it the active window (Figure 2–50).

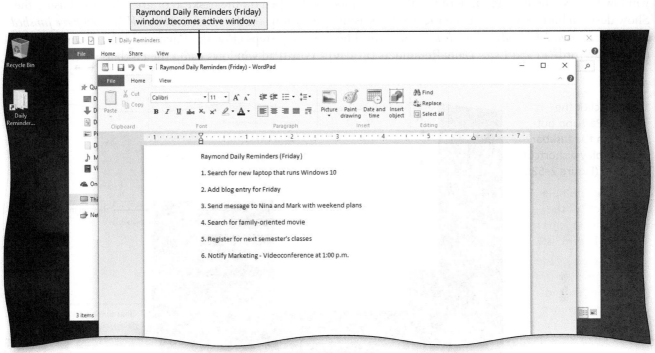

Figure 2–50

3

- When the window opens, position the insertion point at the end of the document, type 7. **Dinner with Jacob Patel - 7:00 p.m., Orlando International Airport** and then press the ENTER key to update the document (Figure 2–51).

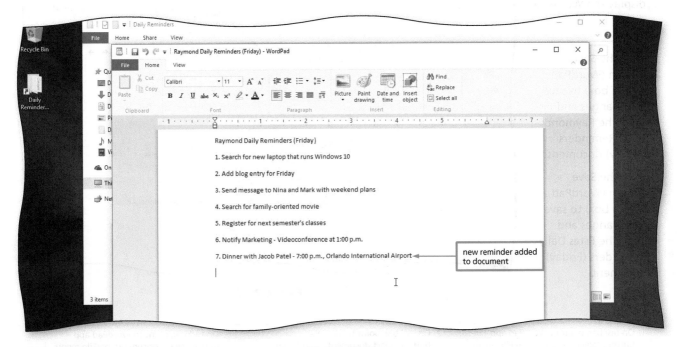

Figure 2–51

To Close Multiple Open Windows and Save Changes Using the Taskbar

If the windows are open on the desktop, you can click the Close button on the title bar of each open window to close them. Regardless of whether the windows are open on the desktop or are minimized using the Show desktop button, you can close the windows using the buttons on the taskbar. ***Why? When you have finished working with multiple windows, you should close them.*** The following steps close the Raymond Daily Reminders (Friday) - WordPad and Estes Daily Reminders (Friday) - WordPad windows using the taskbar.

• Right-click the WordPad app button on the taskbar to display a shortcut menu (Figure 2–52).

Q&A Why do multiple instances of the documents appear in the Recent list?

The list shows the files you recently have edited and does not remove duplicate listings. As a result, a document might appear in the list multiple times.

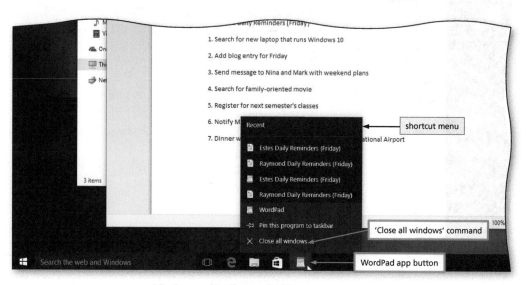

Figure 2–52

2

• Click 'Close all windows' on the shortcut menu to display the WordPad dialog box (Figure 2–53).

• Click the Save button (WordPad dialog box) to save the changes and close the Raymond Daily Reminders (Friday) document.

• Click the Save button (WordPad dialog box) to save the changes and close the Estes Daily Reminders (Friday) document.

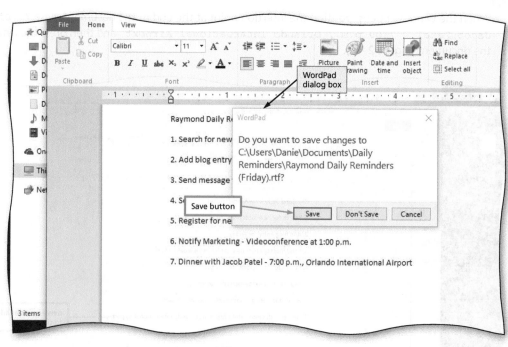

Figure 2–53

Other Ways

1. On taskbar, point to WordPad app button, select document, on File menu click Save (WordPad dialog box), click Close button on title bar

2. On taskbar, point to WordPad app button, select document, on title bar click Close button, click Save button (WordPad dialog box)

3. On taskbar, point to WordPad app button, select document, on File menu click Exit, click Save button (WordPad dialog box)

The Recycle Bin

Occasionally, you will want to delete files and folders from the Documents folder. Windows 10 offers three different techniques to perform this operation: (1) drag the object to the Recycle Bin, (2) right-drag the object to the Recycle Bin, and (3) right-click the object and then click Delete on the shortcut menu.

It is important to understand what you are doing when you delete a file or folder. When you delete a shortcut from the desktop, you delete only the shortcut icon and its reference to the file or folder. The file or folder itself is stored elsewhere on the hard drive or storage device and is not deleted. When you delete the icon for a file or folder (not a shortcut), the actual file or folder is deleted. A shortcut icon includes an arrow to indicate that it is a shortcut, whereas a file or folder does not have the arrow as part of its icon.

When you delete a file or folder, Windows 10 places these items in the Recycle Bin, which is an area on the hard drive that contains all the items you have deleted. If you are running low on hard drive space, one way to gain additional space is to empty the Recycle Bin. Up until the time you empty the Recycle Bin, you can recover deleted files. Even though you have this safety net, you should be careful whenever you delete anything from your computer.

To Move a Text File to the Recycle Bin

The following steps move the file to the Recycle Bin. ***Why?*** *You will not be using the Estes Daily Reminders (Friday) text file, so you will move it to the Recycle Bin.*

1

- If necessary, display the contents of the Daily Reminders folder.

- Drag the Estes Daily Reminders (Friday) text icon to the Recycle Bin. Do not release the mouse button (Figure 2–54).

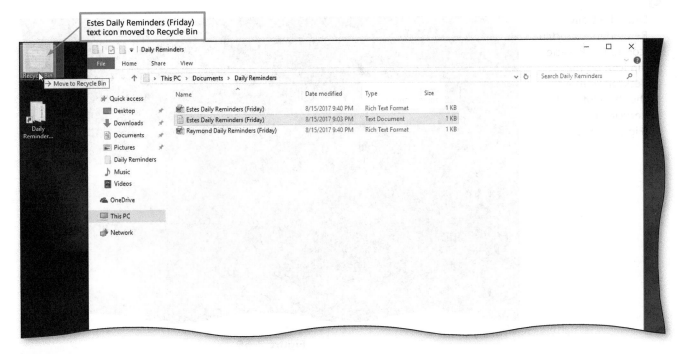

Figure 2–54

2

- Release the mouse button to move the Estes Daily Reminders (Friday) text file to the Recycle Bin (Figure 2–55).

- Click the Close button on the Daily Reminders window's title bar to close the Daily Reminders folder window.

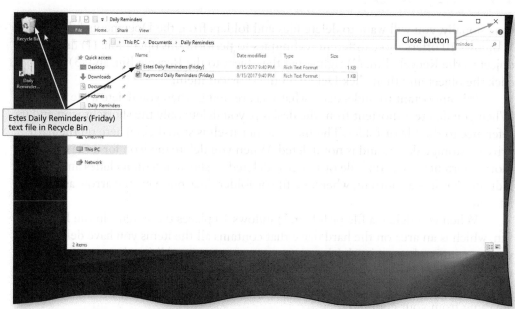

Figure 2–55

Other Ways

1. Select file, press DELETE

To Delete a Shortcut from the Desktop

Why? *You have finished working with the files in the Daily Reminders folder, so you can remove the shortcut from the desktop.* The following step removes the Daily Reminder folder shortcut from the desktop.

1

- Drag the Daily Reminders - Shortcut icon to the Recycle Bin icon on the desktop to move the shortcut to the Recycle Bin (Figure 2–56).

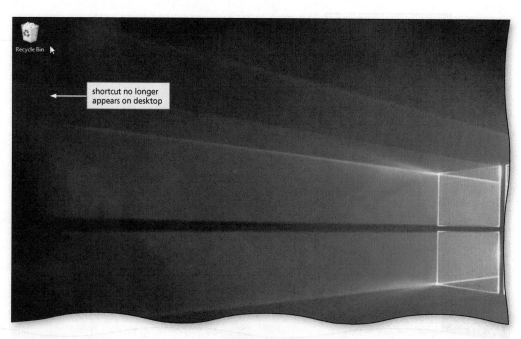

Figure 2–56

To Restore an Item from the Recycle Bin

The following steps restore the Daily Reminders - Shortcut icon to the desktop. *Why? At some point, you might discover that you accidentally deleted a shortcut, file, or folder that you did not want to delete. As long as you have not emptied the Recycle Bin, you can restore deleted files.*

1

- Double-click the Recycle Bin icon to open the Recycle Bin window.

- Click the Daily Reminders - Shortcut icon to select it (Figure 2–57).

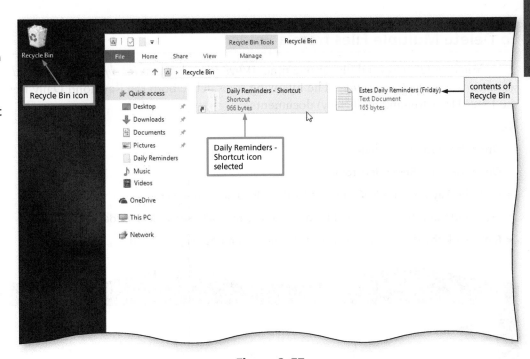

Figure 2–57

2

- Click Manage on the ribbon to display the Recycle Bin Tools Manage tab (Figure 2–58).

- Click the 'Restore the selected items' button to restore the Daily Reminders - Shortcut icon to its previous location. In this case, the icon is restored to the desktop.

- Close the Recycle Bin window.

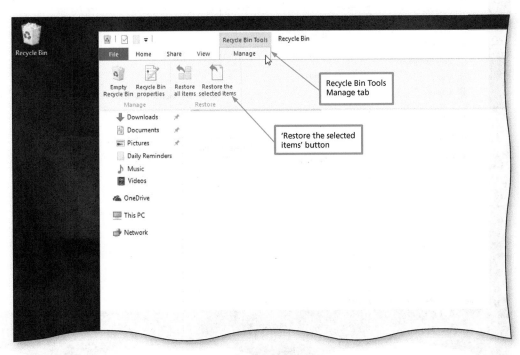

Figure 2–58

To Delete a Shortcut from the Desktop

The following step deletes the Daily Reminders shortcut icon again so that you can leave the desktop how you found it.

 Drag the Daily Reminders - Shortcut icon to the Recycle Bin icon.

To Delete Multiple Files from a Folder

You can delete several files at one time. *Why? If you have several objects you want to delete in the same location, you can delete them all at one time.* The following steps delete both the Raymond Daily Reminders (Friday) and the Estes Daily Reminders (Friday) documents.

1

- Open the Documents folder.

- Open the Daily Reminders folder.

- Click the Raymond Daily Reminders (Friday) document to select it.

- Press and hold the CTRL key and then click the Estes Daily Reminders (Friday) document.

- Right-click the documents to display the shortcut menu (Figure 2–59).

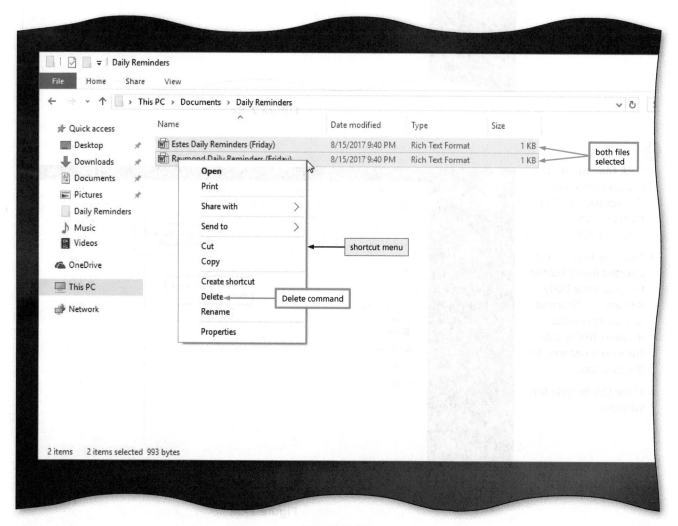

Figure 2–59

②

• Click Delete on the shortcut menu to delete the selected items (Figure 2–60).

Figure 2–60

To Delete a Folder from the Documents Folder and Empty the Recycle Bin

You also can delete folders from the Documents folder using the same method. The following steps delete the Daily Reminders folder and empty the Recycle Bin.

① Click Documents in the Navigation pane.

② Delete the Daily Reminders folder.

③ Close the Documents folder.

④ Right-click the Recycle Bin to display the shortcut menu.

⑤ Click 'Empty Recycle Bin' on the shortcut menu.

⑥ Click the Yes button (Delete Multiple Items dialog box) to delete the contents of the Recycle Bin permanently.

To Sign Out of an Account and Shut Down the Computer

You have completed the work with Windows. The following steps end the session by signing out of your account and then shutting down the computer.

1 Display the Start menu.

2 Click the name identifying your user account and then click Sign out.

3 Click the lock screen to display the sign-in screen.

4 Click the Shut down button.

5 Click the Shut down command on the Shut down menu to shut down the computer.

Summary

In this module, you learned how to create WordPad documents using both the application-centric approach and the document-centric approach. You moved these documents to the Documents folder and then modified and printed them. You created a new folder in the Documents folder and placed documents in the folder. You worked with multiple documents open at the same time. You pinned a folder to the Start menu and added a shortcut on the desktop. Using various methods, you deleted shortcuts, documents, and a folder. Finally, you learned how to work with the Recycle Bin and restore items that have been deleted.

Apply Your Knowledge

Reinforce the skills and apply the concepts you learned in this module.

Creating a Document with WordPad

Instructions: Use WordPad to create the shopping list shown in Figure 2–61.

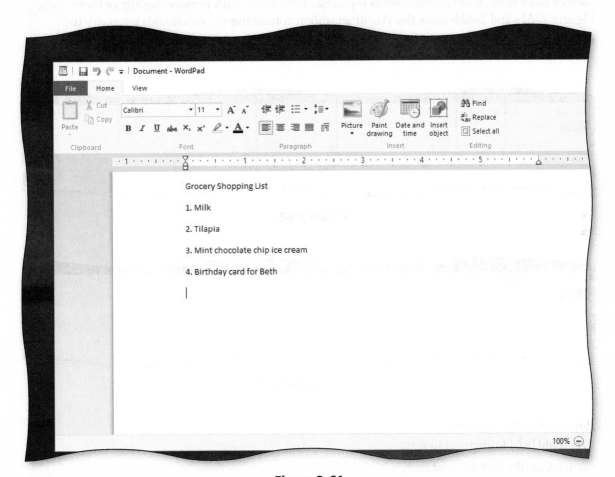

Figure 2–61

Perform the following tasks:
1. Run WordPad.
2. Type **Grocery Shopping List** and then press the ENTER key.
3. Type **1. Milk** and then press the ENTER key.
4. Type **2. Tilapia** and then press the ENTER key.
5. Type **3. Mint chocolate chip ice cream** and then press the ENTER key.
6. Type **4. Birthday card for Beth** and then press the ENTER key.
7. Click the File tab and then click Print to display the Print dialog box. Click the Print button (Print dialog box) to print the document.
8. Click the File tab and then save the file in Rich Text Format.
9. Save the document in the Documents folder with the file name, Shopping List.
10. Exit WordPad, and close any open windows.

Extend Your Knowledge

Extend the skills you learned in this module and experiment with new skills.

Using Help

Instructions: Use WordPad to perform the following tasks. Write the steps you take to perform each of these skills. Use Help resources if you need assistance with performing any of these skills. Figures 2–62a and 2–62b show the WordPad ribbon containing the commands necessary to perform some of the functions listed below.

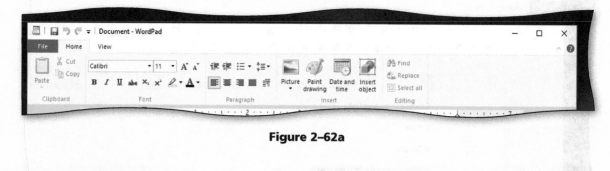

Figure 2–62a

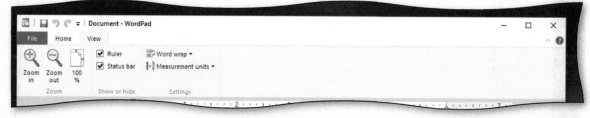

Figure 2–62b

Perform the following tasks:
1. Apply bold formatting to text.
2. Change the font color of text.
3. Right-align text.
4. Insert a picture.
5. Enable and disable wordwrap.
6. Change the font size.
7. Create a bulleted list.
8. Create a numbered list.
9. Insert the date and time.
10. Change the font size of text.
11. Undo the last action.
12. Zoom in.
13. Zoom out.
14. Display information about WordPad.
15. Obtain Help about WordPad.

Expand Your World

Create a solution that uses cloud or web technologies by learning and investigating on your own from general guidance.

Selecting a Smartphone

Instructions: You want to purchase a new smartphone and decide to research them online.

Perform the following tasks:

1. Open a new WordPad document. Save the document in the Documents folder with the file name, Smartphones.
2. Use Microsoft Edge to locate information online about three different smartphones you would consider purchasing.
3. In the WordPad document, record information about each smartphone. For each smartphone, include the operating system (such as Windows, iOS, or Android), the screen size, storage space, supported wireless carrier(s), and price. In addition, include three top features you like about the phone.
4. Save the changes to the document.
5. Print the document.
6. Close the document.

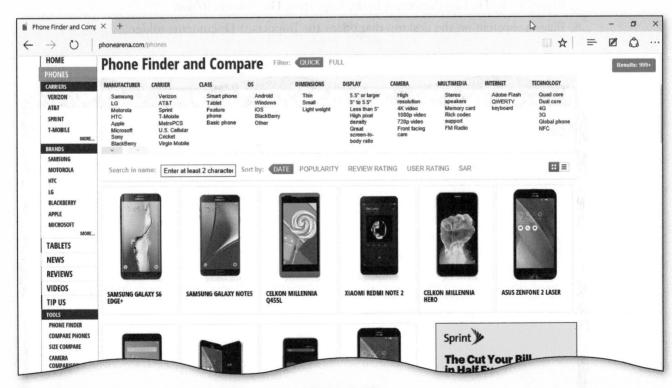

Figure 2–63

In the Labs

Design, create, modify, and/or use files following the guidelines, concepts, and skills presented in this module. Labs 1 and 2, which increase in difficulty, require you to create solutions based on what you learned in the module; Lab 3 requires you to apply your creative thinking and problem-solving skills to design and implement a solution.

Lab 1: Creating a To-Do List

Problem: You have a schedule of tasks to complete today. You decide to use WordPad to create a to-do list.

Perform the following tasks.

1. Open a new WordPad document. Save the document on the desktop using the file name, To-Do List. *Hint:* When saving, save on the desktop.
2. Type the text shown in Figure 2–64.
3. Save changes to the document.
4. Print the document.
5. Close the document.
6. Create a folder in the Documents folder named, Important Documents.
7. Place the To-Do List document in the Important Documents folder.
8. Place a shortcut on the desktop that opens the Important Documents folder.

Figure 2–64

Lab 2: **Creating, Saving, and Printing Automobile Information Documents**

Problem: For eight months, you have accumulated data about your automobile. Some of the information is written on pieces of paper, while the rest is in the form of receipts. You have decided to organize this information using your computer or mobile device. You create the document shown in Figures 2–65 and 2–66 using the application-centric approach and WordPad.

Perform the following tasks:
1. Create a new WordPad document. Save the document in the Documents folder with the file name, Automobile Information.

2. Enter the text shown in Figure 2–65.

3. Save the document.

4. Print the document.

5. Create a folder in the Documents folder called Automobile Documents.

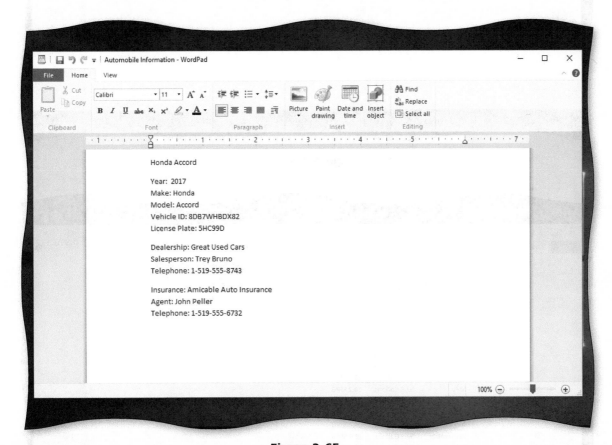

Figure 2–65

6. Move the Automobile Information document to the Automobile Documents folder.

7. Create the Phone Numbers document (Figure 2–66a), the Automobile Gas Mileage document (Figure 2–66b), and the Automobile Maintenance document (Figure 2–66c) on the desktop.

8. Save each document into the Documents folder.

9. Print each document.

10. Place each document in the Automobile Documents folder.

Continued >

In the Labs *continued*

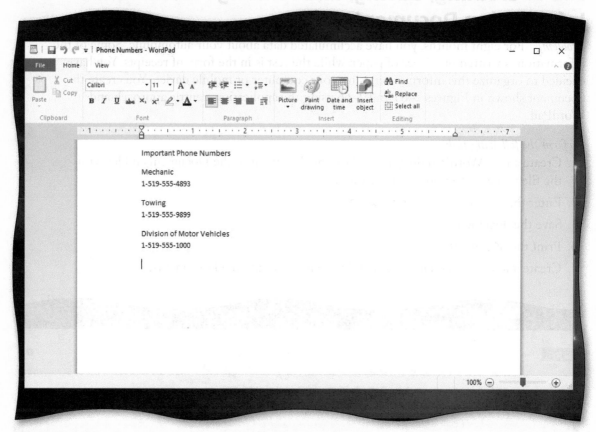

Figure 2–66a

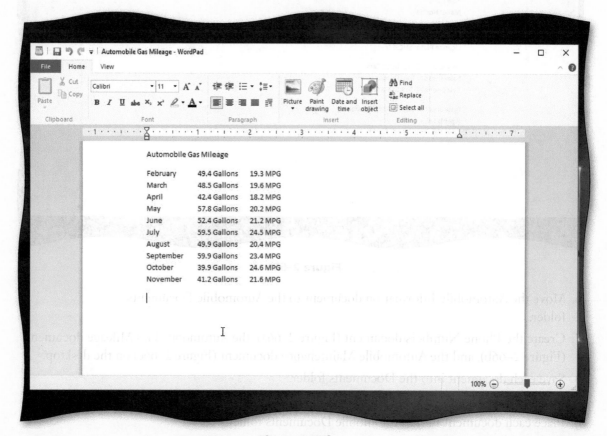

Figure 2–66b

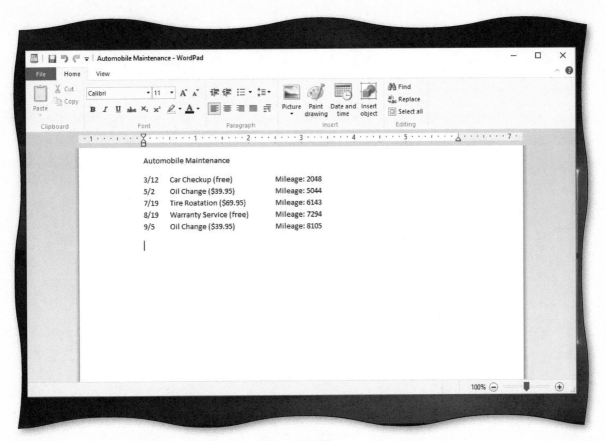

Figure 2–66c

Lab 3: **Consider This: Your Turn**

Posting Company Hiring Procedures

Problem: Your employer is concerned that some people in the company are not uniformly following the same policy when hiring new employees. She has prepared a list of steps she would like everyone to follow when hiring a new employee: (1) determine your department's need for a new employee, (2) justify the need for a new employee to executive management, (3) advertise the position in at least three locations, (4) interview no less than three top candidates, and (5) submit hiring recommendation to executive management and Human Resources department.

Part 1:   Your employer has asked you to use WordPad to prepare a copy of the steps above that outline the hiring process so that it can be posted in every department. Save and print the document. After you have printed one copy of the document, try experimenting with different WordPad features to make the list more eye-catching. Save and print a revised copy of the document.

Part 2:   You made several decisions while performing research for this assignment. What decisions did you make? What was the rationale behind these decisions? How did you learn how to format a WordPad document?

3 File and Folder Management

Objectives

You will have mastered the material in this module when you can:

- View the contents of a drive and folder using the This PC window
- View the properties of files and folders
- Find files and folders from a folder window
- Use Shake and Snap to manipulate windows
- View, copy, and move contents of the Pictures folder

- View and change the properties of a picture
- Run and use the Photos app
- View pictures as a slide show
- Compress a folder and view the contents of a compressed folder
- Back up files and folders using OneDrive

Introduction

In Module 2, you used Windows to create documents on the desktop and work with documents and folders in the Documents folder. Windows also allows you to examine the files and folders on the computer in a variety of other ways, enabling you to choose the easiest and most accessible manner when working with a computer or mobile device. The This PC window and the Documents folder provide two ways for you to work with files and folders. In addition, the Pictures folder allows you to organize and share picture files, and the Music folder allows you to organize and share your music files.

BTW
Managing Windows
Having multiple windows open on the desktop can intimidate some users. Consider working in a maximized window, and when you want to switch to another open window, display that window instead.

This PC Window

As noted in the previous module, the desktop displays the File Explorer button. Clicking the File Explorer button opens the File Explorer window. Using the navigation bar, you can navigate to the This PC window that contains the storage devices that are installed on the computer. Windows uses folder windows to display the contents of the computer. A **folder window** consists of tabs at the top that display the ribbon with multiple commands, an address bar below the ribbon, a toolbar to the left of the address bar that contains buttons to help you navigate your computer's folder structure, a navigation pane on the left below the toolbar, a headings bar and list area on the right below the address bar, and a status bar at the bottom of the window. Depending upon which folder you are viewing — This PC, Documents, Pictures, and so on — the folder window will display the toolbar options that are most appropriate for working with the contents.

To Open and Maximize the This PC Window

The list area of the This PC window groups objects based upon their type. The Folders group lists folders you might access frequently, such as the Desktop, Documents, Downloads, Music, Pictures, and Videos folders. The 'Devices and drives' group contains the Local Disk (C:) icon that represents the hard drive on the computer. The **hard drive** is where you can store files and folders. Storing data on a hard drive is more convenient than storing data on a USB flash drive because the hard drive is readily available and generally has more available storage space. A computer always will have at least one hard drive, which normally is designated as drive C. On the computer represented by the This PC window in Figure 3–1, the icon consists of an image of a hard drive and a **drive label**, or title, Local Disk, and a drive letter (C:). The drive label can change and may differ depending upon the name assigned to the hard drive. For example, some people label their hard drive based upon usage; therefore, it could be called PRIMARY (C:), where PRIMARY is the label given to the hard drive, as it is the drive that houses the operating system and main apps. If you have another type of drive, such as an optical drive, installed in or connected to your computer, the drive also will appear in the 'Devices and drives' group. The Network locations group will appear if you are connected remotely to drives on computers in another location. The following step opens and maximizes the This PC window. *Why? This will allow you to view the computer's content in its entirety.*

- If necessary, sign in to your Windows account.
- Click the File Explorer button to open a File Explorer window.
- Click This PC in the navigation pane to open the This PC window. If necessary, maximize the This PC window (Figure 3–1).

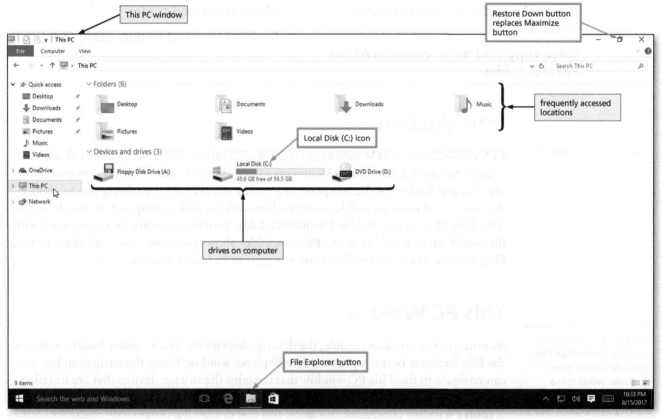

Figure 3–1

To Display Properties for the Hard Drive in the Details Pane

The details pane of a folder window displays the properties of devices, apps, files, and folders, which all are considered to be objects by Windows. Every object in Windows has properties that describe the object. A **property** is a characteristic of an object, such as the amount of storage space on a storage device or the number of items in a folder. The properties of each object will differ, and in some cases, you can change the properties of an object. *Why? For example, in the Local Disk (C:) properties, you could check the file system being used on the drive using the File system property. To determine the drive's capacity, you would view the Total size property.* The following steps display the properties for the Local Disk (C:) in the details pane of the This PC window.

- Click the 'Local Disk (C:)' icon to select the hard drive (Figure 3–2).

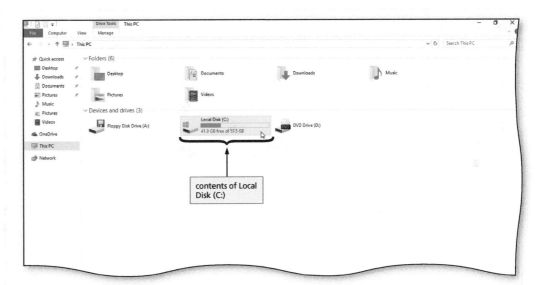

Figure 3–2

②

- Click View on the ribbon to display the View tab (Figure 3–3).

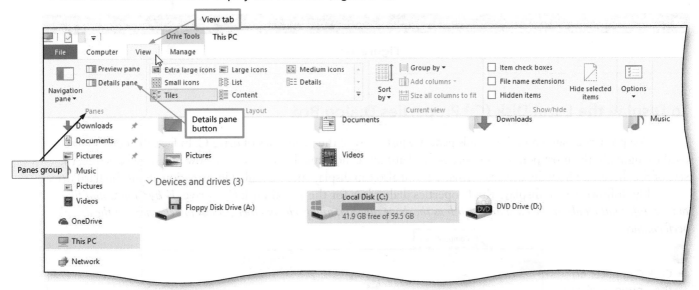

Figure 3–3

3

- Click the Details pane button (View tab | Panes group) to display the details pane (Figure 3–4).

🔍 Experiment

- See what properties are displayed for the other drives and devices shown. Click each one and note what properties appear in the details pane. Click 'Local Disk (C:)' when you are done.

Q&A Why do the properties of my drive differ from those in the figure?

The size and contents of your drive will be different from the one in the figure. As a result, the properties of the drive also will be different. Depending upon what has been installed on the drive and how it is formatted, the Space used, Space free, Total size, and File system properties will vary.

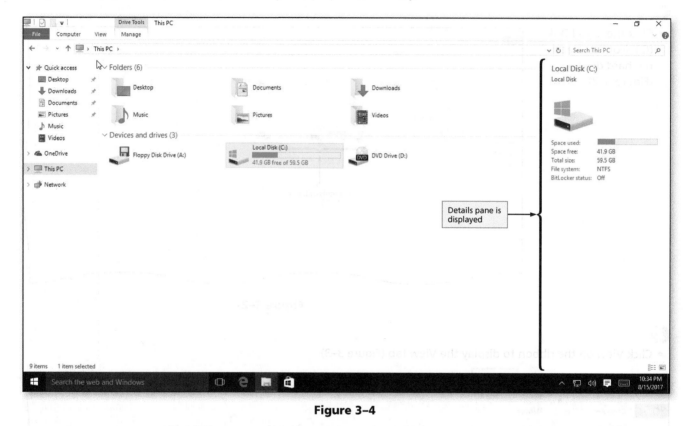

Figure 3–4

To Display the Local Disk (C:) Properties Dialog Box

The properties shown in the details pane are just a few of the properties of drive C. In fact, the details pane is used to highlight the most popular properties of a hard drive: how much space is used, how much space is free, the size of the drive, and how the drive is formatted. You also can display more detailed information about the hard drive.

The following step displays the Properties dialog box for the Local Disk (C:) drive. *Why? You would like to view information about the hard drive, such as the drive capacity, and perform other actions to help increase the drive's performance.*

1

- Click Computer on the ribbon to display the Computer tab (Figure 3–5).

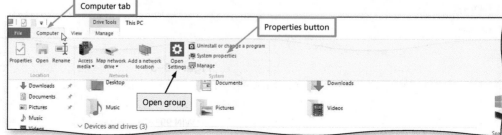

Figure 3–5

2

- Click the Properties button (Computer tab | Location group) to display the Local Disk (C:) Properties dialog box (Figure 3–6).

Q&A What sheets are in the Local Disk (C:) Properties dialog box?

The Tools sheet in the Local Disk (C:) Properties dialog box, accessible by clicking the Tools tab, allows you to check for errors on the hard drive or defragment the hard drive. The Hardware sheet allows you to view a list of all drives, troubleshoot drives that are not working properly, and display the properties for each drive. The Sharing sheet allows you to share the contents of a hard drive with other computer users. To protect a computer from unauthorized access, however, sharing the hard drive is not recommended. The Security sheet displays the security settings for the drive, such as user permissions. The Previous Versions sheet allows you to work with previous versions of files and folders on your hard drive if you have File History enabled or have created restore points. Finally, the Quota sheet can be used to see how much space is being used by various user accounts. Other tabs might be displayed in the Local Disk (C:) Properties dialog box on your computer.

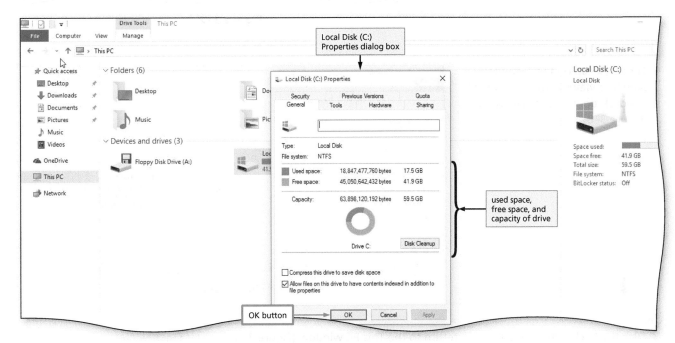

Figure 3–6

3

- Click the OK button (Local Disk (C:) Properties dialog box) to close the dialog box.

Other Ways

1. Right-click Local Disk (C:) icon, click Properties on shortcut menu   2. Select drive icon in right pane, press ALT+ENTER

To Switch Folders Using the Address Bar

Why? *Folder windows contain the address bar, which indicates which folder you are viewing.* A useful feature of the address bar is its capability to allow you to switch to different folder windows by clicking the arrows preceding or following the folder names. Clicking the arrow to the right of the This PC label, for example, displays a menu containing options for showing other drives, as well as other locations and folders, such as the Downloads, Pictures, Music, Desktop, Documents, and Videos folders. The drives and folders that are displayed can vary from computer to computer. The following steps use the address bar to change the folder window from displaying the This PC folder to displaying the desktop and then return to the This PC folder.

1

- Click the This PC arrow on the address bar to display a menu that contains locations in This PC (Figure 3–7). Depending upon your computer's configuration, the list of locations might differ.

Q&A What happens if I click the This PC button instead of the arrow?

Clicking the This PC button will open the This PC window.

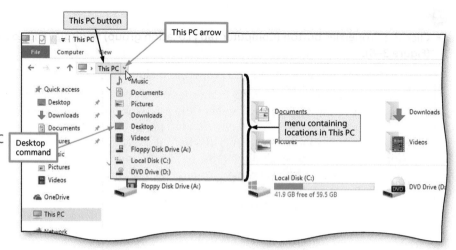

Figure 3–7

2

- Click Desktop on the menu to switch to viewing the contents of the desktop in the folder window (Figure 3–8).

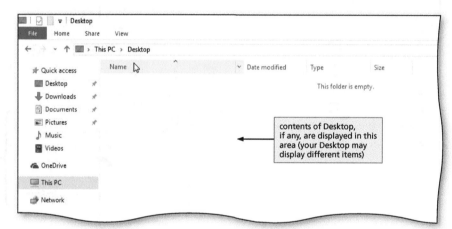

Figure 3–8

3

- Click the Back button two times to return to the This PC window (Figure 3–9).

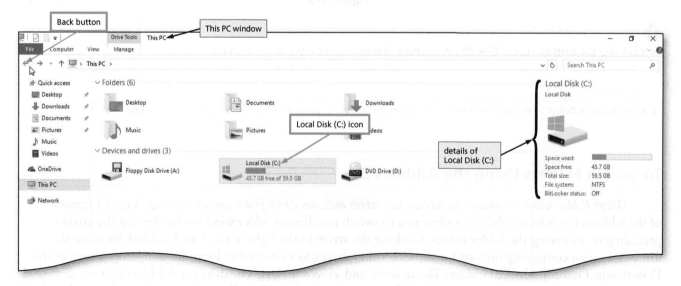

Figure 3–9

To View the Contents of a Drive

In addition to viewing the contents of the Desktop folder, you can view the contents of drives and other folders. In fact, the contents of any folder or drive on the computer will be displayed in a folder window. By default, Windows uses the active window to display the contents of a newly opened drive or folder. The following step displays the contents of drive C in the active window. ***Why?*** *You should know the contents of the drive so that you can see where your information is stored.*

1

- Double-click the Local Disk (C:) icon in the This PC window to display the contents of the Local Disk (C:) drive (Figure 3–10).

 Why do I see different folders?

The contents of the Local Disk (C:) window that appear on your computer can differ from the contents shown in Figure 3–10 because each computer has its own folders, apps, and documents.

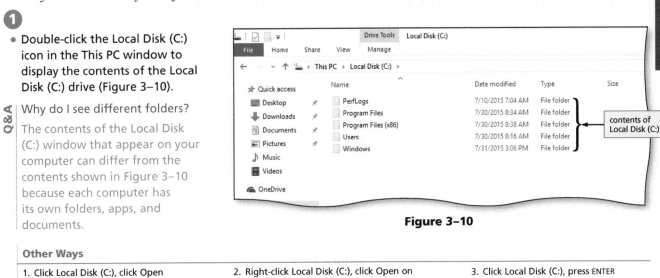

Figure 3–10

Other Ways

1. Click Local Disk (C:), click Open (Computer tab | Location group)
2. Right-click Local Disk (C:), click Open on shortcut menu
3. Click Local Disk (C:), press ENTER

To Preview the Properties of a Folder

Why? *When you move the pointer over a folder icon, a preview of the folder properties will display in a ScreenTip so that you can see information about the folder.* A **ScreenTip** is a brief description that appears when you position the pointer over an object on the screen. ScreenTips do not appear for every object, but when they do, they provide useful information. The properties typically consist of the date and time created, the folder size, and the name of the folder. The Windows folder in the Local Disk (C:) window contains apps and files necessary for the operation of the Windows operating system. As such, you should exercise caution when working with the contents of the Windows folder, because changing the contents of the folder might cause the operating system to stop working correctly. The following step shows a ScreenTip displaying the properties of the Windows folder.

1

- Point to the Windows folder icon to display a ScreenTip displaying the properties of the Windows folder (Figure 3–11).

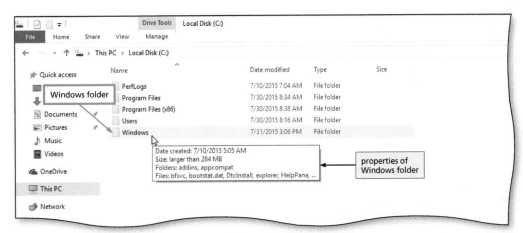

Figure 3–11

To Display Properties for the Windows Folder in the Details Pane

Just like with drives, some properties of folders can be displayed in the details pane. *Why? You want to view the properties of the Windows folder so that you can see how much space it is using on your hard drive.* The following step displays the properties for the Windows folder in the details pane of the This PC window.

1

- Click the Windows folder icon to display the properties in the details pane (Figure 3–12).

Figure 3–12

To Use the Shortcut Menu to Display the Properties for the Windows Folder

Why? If you want to see all of the properties for the Windows folder, you will need to display the Properties dialog box. The following steps display the Properties dialog box for the Windows folder.

1

- Right-click the Windows folder icon to display a shortcut menu (Figure 3–13). (The commands on your shortcut menu might differ.)

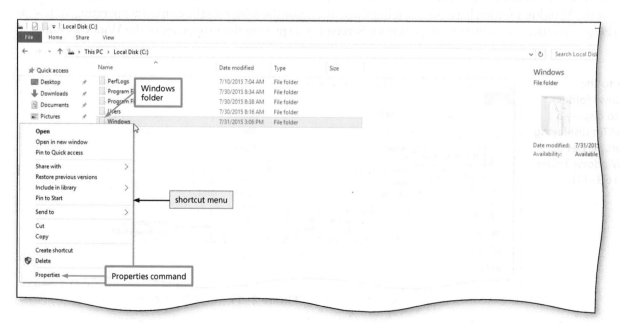

Figure 3–13

2

- Click Properties on the shortcut menu to display the Windows Properties dialog box (Figure 3–14).

🔍 **Experiment**

- Click the various tabs in the Windows Properties dialog box to see the different properties available for a folder.

Q&A Why might I want to look at the properties of a folder?

When you are working with folders, you might need to look at folders' properties to make changes, such as configuring a folder for sharing over a network or hiding folders from users who do not need access to them.

Why are the tabs of the Windows folder properties different from the Local Disk (C:) properties?

Drives, folders, and files have different properties and, therefore, need different tabs. A folder's Properties dialog box typically shows the General, Sharing, Security, and Previous Versions tabs; however, depending upon your Windows 10 edition and installed apps, the tabs may differ. The Properties dialog box always will have the General tab, although what it displays also may differ.

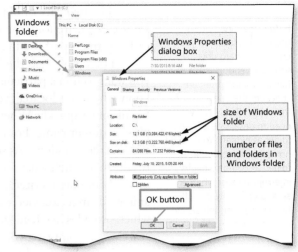

Figure 3–14

3

- Click the OK button (Windows Properties dialog box) to close it.

To View the Contents of a Folder

The following step opens the Windows folder so that you can view its contents. *Why? You will be able see what sort of files your operating system installed.*

1

- Double-click the Windows folder icon to display the contents of the Windows folder (Figure 3–15).

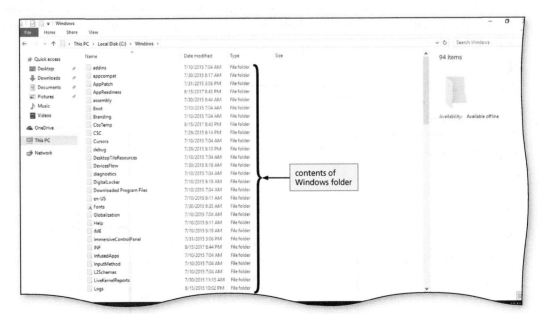

Figure 3–15

Other Ways

1. Click Windows folder, click Open (Home tab | Open group)

2. Right-click Windows folder, click Open on shortcut menu

3. Click Windows folder, press ENTER

Searching for Files and Folders

The majority of objects displayed in the Windows folder, as shown in Figure 3–15, are folder icons. By default, folder icons are displayed in alphabetical order at the top of the file list in a folder window, before the icons for apps or files.

Folders, such as the Windows folder, can contain many files and folders. When you want to find a particular file or folder in the currently displayed folder but do not know where it is located, you can use the **Search box** in the folder window to find the file or folder quickly. When you are in a folder, the Search box displays the word, Search, plus the folder name. For example, in the Windows folder, the Search box contains the text, Search Windows. As soon as you start typing, the window updates to show search results that match what you are typing. As Windows is searching for files or folders that match your search criteria, you will see a searching message displayed in the list area, an animated circle attached to the pointer, and an animated progress bar on the address bar, which provides live feedback as to how much of the search has been completed. When searching is complete, you will see a list of all the items that match your search criteria.

If you know only a portion of a file's name and can specify where the known portion of the name should appear, you can use an asterisk in the name to represent the unknown characters. For example, if you know a file starts with the letters MSP, you can type msp* in the Search box. All files that begin with the letters, msp, regardless of what characters follow, will be displayed. With Windows 10's powerful search capabilities, however, you would get the same results if you did not include the asterisk. If you want to search for all files with a particular extension, you can use the asterisk to substitute for the name of the files. For example, to find all the text files with the extension .rtf, you would type *.rtf in the Search box. Windows will find all the files with the .rtf extension.

To Search for a File and Folder in a Folder Window

The following step uses the Search box to search the Windows folder for all the objects that contain the letters, system, in the file name. **_Why?_** _Sometimes you may forget where a file is stored. Knowing how to search can help you find files faster._

1

• Type **system** in the Search box to search for all files and folders that match the search criteria (Figure 3–16).

How can I stop a search while it is running?

If you decide to stop a search before it is finished running, click the Stop button (the small x) that appears next to the Search box.

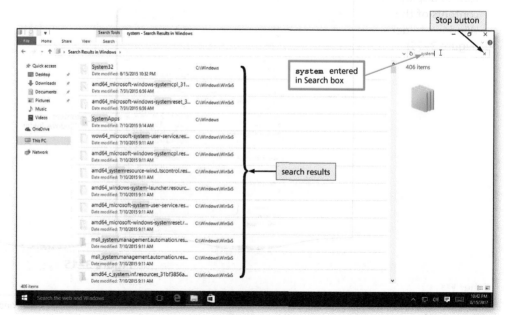

Figure 3–16

To Refine the Search Results

You can refine your search results by specifying properties by which you want to refine them. For example, you can refine search results to display files that were modified within a certain timeframe, certain kinds of files (for example, documents, email messages, or videos), file size, or other properties, such as type, name, folder path, or tags. *Why? If your search returns too many results, you can refine the results to display fewer files and folders.* The following steps refine the search results by file size so that only files between 100 KB (kilobytes) and 1 MB (megabyte) are displayed.

1

- Click the Size button (Search Tools Search tab | Refine group) to display a list of options by which to refine the search by size (Figure 3–17).

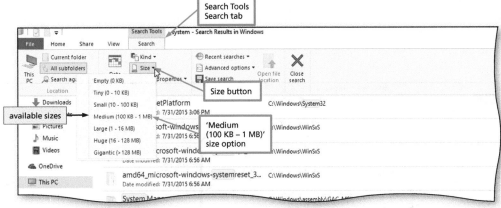

Figure 3–17

2

- Click 'Medium (100 KB – 1 MB)' to refine the search results by size (Figure 3–18).

Q&A Can I refine the search results by more than one property?

Yes.

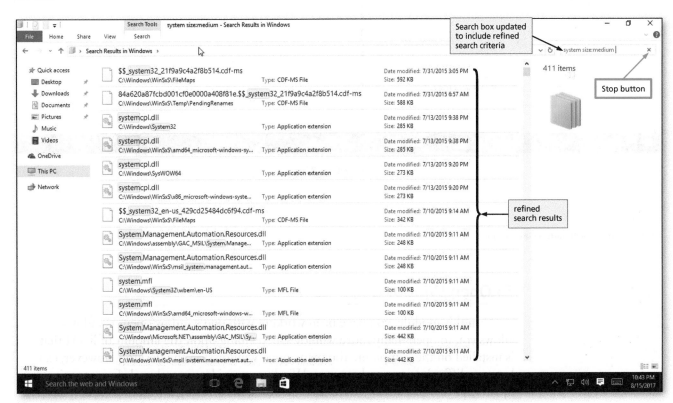

Figure 3–18

Other Ways
1. Type `system size:medium` in Search box, press ENTER

To Clear the Search Box

When you finish searching, you can end the search by clearing the Search box. The following step clears the Search box. *Why? You clear the Search box so that you can resume normal navigation of the folder you are viewing.*

1

- Click the Stop button (denoted with an x in the Search box) to clear the Search box and redisplay all files and folders in the Windows folder (Figure 3–19).

Q&A What happened to the Stop button in the Search box?

The Stop button no longer is displayed when you clear the Search box and search results.

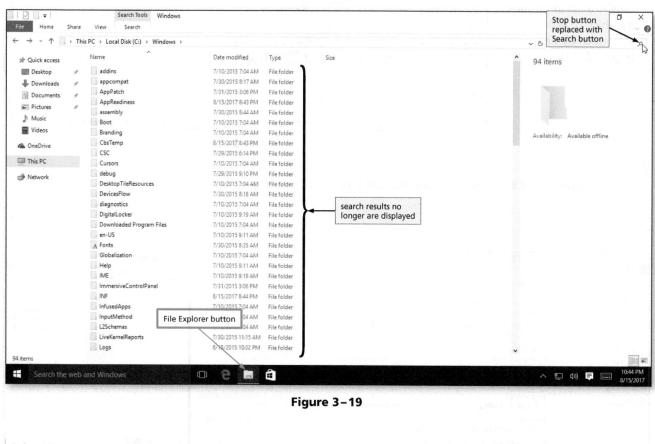

Figure 3–19

Other Ways

1. Click Close search button (Search Tools Search tab)

To Open Windows

In this module, you have been working with one window open. Windows allows you to open many more windows, depending upon the amount of RAM that is installed on the computer. Too many open windows on the desktop, however, can become difficult to use and manage. Windows provides several tools for managing open windows. You already have used one tool, maximizing a window. When you maximize a window, it occupies the entire screen and cannot be confused with other open windows.

Sometimes, it is important to have multiple windows appear on the desktop simultaneously. Windows offers simple commands that allow you to arrange multiple windows in specific ways. The following sections describe the ways that you can manage multiple open windows. The following steps open another File Explorer window.

1 Right-click the File Explorer button on the taskbar.

2 Click File Explorer on the shortcut menu to open another File Explorer window.

3 Double-click the Pictures folder to display its contents.

To Use Shake to Minimize All Background Windows

Shake lets you minimize all windows except the active window and then restore all those windows by shaking the title bar of the active window. ***Why?*** *To reduce clutter on the desktop, you want to quickly minimize all windows other than the window you currently are viewing.* The following steps use Shake to minimize all windows and then restore those windows.

1

- Click the title bar of the Pictures folder window and then shake the title bar (drag the title bar back and forth in short, swift motions several times) to minimize all windows except the Pictures folder (Figure 3–20).

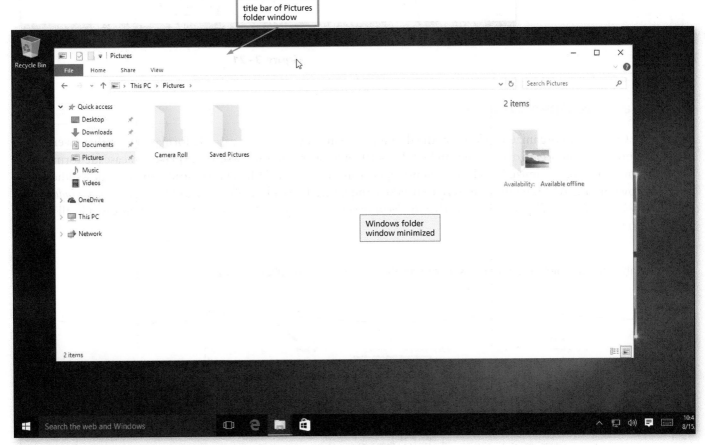

Figure 3–20

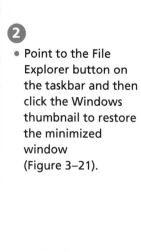

• Point to the File Explorer button on the taskbar and then click the Windows thumbnail to restore the minimized window (Figure 3–21).

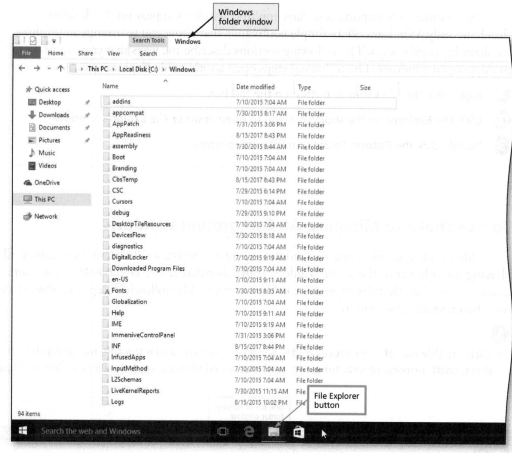

Figure 3–21

To Cascade Open Windows

One way to organize windows on the desktop is to display them in a cascade format, where they overlap one another in an organized manner. In Windows 10, only open windows will be displayed in cascade format; windows that are minimized or closed will not appear in the cascade. When you cascade open windows, the windows are resized to be the same size to produce the layered cascading effect. *Why? Cascading open windows will help you identify all open windows and easily choose the one you want to view.* The following steps cascade all open windows.

• Right-click an open area on the taskbar to display a shortcut menu (Figure 3–22).

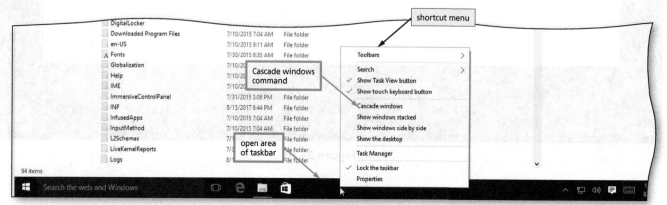

Figure 3–22

2

• Click Cascade windows on the shortcut menu to cascade the open windows (Figure 3–23).

Q&A How do I make a cascaded window the active window?

If a window you want to display is hidden behind another window, simply click that window's title bar to bring that window to the foreground.

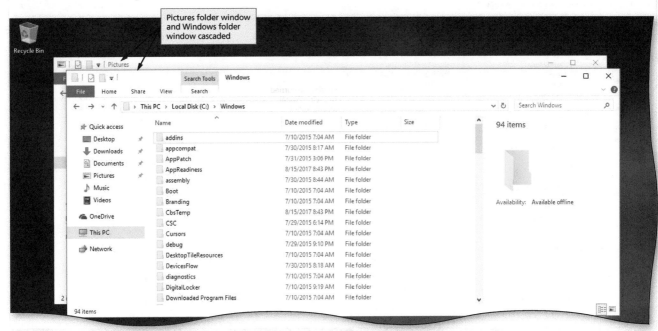

Pictures folder window and Windows folder window cascaded

Figure 3–23

Other Ways

1. Right-click open area on taskbar, press D

To Undo Cascading

Undoing the cascading will return the windows to the original size and location before you cascaded them. **_Why?_** _If you do not like the appearance of the cascaded windows or otherwise want to return the windows to their original size and location, you can undo the cascade effect._ The following steps undo the cascading.

1

• Right-click an open area on the taskbar to display the shortcut menu (Figure 3–24).

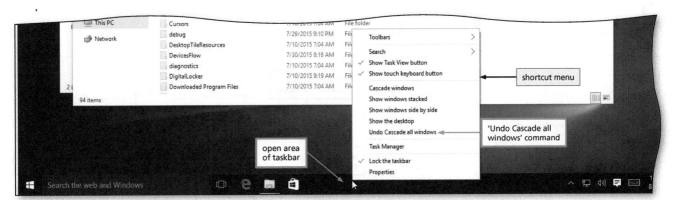

shortcut menu

'Undo Cascade all windows' command

open area of taskbar

Figure 3–24

- Click 'Undo Cascade all windows' on the shortcut menu to return the windows to their original sizes and locations (Figure 3–25).

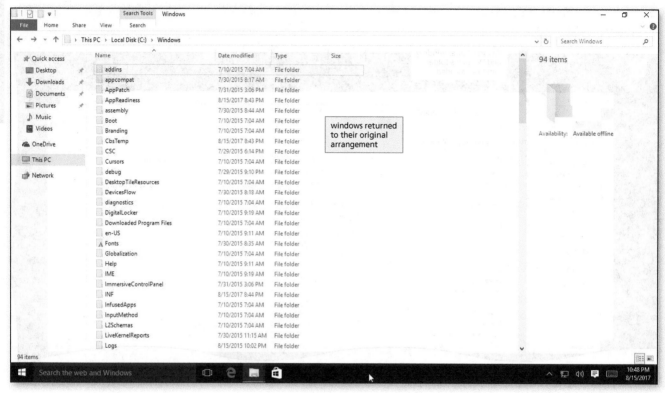

Figure 3–25

Other Ways

1. Right-click open area on taskbar, press U

2. Press CTRL+Z

To Stack Open Windows

Although cascading arranges the windows on the desktop so that each of the windows' title bars is visible, it is impossible to see the contents of each window. **Why?** *Windows 10 also can stack the open windows, which allows you to see partial contents of each window.* When stacking windows, the windows will be resized to the full width of the screen and arranged on top of each other vertically. Each window will be the same size, and you will be able to see a portion of each window. The following steps stack the open windows.

1

- Right-click an open area of the taskbar to display a shortcut menu (Figure 3–26).

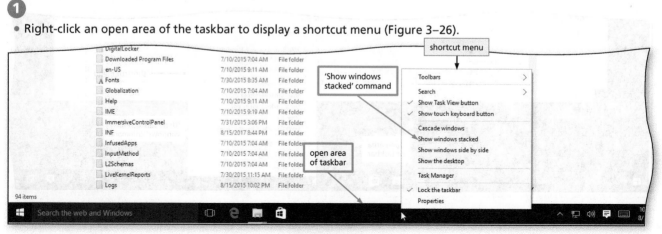

Figure 3–26

2

- Click 'Show windows stacked' on the shortcut menu to stack the open windows (Figure 3–27).

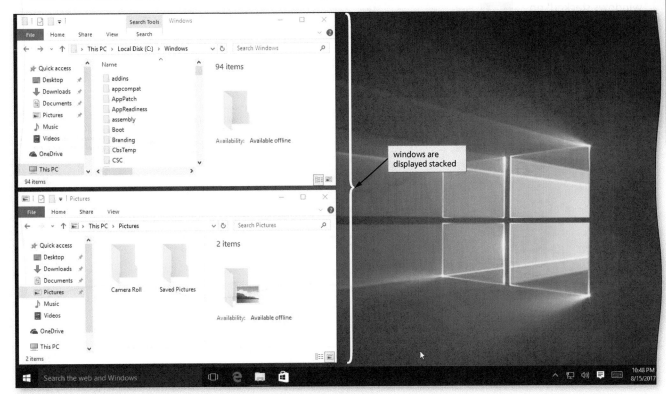

Figure 3–27

To Undo Show Windows Stacked

You will undo the stacking operation to return the windows to the size and position they occupied before stacking. *Why? Although the stacked windows are arranged so that you can view all of them, you find that the reduced size of an individual window makes working in the window difficult.* The following steps return the windows to their original size and position.

1

- Right-click an open area of the taskbar to display the shortcut menu (Figure 3–28).

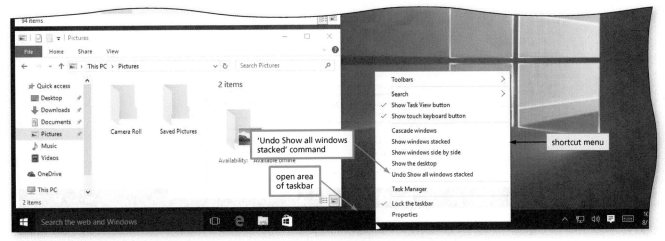

Figure 3–28

● Click 'Undo Show all
windows stacked' on
the shortcut menu to
return the windows
to their original sizes
and locations
(Figure 3–29).

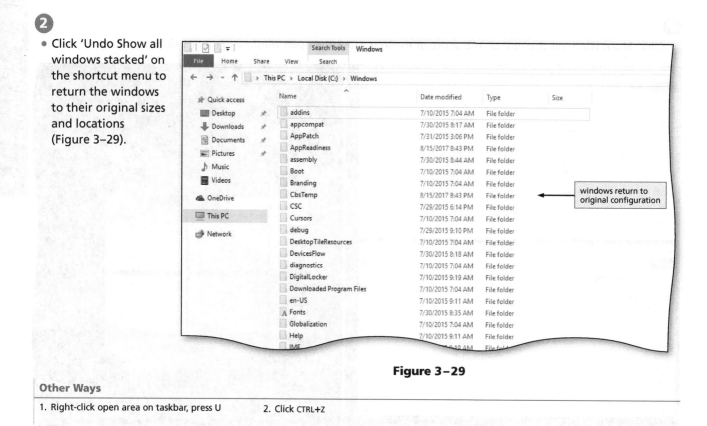

Figure 3–29

Other Ways

1. Right-click open area on taskbar, press U   2. Click CTRL+Z

To Show Windows Side by Side

Although stacking arranges the windows vertically above each other on the desktop, it also is possible to arrange them next to each other. The 'Show windows side by side' command allows you to see partial contents of each window horizontally. *Why? Displaying windows side by side may allow you to see more of each window's contents.* The following steps show the open windows side by side.

● Right-click an open area on the taskbar to display the shortcut menu (Figure 3–30).

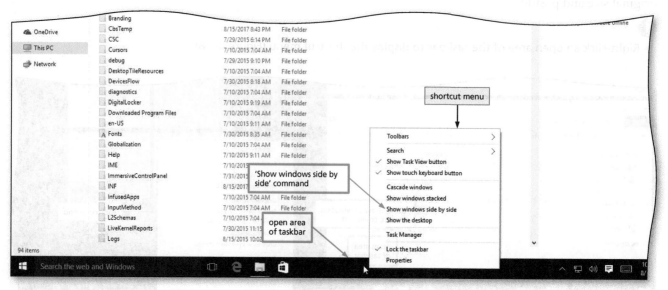

Figure 3–30

2

- Click 'Show windows side by side' on the shortcut menu to display the open windows side by side (Figure 3–31).

Q&A Why does the window layout look the same as when I showed the windows in a stacked configuration?

When you are working with only two open windows, the two layouts look similar. If you have many more windows open, the stacked layout will show the windows slightly overlapping each other.

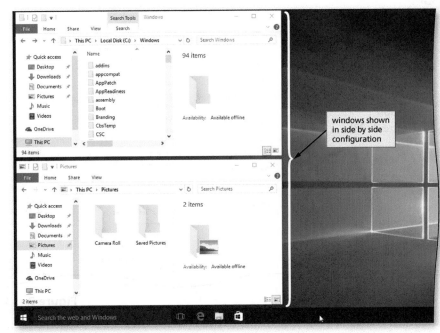

windows shown in side by side configuration

Figure 3–31

Other Ways

1. Right-click open area on taskbar, press I

To Undo Show Windows Side by Side

Why? You want to return the windows to their original size and position. The following steps undo the side by side operation and return the windows to their original arrangement.

1

- Right-click an open area on the taskbar to display the shortcut menu (Figure 3–32).

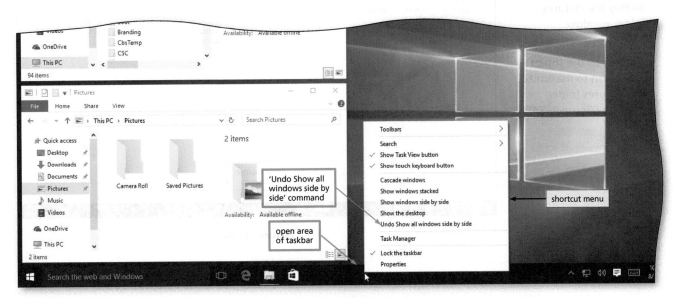

'Undo Show all windows side by side' command

open area of taskbar

shortcut menu

Figure 3–32

● Click 'Undo Show all windows side by side' on the shortcut menu to return the windows to their original size and location (Figure 3–33).

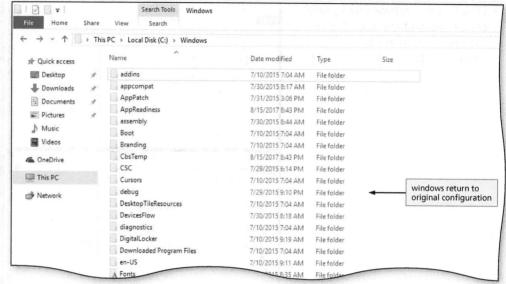

Figure 3–33

Other Ways

1. Right-click open area on taskbar, press U   2. Press CTRL+Z

To Use Snap to Maximize Windows

Why? *Sometimes you want to see a larger portion of a window.* Snap allows you to maximize a window by dragging its title bar to the top of the screen. The following steps maximize the Pictures folder window.

1

● Point to the File Explorer button on the taskbar and then click the Pictures thumbnail to display the Pictures folder window.

● Drag the Pictures folder window to the top of the screen to maximize the Pictures folder window (Figure 3–34).

Q&A

Is Snap used only to maximize windows?

No. If you drag a window's title bar to the right side of the screen, the window will resize to fill the right half of the screen. If you drag the title bar to the left side of the screen, the window will resize to fill only the left half of the screen. When you snap a window to one side of the screen, Windows will display thumbnail images of the remaining open windows on the other side of the screen. Click the thumbnail for the window you want to fill the other side of the screen.

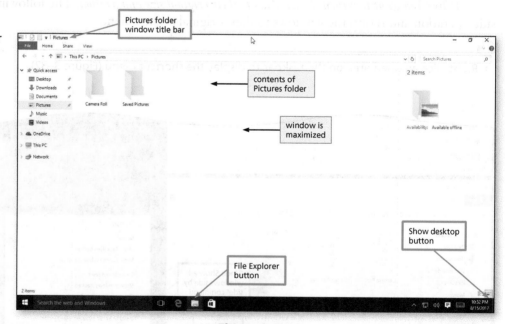

Figure 3–34

To Use the Show Desktop Button to Minimize All Windows

Why? *You need to access an app or file that is on the desktop, so you minimize all open windows so that you can access it.* The following step minimizes all windows to show the desktop.

- Click the Show desktop button (shown in Figure 3–34) on the taskbar to minimize all windows.

To Restore a Window

Why? *To work with one of the windows you previously minimized, you first must restore it.* The following steps switch to the Pictures folder window; however, the steps are the same for any app or folder window currently displayed as a button on the taskbar.

- Point to the File Explorer button on the taskbar to see a live preview of the open File Explorer windows or the window title(s) of the open window(s), depending on your computer's configuration (Figure 3–35).

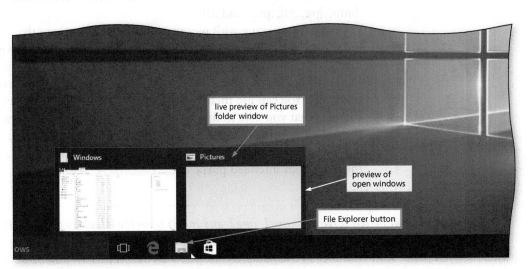

live preview of Pictures folder window

preview of open windows

File Explorer button

Figure 3–35

- Click the live preview of the Pictures folder window to restore the window (Figure 3–36).

Q&A What happens if I click the wrong window?

Click the remaining windows until the Pictures window is displayed in the foreground.

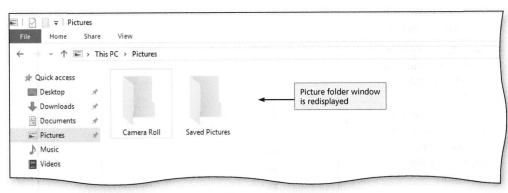

Picture folder window is redisplayed

Figure 3–36

Other Ways

1. Press ALT+TAB until Pictures folder window is selected, release ALT key

The Pictures Folder

You can organize your pictures and share them with others using the Pictures folder. By putting all your pictures in the Pictures folder, you always will know where to find them. When you save pictures from a digital camera, scanner, smartphone, or the Internet, they are saved to the Pictures folder by default.

Windows 10 also includes the Photos app. The **Photos app** is used to view the pictures on your computer. You can use the Photos app to work with your pictures no matter where they are stored on your hard drive.

Using the Pictures folder allows you to organize pictures, preview pictures, share your pictures with others, display your pictures as a slide show, print your pictures, attach your pictures to email messages, or save your pictures on an optical disc.

Many different formats are available for picture files. Some pictures have an extension of .bmp to indicate that they are bitmap files. Other pictures may have the .gif extension, which indicates that they are saved in the Graphics Interchange Format. Too many file types exist to mention them all; however, some common types include .bmp, .jpg, .gif, .png, and .tif.

When working with pictures, you should be aware that most pictures that you did not create yourself, including other multimedia files, are copyrighted. A **copyright** means that a picture belongs to the person who created it. The pictures that come with Windows are part of Windows, and you are allowed to use them; however, they are not yours. You can use them only according to the rights granted to you by Microsoft. Pictures that you take using your digital camera are yours because you created them. Before using pictures and other multimedia files, you should be aware of any copyrights associated with them, and you should know whether you are allowed to use them for your intended purpose.

To Search for Pictures

Why? *You want to copy three files (img1, img2, and img3) from the Windows folder to the Pictures folder, but you have to find these files first.* Because the three files all have the .jpg extension, you can search for them using an asterisk (*) in place of the number in the name, as discussed earlier in this module. The following step opens the Windows folder window and displays the icons for the files you want to copy.

1

- Restore the Windows folder window, and, if necessary, maximize it.

- Type `img*.jpg` in the Search box and then press the ENTER key to search for all files that begin with the characters, img, and that have a .jpg file extension.

- If necessary, scroll down in the Windows folder window until the icons for the img1, img2, and img3 files are visible (Figure 3–37). If one or more of these files are not available, select any of the other picture files.

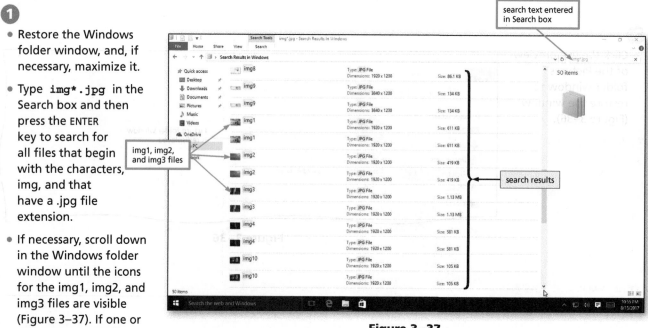

Figure 3–37

Item Check Boxes

When an item is selected, you can see the item check box for that item. By clicking the item check box for several items, you can select them for your use. For example, you can copy multiple files or folders from one location to another.

To Copy Files to the Pictures Folder

A method you can use to copy a file or folder is the **copy and paste method**. When you **copy** a file, you place a copy of the file in a temporary storage area of the computer called the **Clipboard**. When you **paste** the file, Windows copies it from the Clipboard to the location you specify, giving you two copies of the same file.

Why? Because the search results include the pictures you were looking for, you now can select the files and then copy them to the Pictures folder. Once the three files have been copied to the Pictures folder, the files will be stored in both the Pictures folder and Windows folder on drive C. Copying and moving files are common tasks when working with Windows. If you want to move a file instead of copy a file, you use the Cut button on the ribbon to move the file to the Clipboard and the Paste command to copy the file from the Clipboard to the new location. When the paste is complete, the files are moved into the new folder and no longer are stored in the original folder. The following steps copy the img1, img2, and img3 files from the Windows folder to the Pictures folder.

- Click View on the ribbon to display the View tab (Figure 3–38).

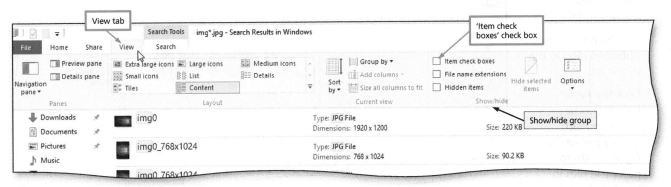

Figure 3–38

- If necessary click the 'Item check boxes' check box (View tab | Show/hide group) to select it.

- Click the item check boxes for the img1, img2, and img3 pictures to select the files (Figure 3–39).

Q&A

Are copying and moving the same?

No. When you copy a file, it is located in both the place to which it was copied and in the place from which it was copied. When you move a file, it is located only in the location to which it was moved.

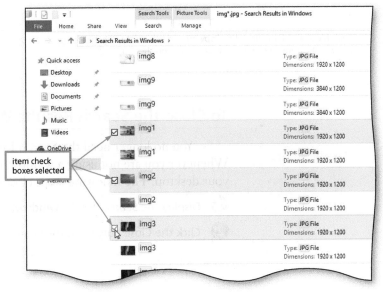

Figure 3–39

- If necessary, click Home on the ribbon to display the Home tab (Figure 3–40).
- Click the Copy button (Home tab | Clipboard group) to copy the files to the Clipboard.

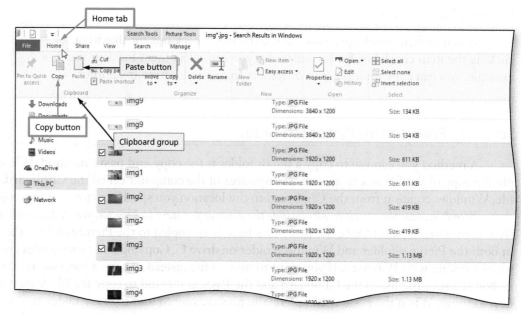

Figure 3–40

- Make the Pictures folder window the active window.
- Click Home on the ribbon to display the Home tab.
- Click the Paste button (Home tab | Clipboard group) (shown in Figure 3–40) to paste the files in the Pictures folder (Figure 3–41).

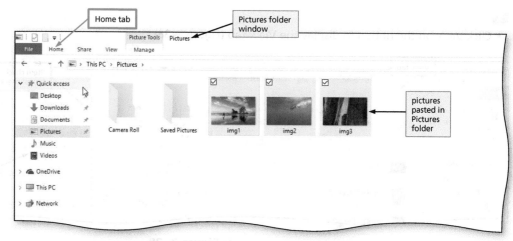

Figure 3–41

Other Ways

1. Select file icons, right-click, click Copy on shortcut menu; display where you want to store files, right-click, click Paste on shortcut menu

2. Select file icons, press CTRL+C, display window where you want to store files, press CTRL+V

To Close the Search Results Window

You no longer need the Search Results window open, so you can close it. Whenever you are not using a window, it is a good idea to close it so as not to clutter your desktop. The following steps close the Search Results window.

1 Display the Search Results window.

2 Click the Close button on the Search Results window's title bar to close the window.

To Create a Folder in the Pictures Folder

Why? *When you have several related files stored in a folder with a number of unrelated files, you might want to create a folder to contain the related files so that you can find and reference them easily.* To reduce clutter and improve the organization of files in the Pictures folder, you will create a new folder in the Pictures folder and then move the pictures you copied into the new folder. The following step creates the Backgrounds folder in the Pictures folder.

- Click the New folder button on the Quick Access Toolbar to create a new folder.

- Type **Backgrounds** in the new folder's text box and then press the ENTER key to assign the name to the new folder (Figure 3–42).

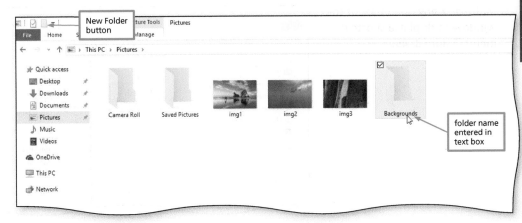

Figure 3–42

Other Ways

1. Right-click folder, point to New, click Folder on shortcut menu
2. Click New folder button (Home tab | New group)
3. Press CTRL+SHIFT+N

To Move Multiple Files into a Folder

Why? *After you create the Backgrounds folder in the Pictures folder, the next step is to move the three picture files into the folder.* The following steps move the img1, img2, and img3 files into the Backgrounds folder.

- If necessary, click the check box for the Backgrounds folder to deselect the folder.

- Click the item check boxes for the img1, img2, and img3 pictures to select the files (Figure 3–43).

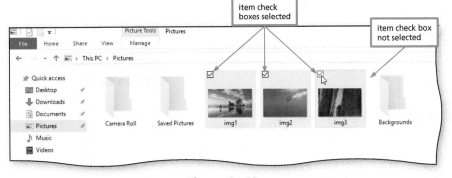

Figure 3–43

- Drag the selected icons to the Backgrounds folder and then release the mouse button to move the files to the Backgrounds folder (Figure 3–44).

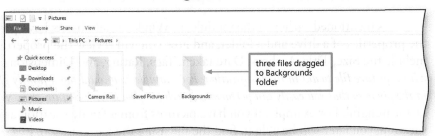

Figure 3–44

Other Ways

1. Drag files individually to folder icon
2. Right-click icon, click Cut on shortcut menu; right-click folder icon, click Paste on shortcut menu

To Refresh the Image on a Folder

Why? *After moving the three files into the Backgrounds folder, it still appears as an empty open folder icon.* To replace the empty folder icon with a preview of the three files stored in the Backgrounds folder (img1, img2, and img3), the Pictures folder must be refreshed. The following steps refresh the Pictures folder to display the preview for the Backgrounds folder.

1

- Right-click any open part of the window to display a shortcut menu (Figure 3–45).

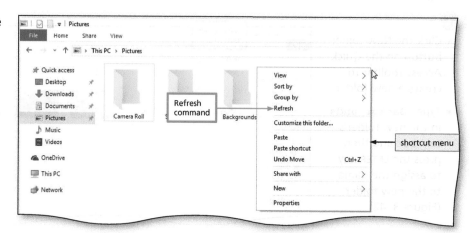

Figure 3–45

2

- Click Refresh on the shortcut menu to refresh the list area (Figure 3–46).

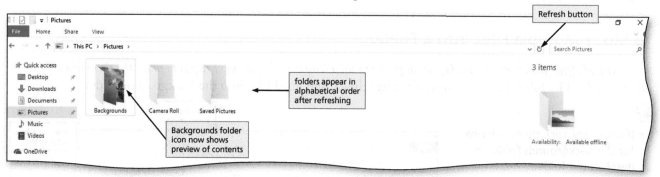

Figure 3–46

Other Ways

1. Press F5	2. Click Refresh button on address bar

To View and Change the Properties of a Picture

As mentioned earlier in the module, in Windows, all objects have properties. You already have explored the properties of a drive and a folder, and now you will review the properties of a picture. Picture properties include the Size, Title, Authors, Date taken, Tags, Rating, and Dimensions. *Why? Tags are keywords you associate with a picture file to aid in its classification. For example, you could tag a family photo with the names of the people in the photo so that you easily can perform a search for photos with certain tags.* When you create a tag, it should be meaningful. For example, if you have pictures from a family vacation at the beach and you add the title, vacation, you later will be able to find the file using the tag, vacation, in a search. Be aware that you can search only for tags that you already have created. If your family vacation photo was saved as photo1.jpg and tagged with the tag, vacation, you will not find it by searching for the word, beach, as it is not part of the name or tag. Rating refers to the ranking, in stars, that you assign to a picture. You can rate a picture from zero to five stars.

Date taken, Tags, and Rating all can be changed using the details pane. Because you do not know when the Background pictures were created, you will change only the Tags and Rating properties. Windows will allow you to set properties, such as Tags and Rating, only for certain image types. These properties might not be available for other image types. The following steps display and change the Tags and Rating properties of the img1 image in the Backgrounds folder.

- Display the contents of the Backgrounds folder.
- Click the img1 icon to select it.
- Click the 'Add a tag' text box in the details pane to activate it (Figure 3–47).

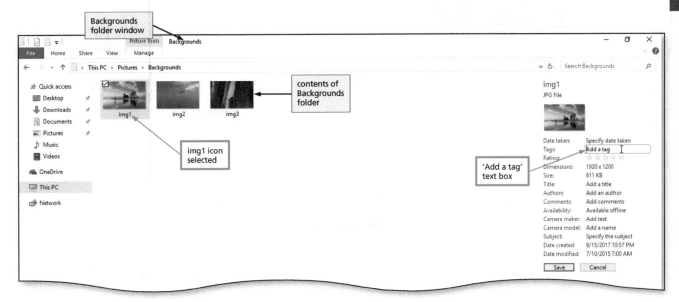

Figure 3–47

- Type **Beach** in the text box to create a tag for the picture.
- Click the fourth star next to the Rating heading in the details pane to assign a four-star rating to the picture (Figure 3–48).

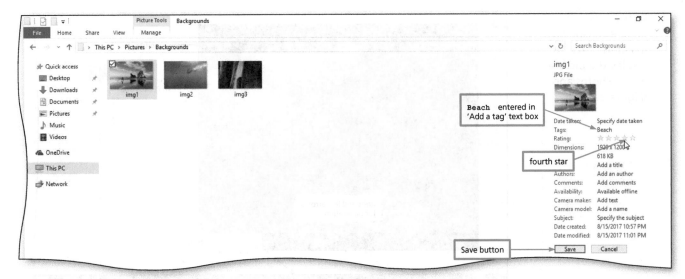

Figure 3–48

Can I add more than one tag to a picture?

Yes. After typing the first tag, click to the right of the semicolon and add an additional tag. Repeat this step to add additional tags.

3

- Click the Save button (shown in Figure 3–48) in the details pane to save the changes to the Tags and Rating properties (Figure 3–49).

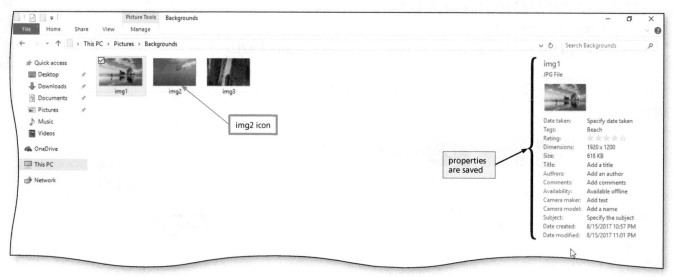

Figure 3–49

Other Ways

1. Right-click icon, click Properties on shortcut menu, click Details tab (img Properties dialog box), click desired rating, enter desired tag(s), click OK button

To View a Picture in the Photos App

Why? *You can view the images in a folder in the Photos app or as a slide show.* The **Photos app** allows you to view, print, burn, send via email, and open the pictures in your Pictures folder. The following steps display the img2 picture in the Backgrounds folder in the Photos app.

1

- Double-click the img2 icon (shown in Figure 3–49) to display the picture in the Photos app (Figure 3–50).

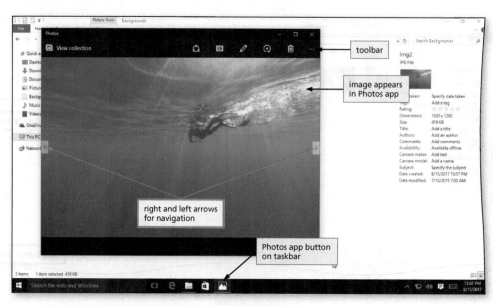

Figure 3–50

• Click the right
arrow (shown in
Figure 3–50) to
navigate to the next
picture in the folder
(Figure 3–51).

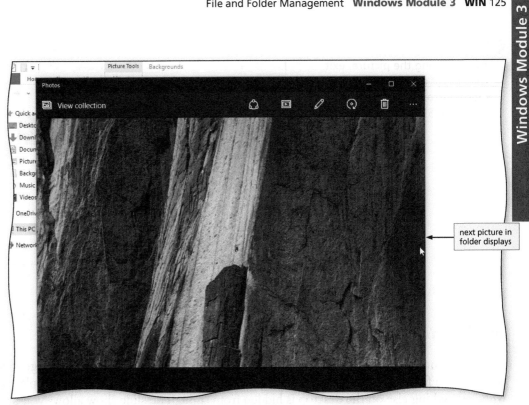

next picture in
folder displays

Figure 3–51

• Click the left arrow two times to navigate back two pictures in the folder (Figure 3–52).

Close button

first picture in
folder is displayed

Figure 3–52

4

- After viewing the picture, exit the Photos app by clicking the Close button on the title bar (Figure 3–53).

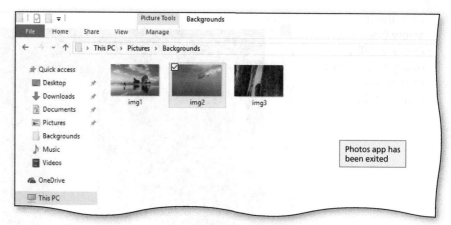

Figure 3–53

To View Your Pictures as a Slide Show

In Windows, you can view pictures as a **slide show**, which displays each image in the folder in a presentation format on the computer screen. The slide show automatically will display one picture at a time while everything else on the desktop is hidden from sight. The slide show allows you to select whether the pictures will loop in order or will be shuffled to appear in random order. You also can select the speed at which the pictures are displayed, pause the slide show, and exit the slide show. The following steps view the images in the Backgrounds folder as a slide show. *Why? Viewing pictures as a slide show makes it easy to display pictures on the full screen so that you can show them to others.*

1

- If necessary, display the Backgrounds folder window.

- Click Picture Tools Manage on the ribbon to display the Picture Tools Manage tab (Figure 3–54).

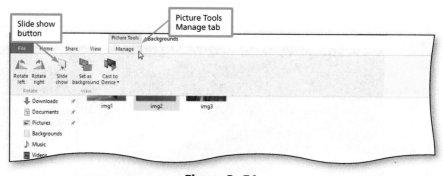

Figure 3–54

2

- Click the Slide show button (Picture Tools Manage tab | View group) to view the selected files as a slide show (Figure 3–55).

- Watch the slide show for a few seconds while the pictures change.

Q&A Can I change the slide show speed?

Yes, you can right-click and then select speeds of Slow, Medium, and Fast on the shortcut menu.

Figure 3–55

To End a Slide Show

When you are done viewing the slide show, the next step is to end it. The following step ends the slide show.

 Press the ESC key to end the slide show.

Compressing Files and Folders

Sometimes when working with files, you may need to send them via email, post them online, or even transfer them to another computer. If the files are large or numerous, you can make it easier to manage by compressing the files. Compressing (zipping) a file or files creates a **zipped file** that will contain compressed copies of the files. You also can compress folders so that your compressed file has a copy of your folder in it.

To Compress (Zip) a Folder

Why? *You want to send the pictures to a friend via an email message, but you want to attach only one file, not three separate ones.* The following step compresses the Backgrounds folder.

- Navigate to the Pictures folder.

- If necessary, select the Backgrounds folder.

- Click Share on the ribbon to display the Share tab.

- Click the Zip button (Share tab | Send group) to create a zipped file (Figure 3–56). Press the ENTER key to accept the file name Windows assigned to the file.

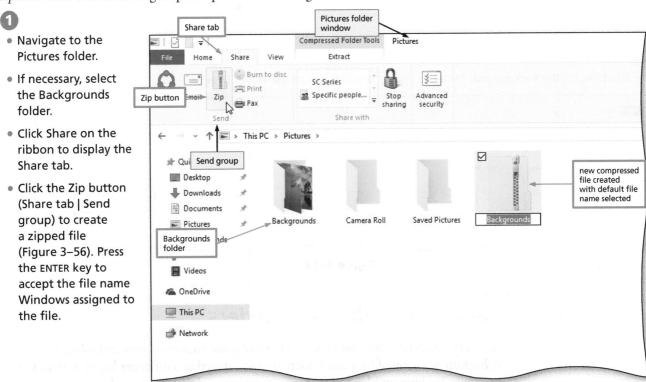

Figure 3–56

Other Ways

1. Right-click folder, point to Send to on shortcut menu, click 'Compressed (zipped) folder' on Send to submenu

To View the Contents of a Compressed Folder

Why? *You want to verify that the files are in the compressed folder before you share it.* You can open a compressed folder and then view the contents as if you were browsing a regular folder. The following steps display the contents of the Backgrounds compressed folder.

1

- Double-click the Backgrounds compressed (zipped) folder icon to display the contents of the folder (Figure 3–57).

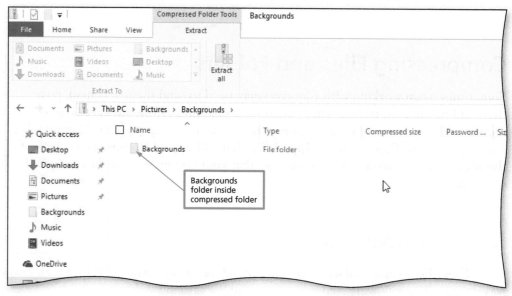

Figure 3–57

2

- Double-click the Backgrounds folder to display the contents of the folder (Figure 3–58).

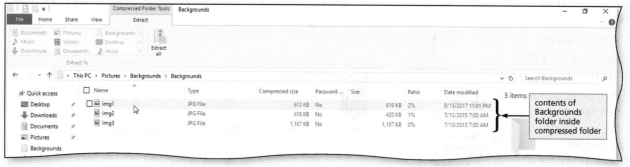

Figure 3–58

Backing Up Files and Folders

It is very important that you make backups of your important files and folders. A **backup** is a copy of files and folders that are stored at a different location than the originals. Backing up files and folders is a security aid; if something happens to the primary copy of a file or folder, you can restore it from the backup.

Although you can back up files and folders on the same drive where they were created, it is not considered as safe as backing them up to a separate drive. For example, you should not back up the files and folders on your primary hard drive to the same hard drive. If something goes wrong with this drive, it would affect any backups stored there, as well. Depending upon the size of the files and folders you are backing up, you might use a USB flash drive, an optical disc, an external hard drive, cloud storage, or any other available storage device to back up your files. You might even consider creating a scheduled backup. A **scheduled backup** is a backup that is made according to predetermined dates and times.

After you have created a backup, you should store your backup away from the computer. Many people store their backups right by their computer, which is not a good practice. If a mishap occurs where the computer area is damaged, someone steals the computer, or any other number of events occurs, the backup still will be safe if it is stored in a different location. Most corporations make regular backups of their data and store the backups off-site.

When you **restore** files or folders from a backup, you copy the files or folders from the backup location to the original location. If your hard drive crashes, a virus infects your computer, or an electrical surge damages your computer, you can restore the files and folders that you have stored on the backup. Before restoring files or folders, make sure that the location where you are restoring the files is now secure. For example, before restoring files on a hard drive that has been infected by a virus, first make sure the virus is gone.

You will copy the compressed (zipped) Backgrounds folder to OneDrive so that the files are stored somewhere other than your primary hard drive. **OneDrive** is a cloud storage location used for storing files on the Internet and for sharing files with other users. Storing these files on OneDrive also will allow you to access these files from any computer or mobile device you use to sign in to your OneDrive account. Similar to previous steps in this text, these steps assume you are signed in to Windows using a Microsoft account. If you are not signed in with a Microsoft account, read the steps in this section without performing them.

To Copy a File to OneDrive

Why? *You want to create a backup of your Backgrounds folder on OneDrive so that you have an extra copy of the files in case you lose the files on your hard drive.* The following steps copy the compressed (zipped) Backgrounds folder to OneDrive.

1

- If necessary, display the Pictures folder.

- Click to select the compressed (zipped) Backgrounds folder.

- If necessary, display the Home tab.

- Click the Copy button (Home tab | Clipboard group) to copy the compressed (zipped) folder to the Clipboard (Figure 3–59).

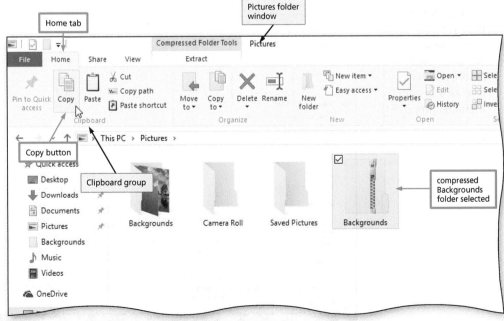

Figure 3–59

- Click OneDrive in the Navigation pane to display the files and folders you currently have stored on OneDrive.

- Click the Paste button (Home tab | Clipboard group) to copy the compressed (zipped) file to OneDrive (Figure 3–60).

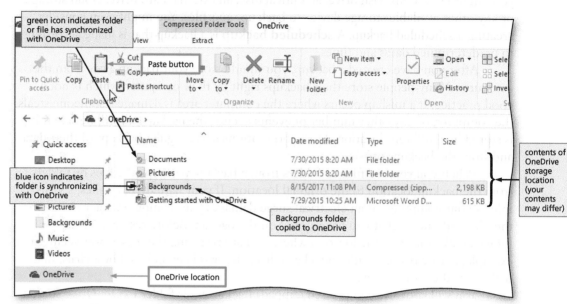

Figure 3–60

Other Ways

1. Select files to copy, right-click, click Copy on shortcut menu; navigate to OneDrive folder, right-click empty area of folder window, click Paste on shortcut menu

2. Select files to copy, press CTRL+C, navigate to OneDrive folder, press CTRL+V

To Rename a Folder

The compressed (zipped) folder on OneDrive is a backup copy of the original folder, so it is a good idea to change its name to reflect that it is a backup. *Why? It is a good idea to assign a unique name to the backup file so that if you have to restore it, it does not try to overwrite existing files that might be stored in the same location on your hard drive.* The following steps rename the compressed (zipped) folder on OneDrive to indicate that it is a backup.

- Right-click the Backgrounds compressed (zipped) folder (shown in Figure 3–60) to display a shortcut menu (Figure 3–61).

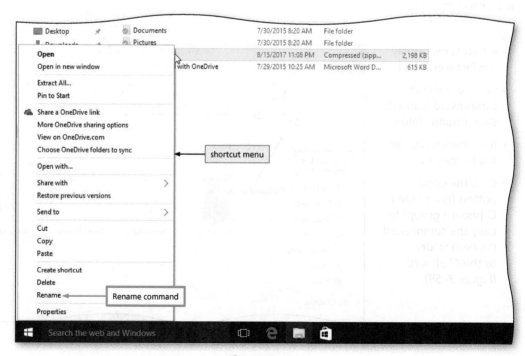

Figure 3–61

2

- Click Rename on the shortcut menu to open the name of the folder in a text box (Figure 3–62).

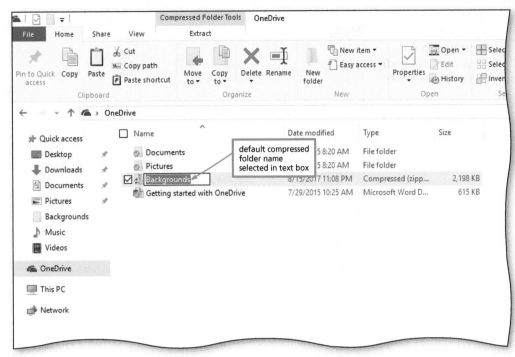

Figure 3–62

3

- Type **Backgrounds – Backup** as the new compressed folder name (Figure 3–63).

Q&A

What if the extension (.zip) displays in the text box as I rename the compressed folder?

This might happen if your computer is configured to display file name extensions. If the extension (.zip) is displayed, do not remove it. If you do, you might not be able to access the compressed folder until you restore the extension.

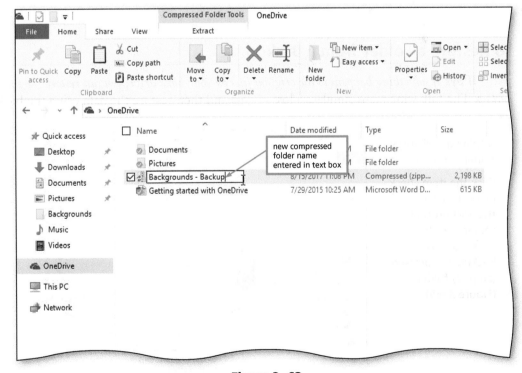

Figure 3–63

- Press the ENTER key to apply the new name to the compressed (zipped) folder (Figure 3–64).

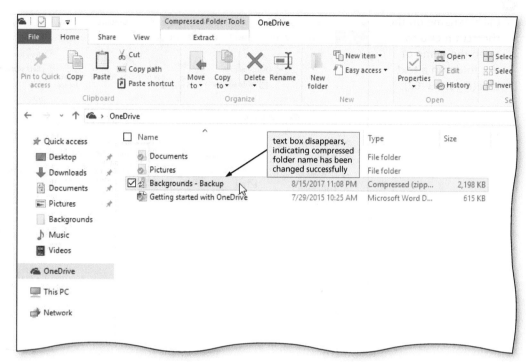

Figure 3–64

Other Ways

1. Select folder to rename, press F2, type new name in text box, press ENTER

2. Click folder name two times (do not double-click), type new name, press ENTER

To Restore a Folder from a Backup

Why? *If something happens to the original files on your hard drive, you can restore the files or folders from the backup.* The following steps simulate a loss of data and then restore the data using the backup on OneDrive.

- Display the Pictures folder window.

- Click the item check boxes to select the Backgrounds folder and the Backgrounds - Backup compressed (zipped) folder (Figure 3–65).

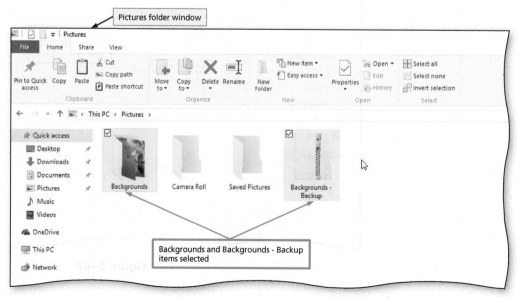

Figure 3–65

2

- Press the DELETE key to move the items to the Recycle Bin (Figure 3–66).

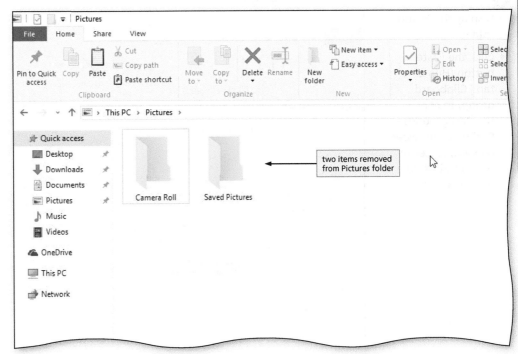

Figure 3–66

3

- Click OneDrive in the Navigation pane to display the contents of the OneDrive folder.

- Click the Backgrounds - Backup compressed (zipped) folder to select it.

- Click the Copy button (Home tab | Clipboard group) to copy the backup file to the Clipboard (Figure 3–67).

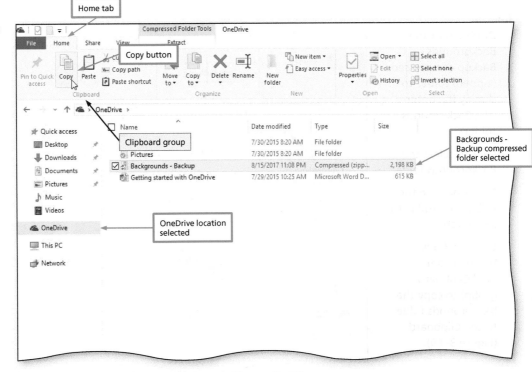

Figure 3–67

4

- Display the Pictures folder.
- Click the Paste button (Home tab | Clipboard group) to copy the Backgrounds - Backup compressed (zipped) folder to the Pictures folder (Figure 3–68).

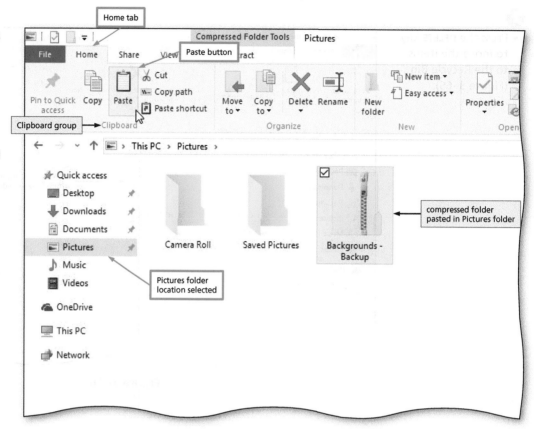

Figure 3–68

5

- Double-click the Backgrounds – Backup compressed (zipped) folder to display its contents (the Backgrounds folder).
- Click to select the Backgrounds folder.
- Click Home on the ribbon to display the Home tab.
- Click the Copy button (Home tab | Clipboard group) to copy the Backgrounds folder to the Clipboard (Figure 3–69).

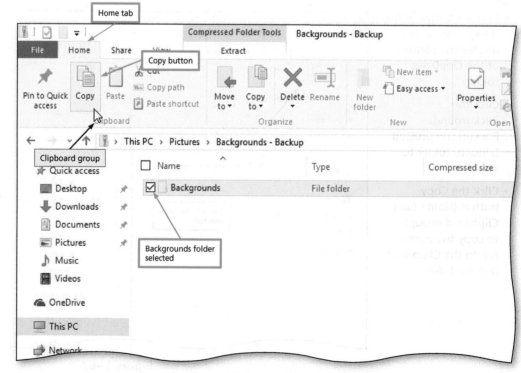

Figure 3–69

6

- Display the Pictures folder.

- Click the Paste button (Home tab | Clipboard group) to copy the Backgrounds folder to the Pictures folder (Figure 3–70).

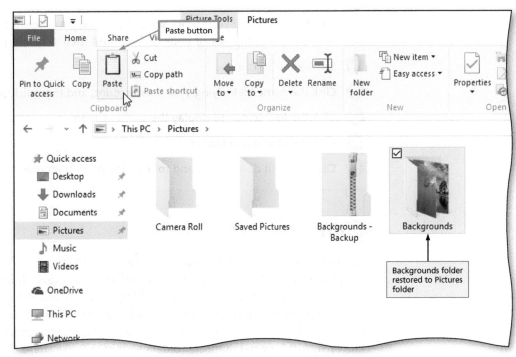

Figure 3–70

Other Ways
1. Select files to restore, right-click, click Copy on shortcut menu; navigate to original folder, right-click empty area of folder window, click Paste on shortcut menu
2. Select files to restore, press CTRL+C, navigate to original folder, press CTRL+V

To Delete Folders from the Pictures Folder and from OneDrive

To return the Pictures folder to its original state, you will delete the Backgrounds folder and the Backgrounds compressed (zipped) folder. The following steps delete the Backgrounds folder and the Backgrounds compressed (zipped) folder.

1 If necessary, navigate to the Pictures folder.

2 Select the Backgrounds folder, display the Home tab, and then click the Delete button (Home tab | Organize group) to delete the Backgrounds folder.

3 Select the Backgrounds zipped folder, display the Home tab, and then click the Delete button (Home tab | Organize group) to delete the Backgrounds compressed (zipped) folder.

4 Click OneDrive in the Navigation pane to display the contents of your OneDrive folder.

5 Select the Backgrounds – Backup compressed (zipped) folder, display the Home tab, and then click the Delete button (Home tab | Organize group) to delete the Backgrounds – Backup compressed (zipped) folder.

6 Close the OneDrive folder window.

To Sign Out of Your Account and Shut Down the Computer

After completing your work with Windows, you should follow these steps to end your session by signing out of your account and then shutting down the computer.

1 Display the Start menu.

2 Click the name identifying your user account, and then click Sign out.

3 Click the lock screen to display the sign-in screen.

4 Click the Shut down button.

5 Click the Shut down command to shut down the computer.

Summary

In this module, you have learned about the This PC window. You learned how to view the properties of drives and folders, as well as how to view their content. You worked with files and folders in the Pictures folder, reviewed and changed their properties, and viewed images in the Photos app and as a slide show. As part of this process, you also learned how to copy and move files, as well as how to create folders. You gained knowledge of how to compress folders so that you can share them. You also learned how to back up files and folders and then restore them using OneDrive.

Apply Your Knowledge

Reinforce the skills and apply the concepts you learned in this module.

File Properties

Instructions: You want to demonstrate to a friend how to display the properties of an image, display the image using the Paint app instead of the Photos app, and print the image. You also want to demonstrate how to display the properties of the folder containing the image.

Part 1: Displaying File Properties

1. Display the desktop and then click the File Explorer button to open the File Explorer window.

2. Click This PC in the navigation pane to display its contents (Figure 3–71).

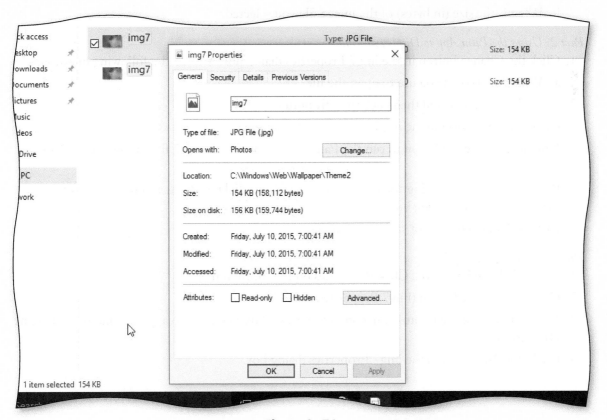

Figure 3–71

3. Double-click the 'Local Disk (C:)' icon.

4. Double-click the Windows folder.

5. Search for the img7 picture file. If the img7 file is not available on your computer, find another image file.

Continued >

Apply Your Knowledge *continued*

6. Right-click the img7 icon. Click Properties on the shortcut menu. Answer the following questions about the img7 file:

    a. What type of file is img7?

    b. What app is used to open the img7 image?

    c. What is the path for the location of the img7 file?

    d. What is the size (in bytes) of the img7 file?

    e. When was the file created?

    f. When was the file last modified?

    g. When was the file last accessed?

7. Search for another image file in the Windows folder and answer the following questions:

    a. What is the name of the image file you selected?

    b. What is the size (in bytes) of the image file you selected?

Part 2: Using the Paint App to Display an Image

1. Click the Change button in the img7 Properties dialog box. Answer the following question:

    a. Which app(s) can you use to open the file?

2. Click the Paint icon and then click the OK button.

3. Click the OK button in the img7 Properties dialog box.

4. Double-click the img7 icon to run the Paint app and open the img7 file in the img7 - Paint window.

5. Print the image by clicking the File tab on the ribbon, clicking Print, and then clicking the Print button (Print dialog box).

6. Exit the Paint app. Do not save any changes.

Part 3: Resetting the App Selection

1. Right-click the img7 icon. Click Properties on the shortcut menu.

2. Click the Change button (img7 Properties dialog box).

3. If necessary, click the Photos app icon in the dialog box to select the app icon and then click the OK button.

4. Click the OK button in the img7 Properties dialog box.

Extend Your Knowledge

Extend the skills you learned in this module and experiment with new skills.

Creating a Picture

Instructions: You want to use Paint to design a get well soon greeting for a friend and then print the message. Because you do not know the location of the Paint app, you first will search to find it.

Part 1: Searching for the Paint App

1. Type **paint** in the search box on the taskbar.

2. Click Paint in the search results to run the Paint app (Figure 3–72).

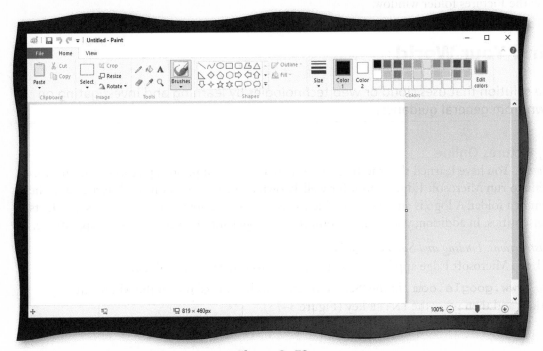

Figure 3–72

Part 2: Creating a Bitmap Image

1. Use the Pencil button to write the message, Get Well Soon! *Hint:* Hold down the left mouse button to write and release the left mouse button to stop writing. If you make a mistake and want to start over, click the Undo button on the Quick Access Toolbar.

2. If requested by your instructor, use the Pencil to write "From" and then your first name.

3. Click the File tab on the ribbon and then click Save as in the Backstage view. When the Save As dialog box is displayed, type **Get Well Soon** in the File name text box, if necessary click the Pictures folder in the navigation pane, and then click the Save button (Save As dialog box) to save the file in the Pictures folder.

4. Exit Paint.

Part 3: Viewing and Printing the Get Well Soon Image

1. Open the Pictures folder.

2. Double-click the 'Get Well Soon' icon in the Pictures folder window to open the picture in the Photos app.

3. After viewing the image in the Photos app, exit the Photos app and return to the Pictures folder window.

4. Display the Share tab and then click the Print button (Share tab | Send group) to display the Print Pictures dialog box.

5. Click the Print button (Print Pictures dialog box) to print the image.

6. Close the Print Pictures dialog box.

Continued >

Extend Your Knowledge *continued*

Part 4: Deleting the Get Well Soon Image

1. Click the Get Well Soon icon to select the file.

2. Click the Delete button (Home tab | Organize group).

3. Close the Pictures folder window.

Expand Your World

Create a solution that uses cloud or web technologies by learning and investigating on your own from general guidance.

Finding Pictures Online

Instructions: You have learned that the Internet is a great source of photos, pictures, and images. You decide to run Microsoft Edge, search for well-known company logos on the Internet, and then save them in a folder. A logo is an image that identifies businesses, government agencies, products, and other entities. In addition, you want to compress the logos into one compressed (zipped) file.

Part 1 Instructions: Finding and Saving Logo Images

1. Click the Microsoft Edge app button on the taskbar to run Microsoft Edge.

2. Type **www.google.com** in the 'Search or enter web address' box in the Microsoft Edge window, and then press the ENTER key (Figure 3–73).

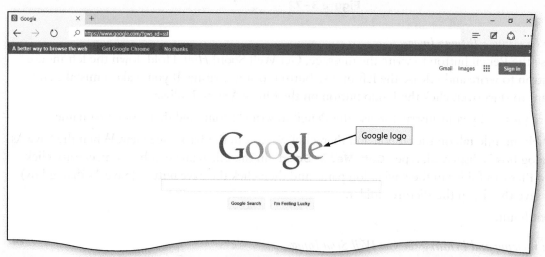

Figure 3–73

3. Locate the Google logo. Right-click the icon, click Save picture on the shortcut menu, name the file Google logo, and then click the Save button (Save As dialog box) to save the logo in the Pictures folder. If you are unable to save this image, contact your instructor for an alternate image to save for this step.

4. Type **www.microsoft.com** in the address bar and then press the ENTER key. Locate the Microsoft logo and use the file name, Microsoft logo, to save the Microsoft logo in the Pictures folder.

5. Exit Microsoft Edge.

6. Make the File Explorer window the active window and navigate to the Pictures folder. The Google logo and Microsoft image appear in the Pictures folder window.

Part 2 Instructions: Displaying File Properties

1. Right-click each logo file in the Pictures folder, click Properties on the shortcut menu, answer the following questions about the logos, and then close the Properties dialog box.

   a. What type of file is the Google logo file?

   b. What type of file is the Microsoft logo file?

2. Click an open area of the Pictures folder to deselect the logo file.

Part 3 Instructions: Creating the Logos Folder in the Pictures Folder

1. Create a new folder in the Pictures folder, type **Logos** in the new folder's text box, and then press the ENTER key.

2. Drag the each logo file to the Logos folder.

3. Refresh the image on the Logos folder.

Part 4 Instructions: Compressing the Logo Images

1. Right-click the Logos folder to display a shortcut menu.

2. Click Share on the ribbon to display the Share tab.

3. Click the Zip button (Share tab | Send group) to create a compressed (zipped) file.

4. Type **Logos Backup** as the file name and then press the ENTER key.

In the Labs

Design, create, modify, and/or use files following the guidelines, concepts, and skills presented in this module. Labs 1 and 2, which increase in difficulty, require you to create solutions based on what you learned in the module; Lab 3 requires you to apply your creative thinking and problem-solving skills to design and implement a solution.

Lab 1: **Using Search to Find Picture Files**

Problem: You know that searching is an important feature of Windows. You decide to use the Search box to find images on the hard drive. You will store the files in a folder in the Pictures folder and then print the images.

Part 1 Instructions: Searching for Files in the Search Results Window

1. If necessary, start Windows and sign in to your account.

2. Display the desktop.

3. Click the File Explorer button. Navigate to the This PC window. Maximize the This PC window.

4. Double-click Local Disk (C:), and then double-click the Windows folder to open it.

Continued >

In the Labs *continued*

5. In the Search box, type **garden** as the entry (Figure 3–74).

6. Copy the image to the Pictures folder.

Figure 3–74

Part 2 Instructions: Searching for Groups of Files

1. Navigate to the This PC window. Maximize the This PC window.

2. Double-click Local Disk (C:) and then double-click the Windows folder to open it.

3. In the Search box of the Windows folder, type **img1*** as the search text.

4. Answer the following question:

   a. How many files were found?

5. Click the img101 icon to select the icon. If the img101 icon does not appear, select another icon.

6. Copy the image to the Pictures folder.

Part 3 Instructions: Creating the More Backgrounds Folder in the Pictures Folder

1. If necessary, navigate to the Pictures folder. Click the New folder button on the Quick Access Toolbar, type **More Backgrounds** in the new folder's text box, and then press the ENTER key.

2. Select the icons of the images you copied to the Pictures folder and then move the images to the More Backgrounds folder.

3. Right-click an open area of the window and refresh the image on the More Backgrounds folder.

Part 4 Instructions: Printing the Images

1. Open the More Backgrounds folder.

2. Select the pictures.

3. Display the Share tab, click the Print button (Share tab | Send group) and then click the Print button (Print Pictures dialog box) to print the photos.

4. Delete the More Backgrounds folder from the Pictures folder.

5. Close the Pictures folder window.

Lab 2: **Backing Up Your Files**

Problem: Several files exist on your computer that you would like to store in their own compressed folder and then back up to OneDrive.

Perform the following tasks:
1. Click the File Explorer button on the taskbar to open the File Explorer window.
2. Display the This PC window.
3. Display the Local Disk (C:) window (or the window for your primary hard drive).
4. Display the contents of the Windows folder.
5. Perform a search for all files with the file name extension, .jpg. *Hint:* Search for *.jpg (Figure 3–75).

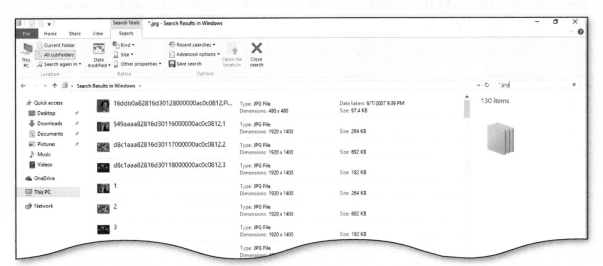

Figure 3–75

6. Copy five images of your choice to the Pictures folder.
7. Navigate to the Pictures folder window.
8. Create a new folder named, Important Pictures - Backup, and copy the five images to it.
9. Compress the Important Pictures - Backup folder.
10. Copy the Important Pictures - Backup compressed (zipped) folder to OneDrive.
11. Delete the Important Pictures - Backup folder and the Important Pictures - Backup compressed (zipped) folder from the Pictures folder.
12. Display the contents of the OneDrive folder, and copy the compressed (zipped) Important Pictures - Backup folder to the Pictures folder.
13. Copy the Important Pictures - Backup folder from the compressed (zipped) folder to the Pictures folder.
14. Delete the Important Pictures - Backup compressed (zipped) folder from the Pictures folder.

Continued >

In the Labs *continued*

Lab 3: **Consider This: Your Turn**

Researching Data Security

Problem: Stored data stored is one of a company's most valuable assets. If that data were to be stolen, lost, or compromised so that it could not be accessed, the company could go out of business. Therefore, companies go to great lengths to protect their data.

Part 1:   Working with classmates, research how the companies where you each work handle their backups. If you are unable to determine this information from the company where you work, contact another local company for information.

Part 2:   Find out how each company protects its data against malware, unauthorized access, and even against natural disasters, such as fire and floods. Prepare a brief report that describes the companies' procedures. In your report, point out any areas where you find a company has not protected its data adequately.

4 | Personalizing Your Work Environment

Objectives

You will have mastered the material in this module when you can:

- Differentiate among the various types of user accounts
- Create user accounts
- Create a picture password
- Personalize the lock screen
- Customize the Start screen
- Work with multiple desktops
- Work with and customize the taskbar
- Display the Action Center
- View and modify folder options

Introduction

One of the best ways to improve productivity while using a computer is to personalize your work environment. For example, you can change your desktop's appearance, screen resolution, screen saver, taskbar, and folder options to best suit how you work. Similarly, users often personalize their computers by adding unique touches. This includes changing their lock screen and Start menu to display the apps and colors relevant to them. By personalizing the work environment, users feel more in tune with their computers, which can put them more at ease and lead to improved productivity.

User Accounts

A **user account** is a collection of information that Windows requires about a computer user. When you are signed in to an account, the Start menu displays the user account that is signed in at the upper-left corner of the menu. Information is saved for each user account, including the user name, password, picture, and rights and permissions the user has for accessing a computer or network resources. User accounts make it possible for each user to perform tasks, such as sign in to the computer, keep information confidential and computer settings protected, customize Windows, store files in unique folders, and maintain a personal list of favorite websites.

Normally, user accounts operate in standard user mode, which allows you to use most of the capabilities of the computer. A standard user cannot install software that affects other users or change system settings that affect security. An administrator account has full control of the computer and operating system and can change user permissions, install software that affects all users, and change all system settings. When a task requires administrator access, depending on how Windows is configured, the User Account Control feature might prompt you to authorize the task. By default, you are asked for permission only when apps attempt to make a change to the computer. Once authorized, the user has temporary administrator privileges. After the task is finished, the user returns to standard user mode. User Account Control is designed to prevent malicious software from being installed inadvertently, even by administrators. For standard user accounts, the user needs to know an administrator account user name and the password to authorize User Account Control. Only administrators are prompted to continue without requiring a user name and password. Table 4–1 provides a list of the different privileges for the account types.

Table 4–1 User Accounts and Privileges	
User Account Type	**Privileges**
Administrator	Create, change, and delete user accounts
	Install programs and apps
	Set folder sharing
	Set permissions
	Access all files
	Take ownership of files
	Grant rights to other user accounts and to their own accounts
	Install or remove hardware devices
	Sign in using safe mode
Standard	Change the password and picture for their own user accounts
	Use programs that have been installed on the computer
	View permissions
	Create, change, and delete files in their libraries
	View files in shared document folders

Local Accounts

Windows supports Microsoft accounts and local accounts. A **local account** is an account that works on only one computer. A local account can be either an administrative or a standard account. A local account does not integrate automatically with the cloud, which enables features such as saving files and synchronizing your Windows settings on OneDrive. Recall in Module 3 that you copied a file to OneDrive.

Microsoft Accounts

If you create a Microsoft account on Microsoft's website, you can have access to email, OneDrive, and Microsoft Office Online. When you are signed in with a Microsoft account, you can access the services provided on the web for Microsoft account holders. Apps that support Microsoft accounts will allow you to use the associated services that a local account may not be able to use, such as OneDrive. When you add a Microsoft account to your computer, as is the case with a local account, it can be an administrative or a standard account.

When using a Microsoft account, your sign-in settings can be saved on the Internet. When you sign in to Windows on another computer, your settings will be used from your Microsoft account. You can sync your account to the web, which allows you to carry your settings from computer to computer automatically. If you are signed in to Windows with a Microsoft account and you save your files to OneDrive, your files will be readily available if you sign in to another computer using the same Microsoft account. In some lab settings, you may not be able to use your Microsoft account if the lab does not allow you to sign in without a local account. Your instructor can tell you if you can sign in using your Microsoft account.

To Create a Microsoft Account

Why? *You might want to have a Microsoft account so that you can save files on OneDrive and synchronize your user settings.* The following steps create a Microsoft account. If you already have a Microsoft account or do not wish to create a Microsoft account, read these steps without performing them.

1

- Type **https://signup.live.com** in the search box on the taskbar and then press the ENTER key to display the Create an account webpage in the Microsoft Edge browser (Figure 4–1).

Q&A Why did a Sign In webpage appear instead of the Create an account webpage?

If you already are signed in to Windows with a Microsoft account, the Sign In webpage might be displayed. To continue creating a Microsoft account, click the links on the page to sign in with a different Microsoft account and then to create a new Microsoft account.

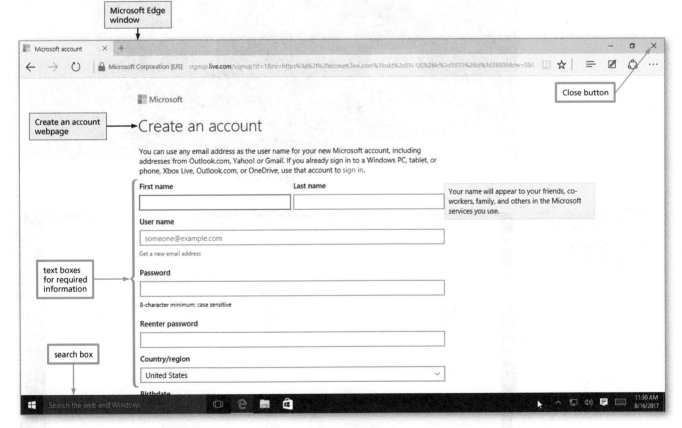

Figure 4–1

2

- Complete the requested information and follow the required steps to create your account.

- When the account has been created, click the Close button to close Microsoft Edge and return to the desktop.

Setting Up User Accounts

Windows users who want to allow multiple people use of their computer can add an account for each user. When adding an account, you can add either a local or Microsoft account. For the Microsoft account to be used, the computer should have an Internet connection. Once you have added the accounts, different users then can sign in to their account by selecting it on the sign-in screen. To add an account, you first must run the Settings app.

To Add a Local Account

Why? *You have decided to let another person use your computer.* The following steps add a local account with the user name, SC Student.

- Display the Start menu (Figure 4–2).

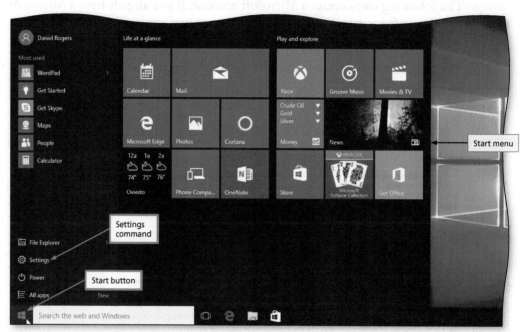

Figure 4–2

- Click Settings on the Start menu to run the Settings app (Figure 4–3).

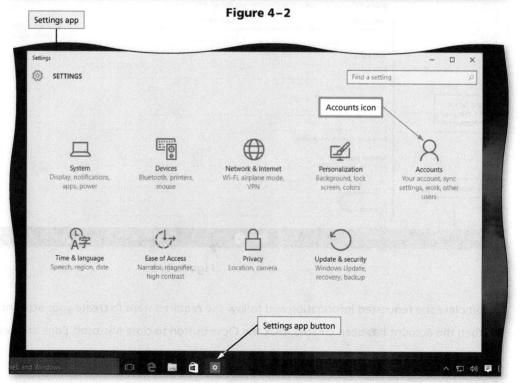

Figure 4–3

3

- Click the Accounts icon to view the Accounts page and related settings (Figure 4–4).

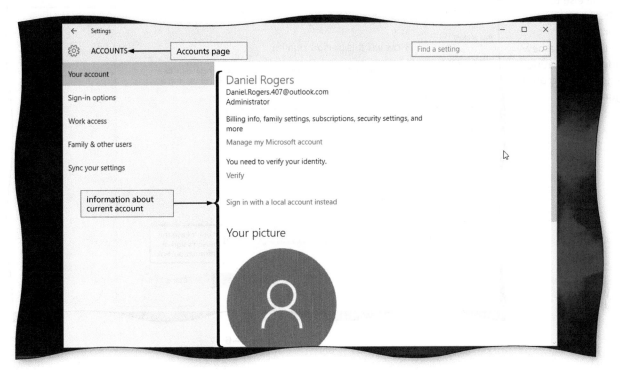

Figure 4–4

4

- Click the 'Family & other users' tab to display the page allowing you to add accounts to Windows (Figure 4–5). If necessary, click the Yes button in the User Account Control dialog box.

Q&A What if I do not see the 'Family & other users' option?

You might not be signed in to Windows using an Administrator account. Recall that Standard user accounts are unable to add accounts to the computer. If you are unable to sign in to the computer with an Administrator account, read these steps without performing them.

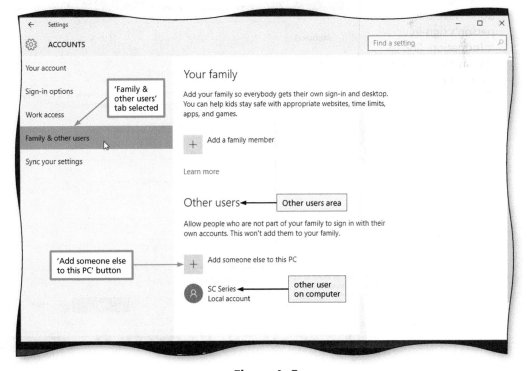

Figure 4–5

5

- Click the 'Add someone else to this PC' button in the Other users area to display a new window for creating the new user account (Figure 4–6).

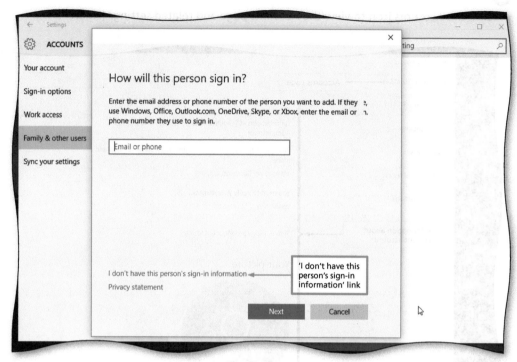

Figure 4–6

6

- Click the 'I don't have this person's sign-in information' link to display the account creation page (Figure 4–7).

Q&A Can I also create a Microsoft account on this page?

Yes. You can create a Microsoft account at the same time you add a Microsoft account to your computer, if desired.

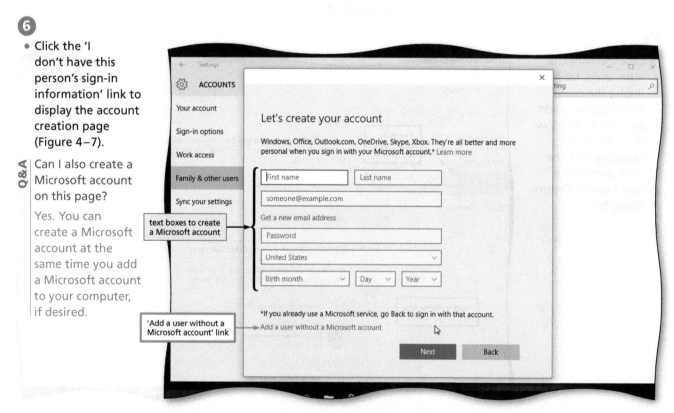

Figure 4–7

7

- Click the 'Add a user without a Microsoft account' link to display several text boxes prompting you for account information.

- Type **SC Student** in the User name text box.

- Type **Windows10** in the Enter password text box.

- Type **Windows10** in the Re-enter password text box.

- Type **Standard password** in the Password hint text box (Figure 4–8).

Q&A What password should I use when creating user accounts on my computer?

Whether you are creating a Microsoft account or a local account, you should create a secure password. Secure passwords have more than eight characters, both uppercase and lowercase letters, numbers, and special characters (such as a question mark, exclamation mark, asterisk, or ampersand). The longer your password and the more of these different types of characters, the more secure your account will become.

Why do I have to type a password hint?

In the event you forget your password, the hint might help you remember it. However, this hint can be seen by anyone attempting to sign in to your account, so make sure it is not helpful enough for someone else to determine the password.

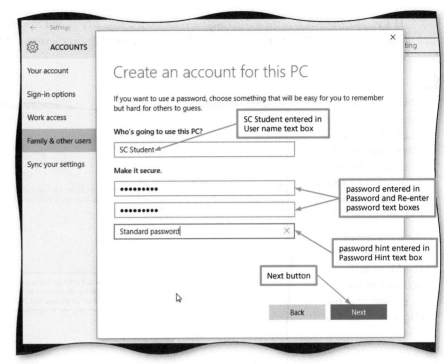

Figure 4–8

8

- Click the Next button to create the account. If necessary, scroll to view the SC Student user account (Figure 4–9). If necessary, click the Yes button in the User Account Control dialog box.

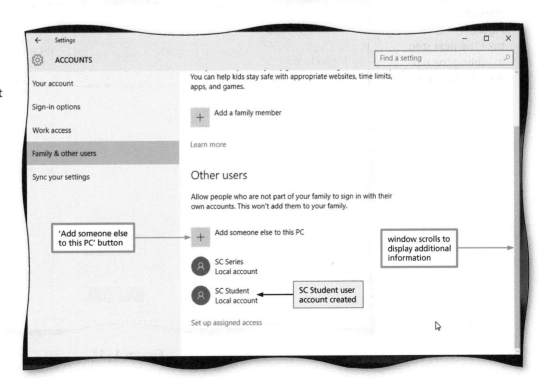

Figure 4–9

To Add a Microsoft Account

Why? *You recently created a Microsoft account and would like to add it so that you easily can integrate features, such as OneDrive and Office Online, while working with your Windows account.* The following steps add a Microsoft account.

- With the 'Family & other users' settings displayed, click the 'Add someone else to this PC' button to prepare to add a Microsoft account to the computer.

- Type the email address for the Microsoft account in the 'Email or phone' text box (Figure 4–10).

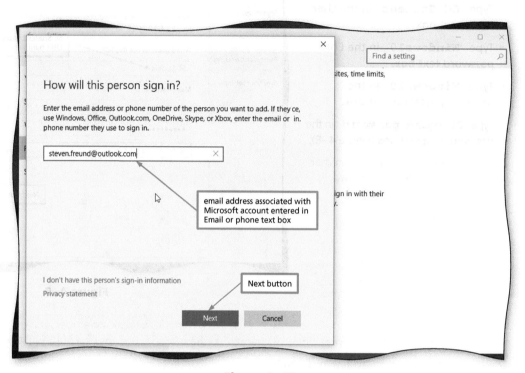

Figure 4–10

- Click the Next button (shown in Figure 4–10) to take the next step in adding the new account (Figure 4–11).

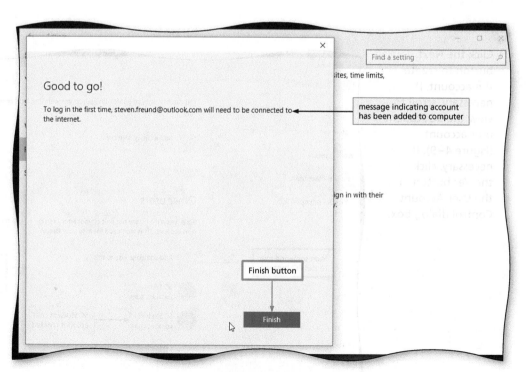

Figure 4–11

3

- Click the Finish button to add the Microsoft account to the computer (Figure 4–12).

- Click the Close button to exit the Settings app.

Q&A Why did I not have to specify a user name or password when creating the Microsoft account?

When you sign in to Windows with a Microsoft account, the email address associated with the account is the user name. The password is the same password you specified when creating the Microsoft account. If you ever change your Microsoft account password, you will need to sign in to Windows using the new password.

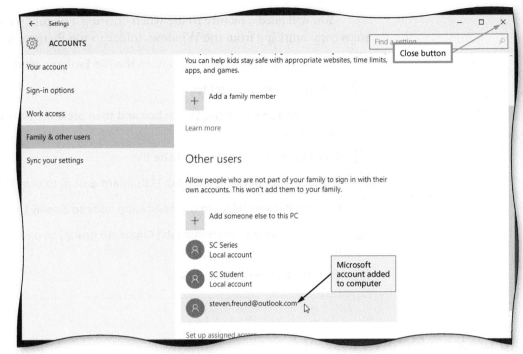

Figure 4–12

If I currently am using a local account with Windows, can I convert it to a Microsoft account?

Yes. To convert a local account to a Microsoft account, click the Start button, click Settings on the Start menu, click the Accounts icon in the Settings window, and, with Your account selected, click the 'Sign in with a Microsoft account instead' link and follow the steps to convert your local account to a Microsoft account.

To Sign In to a Microsoft Account

After creating a Microsoft account and adding it to your computer, you can sign in to your computer using the Microsoft account. If you wanted to sign in to your computer with the newly created Microsoft account, you would perform the following steps.

1. If necessary, sign out of your existing account.
2. Click the lock screen to display the sign-in screen.
3. Click the name and email address associated with your Microsoft account.
4. Type your Microsoft account password in the text box and then press the ENTER key to sign in to Windows.

Picture Passwords

Instead of using a password that you have to type in, Windows allows you to use a picture password. A **picture password** involves you selecting a picture and then adding gestures to use for your password. A gesture can be a circle, a straight line, or a click. When you sign in to your account, you will use those gestures to sign in, rather than a password. You always can go back and remove the picture password should you no longer want to use it. Also, you can change your picture password to use a different picture or different gestures. While a picture password can be difficult for others to guess, beware of individuals looking over your shoulder as you enter the picture password, as it may be easy for them to remember.

BTW

Picture Passwords
Picture passwords are easiest to use when you are using Windows on a computer with a touch screen, so that you can draw the gestures directly on the screen using your finger. If you are using a keyboard and mouse with your computer, it might be easier just to type a password instead of using a picture password.

To Copy a Picture

You will need a picture to use when creating a picture password. The following steps copy img1.jpg from the Windows folder to the Pictures folder.

1 Click the File Explorer button to open the File Explorer window.

2 Display the Windows folder.

3 Type **img1.jpg** in the Search box and then press the ENTER key to search for the img1 picture.

4 Click the img1 picture to select the file.

5 Click the Copy button (Home tab | Clipboard group) to copy the file to the Clipboard.

6 Click the Pictures folder in the navigation pane to display the Pictures folder.

7 Click the Paste button (Home tab | Clipboard group) to paste the file in the Pictures folder.

8 Close the Pictures folder window.

To Create a Picture Password

Why? *You want to use a picture password so that it is easier to enter on a touch-enabled device.* Once you create the gestures, you will have to repeat them to make sure you are using the same exact gestures. If you recognize that you have made a mistake, you can click the Start over button (Picture password dialog box) to begin again. Should you fail to enter them correctly the second time, you will be prompted to try again. The following steps create a picture password.

- Display the Start menu.

- Click Settings to run the Settings app.

- Click the Accounts icon in the Settings window to display the account options.

- Click the Sign-in options tab in the left pane to display the sign-in options for the current account (Figure 4–13).

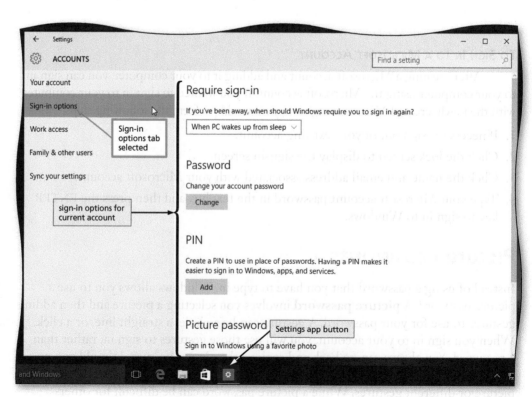

Figure 4–13

2

- If necessary, scroll in the right pane to display the Add button in the Picture password area (Figure 4–14).

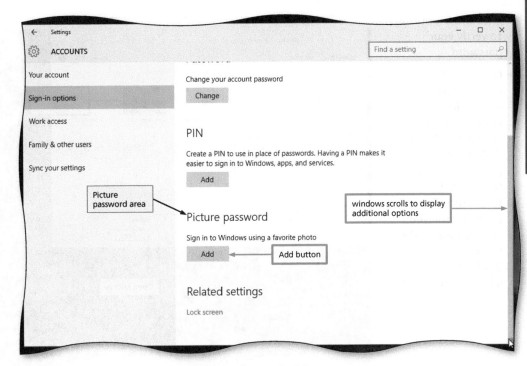

Figure 4–14

3

- Click the Add button below the Picture password heading to display the Create a picture password dialog box.

- Type your current Windows password in the Password text box (Figure 4–15).

Q&A

Why do I have to type my Windows password?

You have to type your Windows password as a safety precaution. If you are signed in to your Windows account and leave your computer unattended, this measure will prevent people from sitting at your computer and quickly changing your password to something else.

Figure 4–15

4

- Click the OK button to verify your password.

- Click the Choose picture button (shown in Figure 4–15) to display the Open dialog box (Figure 4–16). If the contents of the Pictures folder are not displayed, click Pictures in the navigation pane to display the contents of the Pictures folder.

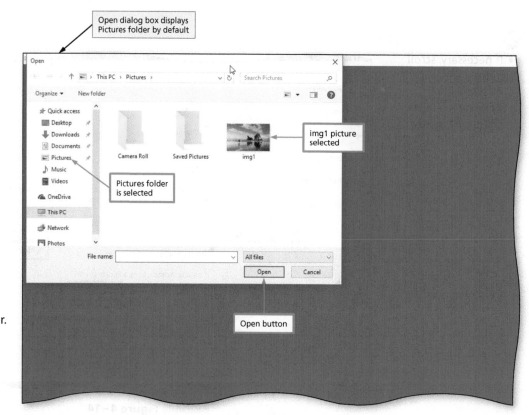

Open dialog box displays Pictures folder by default

img1 picture selected

Pictures folder is selected

Open button

Figure 4–16

5

- Click the img1 picture to select it.

- Click the Open button (shown in Figure 4–16) to select the img1 image (Figure 4–17).

How's this look?

Drag your picture to position it the way you want.

Use this picture

'Use this picture' button

Choose new picture

'Choose new picture' button allows you to choose a different picture

preview of selected picture

Cancel

Search the web and Windows

11:42 AM
8/16/2017

Figure 4–17

6

- Click the 'Use this picture' button to select this picture for use (Figure 4–18).

Figure 4–18

7

- Perform three gestures of your choice either using your mouse or finger (if you have a touch screen). Gestures might include tapping or clicking, or dragging to create a curved or straight line or a shape. If you make a mistake, click the Start over button (shown in Figure 4–18).

- Perform the three gestures again to confirm them (Figure 4–19).

Q&A What happens if I forget my picture password?

Your original password still exists, so you still have the option of signing in to Windows using that password.

8

- Click the Finish button to save the picture password.

- Exit the Settings app.

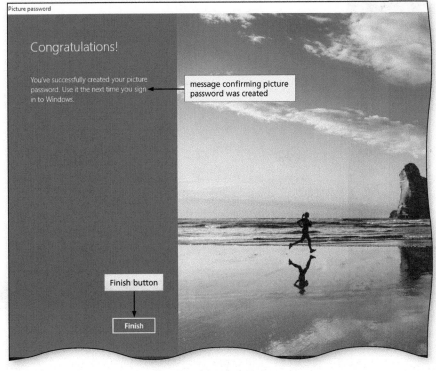

Figure 4–19

Personalization

One way to personalize your Windows settings is to change the appearance of the desktop, lock screen, and Start menu. Personalization settings that you can apply to the desktop include changing the background and accent color. For the lock screen, you can change the apps that are displayed to the apps that you want or use most frequently. They will run in the background and be available whenever the lock screen is displayed. You also can change settings, such as the screen resolution and screen saver. You can change most personalization settings using the Settings app.

To Change the Desktop Background

Windows allows you to specify one of three settings for the desktop background. In this textbook, all figures showing the desktop show the default Windows background image; however, you can change the desktop background to a different picture, a solid color, or a slideshow consisting of two or more pictures that change at a set interval. *Why? You want to change the desktop background to show something that is of interest to you.* The following steps change the desktop background using a picture, solid color, and slideshow.

- Display the Start menu.
- Click Settings on the Start menu to run the Settings app (Figure 4–20).

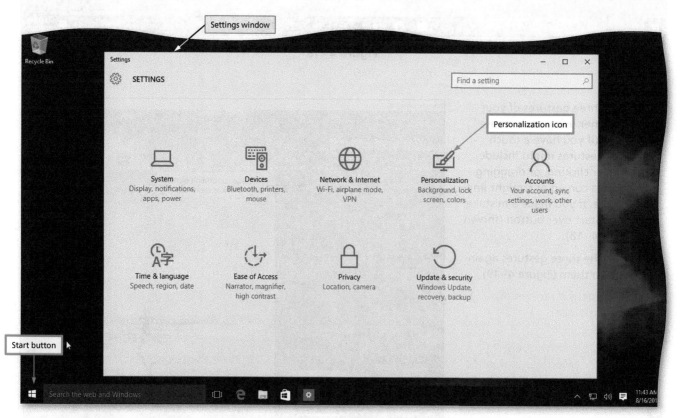

Figure 4–20

2

● Click the Personalization icon in the Settings window to display the Personalization page and its related settings (Figure 4–21).

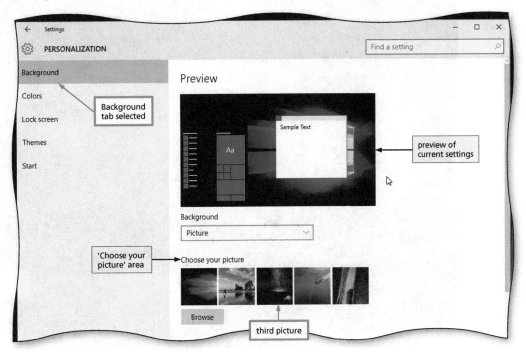

Figure 4–21

3

● Make sure the Background tab is selected in the left pane.

● Click to select the third picture (shown in Figure 4–21) in the Choose your picture area to change the desktop background (Figure 4–22).

Q&A Can I use a picture other than the ones shown?

Yes. If you want to use your own picture, click the Browse button and then navigate to and select the picture you want to use.

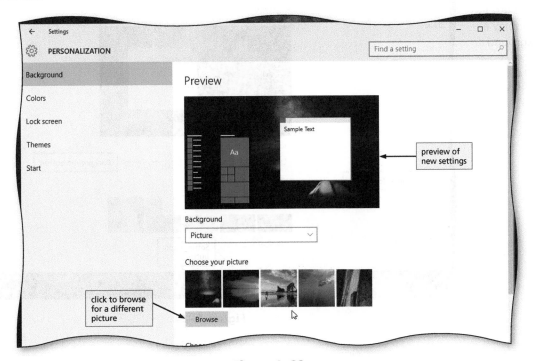

Figure 4–22

4

- Click the Show desktop button to minimize all open windows and preview the new desktop background (Figure 4–23).

Figure 4–23

5

- Click the Settings app button on the taskbar to view the Settings window.

- Click the Background button to display a list of background options (Figure 4–24).

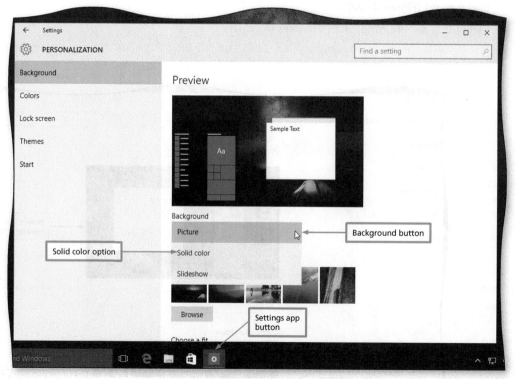

Figure 4–24

- Click Solid color in the Background list to display a list of available background colors.

- Click the red background color to change the desktop background to a solid color (Figure 4–25).

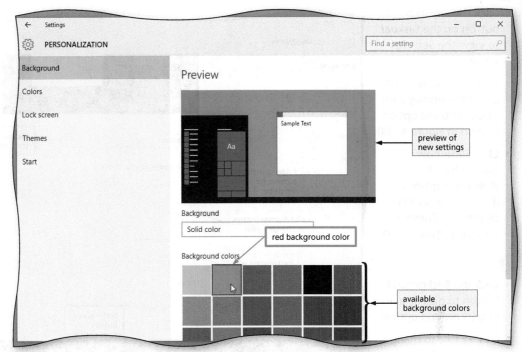

Figure 4–25

- Click the Show desktop button to minimize all windows so that you can preview the solid background color (Figure 4–26).

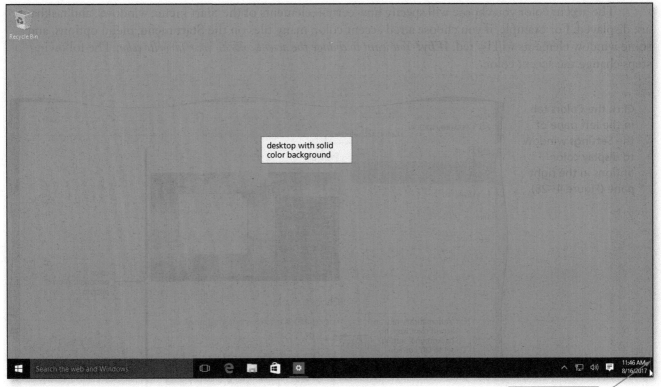

Figure 4–26

Show desktop button

- Click the Settings app button on the taskbar to view the Settings window.

- Click the Background button to display a list of background options (shown in Figure 4–24).

- Click Slideshow to show a list of slideshow options. If necessary, scroll to display all slideshow options (Figure 4–27).

- Click the Background button to display a list of background options.

- Click Picture to change the desktop background to a picture.

- Choose the third picture in the Choose a picture area to change the desktop background again.

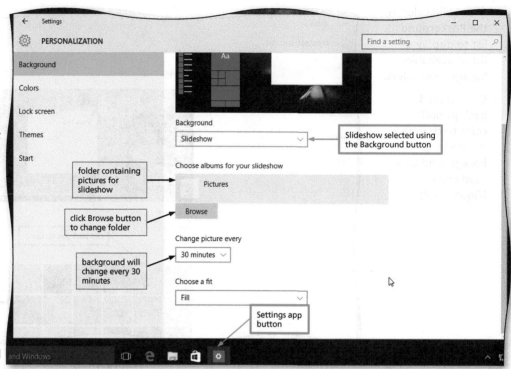

Figure 4–27

To Change the Accent Color

The accent color you choose will specify how certain elements of the Start menu, windows, and taskbar are displayed. For example, if you choose a red accent color, many tiles on the Start menu, menu options, and some window elements will be red. *Why? You want to change the accent color to your favorite color.* The following steps change the accent color.

- Click the Colors tab in the left pane of the Settings window to display color options in the right pane (Figure 4–28).

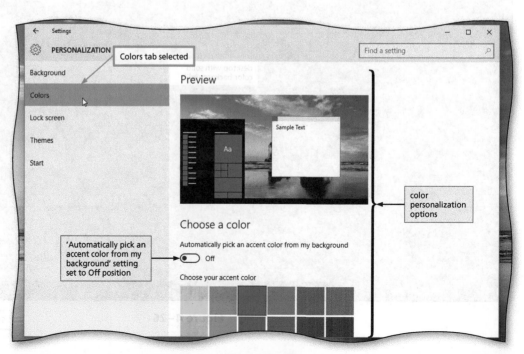

Figure 4–28

2

- Scroll to display the palette of available accent colors (Figure 4–29).

- Make a note of the accent color currently selected. The selected accent color is identified by a thin border surrounding the color.

Q&A Why are no accent colors being displayed?

The 'Automatically pick an accent color from my background' setting might be set to the On position. This feature will determine an accent color that matches your desktop background and apply it automatically. To see the palette of accent colors, change this setting to Off by clicking it.

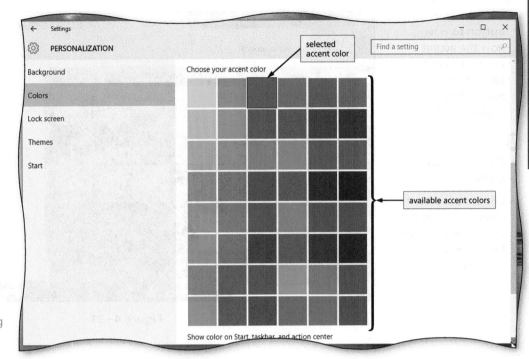

Figure 4–29

3

- Click the orange accent color to change the accent color (Figure 4–30).

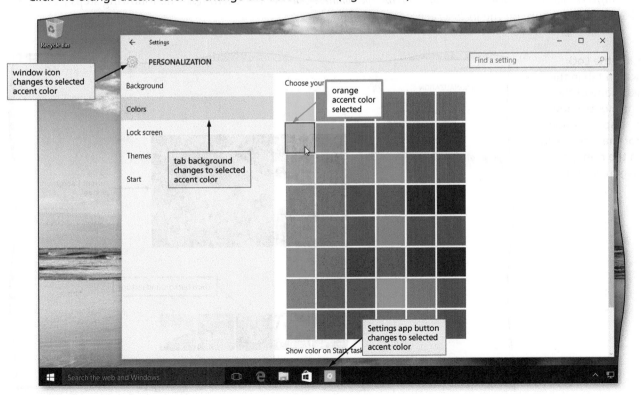

Figure 4–30

4

- Click the Start button to view how the accent color changes the appearance of the Start menu (Figure 4–31).

5

- Close the Start menu.

- Choose the accent color you made note of in Step 2 to revert back to your original settings.

tiles, icons, and buttons use new accent color

Figure 4–31

To Change the Appearance of the Lock Screen

As you have learned, the lock screen is the screen that appears when you first start Windows or after you sign out of your Windows account. Clicking or swiping the lock screen then displays the sign-in screen. Similar to changing the desktop background, you also can personalize the lock screen background. *Why? You would like to use a different picture for your lock screen to further personalize your Windows settings.* The following steps change the background picture on the lock screen.

1

- Click the Lock screen tab in the left pane of the Settings window to display options for the lock screen in the right pane (Figure 4–32).

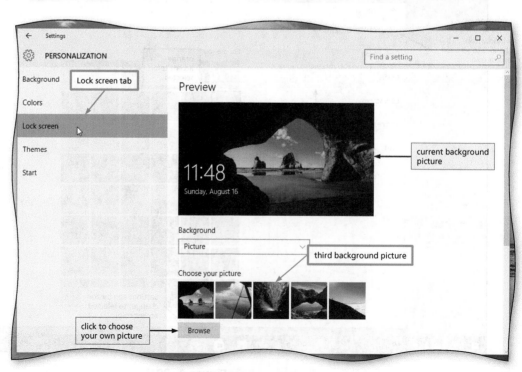

Lock screen tab

current background picture

third background picture

click to choose your own picture

Figure 4–32

2

- Make note of the background picture currently being displayed.

- Click the third background picture to change the background on the lock screen (Figure 4–33).

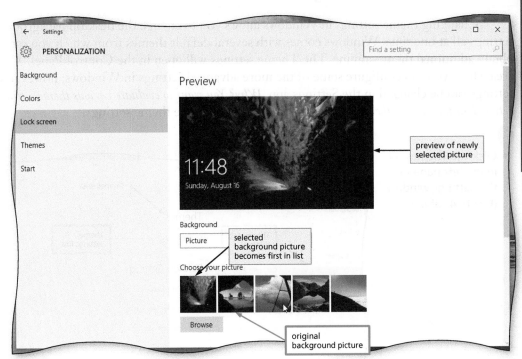

Preview

preview of newly selected picture

Background

Picture

selected background picture becomes first in list

Choose your picture

Browse

original background picture

Figure 4–33

3

- Click the background picture you made note of in Step 2 to revert the lock screen background to its original setting.

- Scroll the right pane to view additional lock screen settings (Figure 4–34).

Q&A

What other options are available for personalizing the lock screen?

Many options are available. You can use a different picture by clicking the Browse button and then navigating

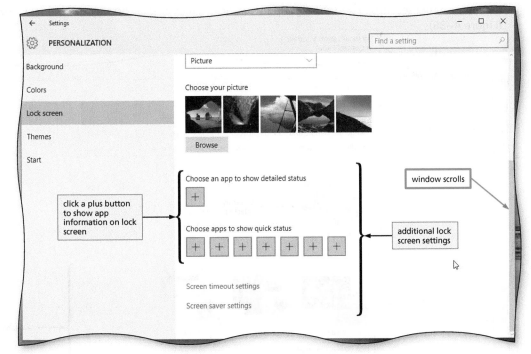

Picture

Choose your picture

Browse

Choose an app to show detailed status

click a plus button to show app information on lock screen

Choose apps to show quick status

Screen timeout settings

Screen saver settings

window scrolls

additional lock screen settings

Figure 4–34

to and selecting the picture of your choice, you can view a slideshow of images as your lock screen background, and you can display information from selected apps on the lock screen. For example, if you have an email account configured on your computer, you can configure the lock screen to show how many new email messages are awaiting your attention.

To Change Theme Settings

Changing theme settings in Windows allows you to change the desktop background, colors, and sound settings all at one time. Windows comes with several default themes from which you can choose, or you can obtain additional themes online. The Theme settings will open in the Control Panel. The **Control Panel** is an area where you can configure some of the more advanced settings in Windows; however, you will find that most settings can be changed in the Settings app. *Why? You want to evaluate various theme settings to see if you like any better than the current theme.* The following steps change the theme settings.

1

● Click the Themes tab in the left pane of the Settings window (Figure 4–35).

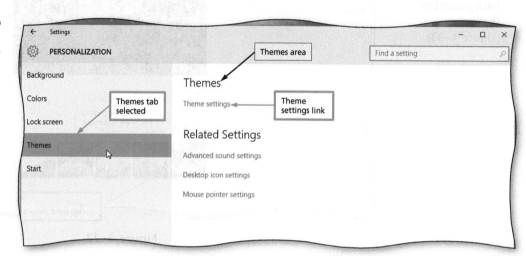

Figure 4–35

2

● Click the Theme settings link in the right pane in the Themes area to display the theme settings in the Control Panel (Figure 4–36).

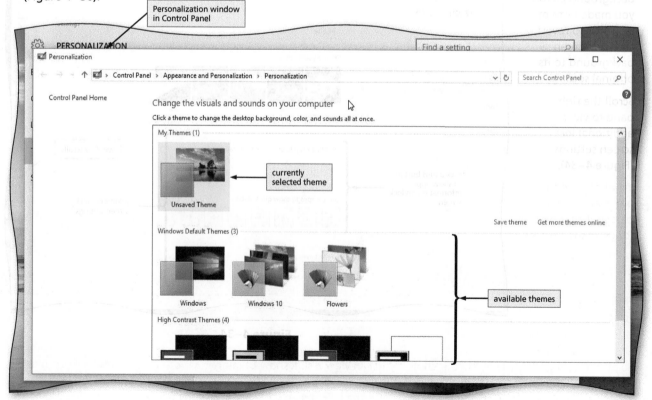

Figure 4–36

- Make a note of the theme that currently is selected.

- Click the Flowers theme to change the theme to Flowers (Figure 4–37).

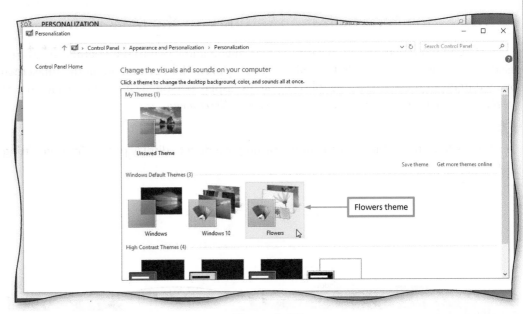

Figure 4–37

- Click the Show desktop button to minimize all windows and view the changes (Figure 4–38).

Q&A What changed when I selected the Flowers theme?
Visible changes include a different desktop background and updated colors.

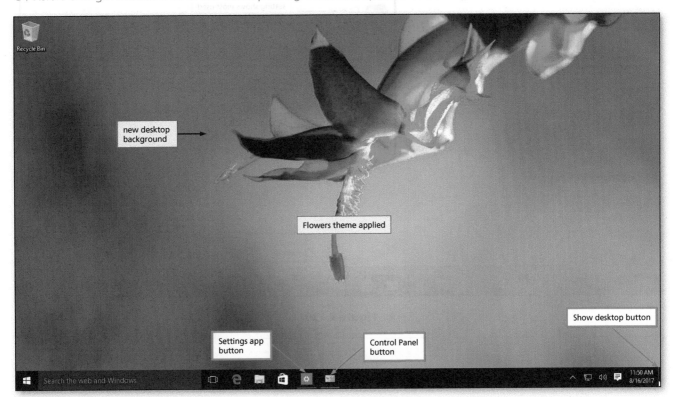

Figure 4–38

- Click the Control Panel button on the taskbar to display the Control Panel.
- Click the theme you recorded from Step 3 to restore the theme to the previous setting.
- Click the Close button to close the Control Panel.
- Click the Settings app button on the taskbar to display the Settings app.

To Display the Personalization Settings for the Start Menu

The Personalization settings for the Start menu allow you to set whether the Start menu shows the most used apps, shows recently added (installed) apps, displays the Start menu on the full screen, or shows recently opened items in Jump Lists. The following steps display personalization settings for the Start menu. *Why? You would like to see the settings you can customize for your Start menu.*

1

- Click the Start tab in the left pane of the Settings window to display personalization settings for the Start menu (Figure 4–39).

Q&A

What is a Jump List?

If a command on the Start menu has a Jump List, an arrow will appear next to the command. When you click the arrow, the Jump List is displayed and will contain a list of recently viewed files or webpages using that app. Clicking an item on the Jump List will open the selected file or webpage in its respective app.

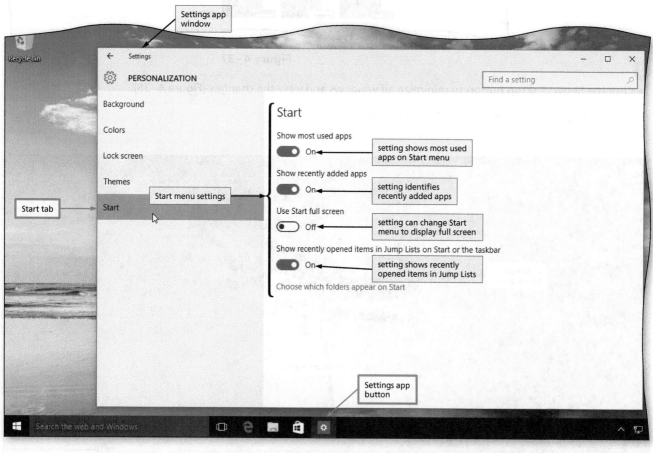

Figure 4–39

To Display the Control Panel

Why? You might need to display the Control Panel in some instances where you would like to access and change settings you are unable to find in the Settings app. The following steps display the Control Panel.

1

- Type **control panel** in the search box to display the search results (Figure 4–40).

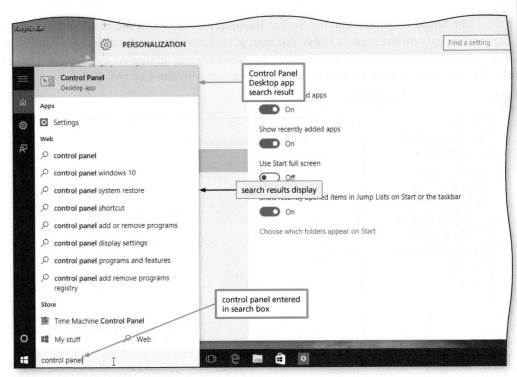

Figure 4–40

2

- Click the Control Panel Desktop app search result to display the Control Panel (Figure 4–41).

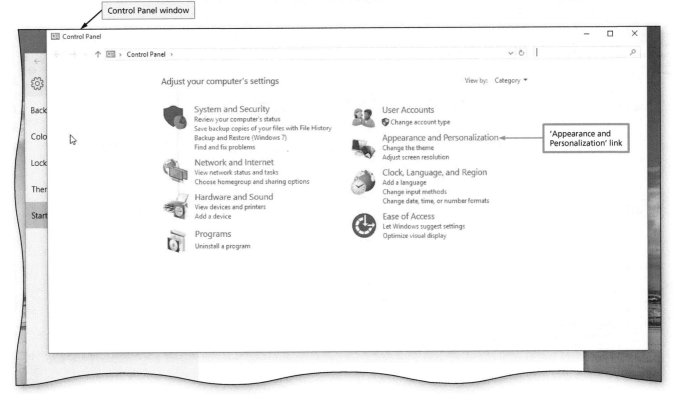

Figure 4–41

To View the Display Window and the Screen Resolution Window

The Display window and the Screen Resolution window in the Control Panel enable you to change how content appears on the screen. *Why? You want to view the settings available that can adjust brightness, calibrate color, and change the screen resolution (which affects how much content displays on the screen at once).* The following steps view the Display window and the Screen Resolution window in the Control Panel.

1

- Click the 'Appearance and Personalization' link (shown in Figure 4–41) in the Control Panel window to display the Appearance and Personalization settings (Figure 4–42).

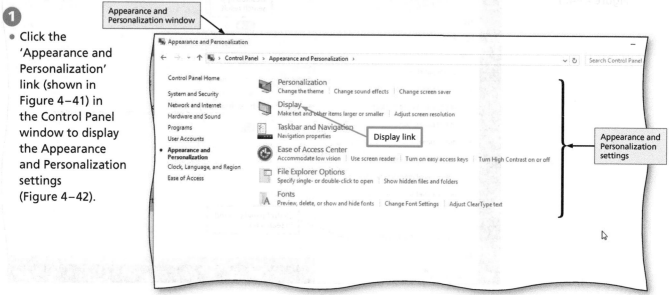

Figure 4–42

2

- Click the Display link (shown in Figure 4–42) to display the Display settings (Figure 4–43).

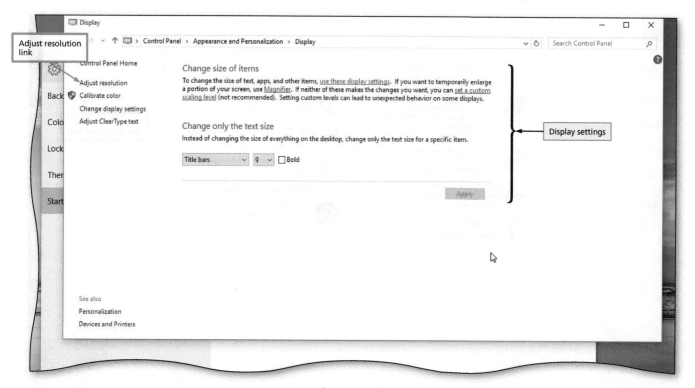

Figure 4–43

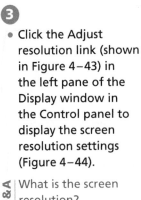

• Click the Adjust resolution link (shown in Figure 4–43) in the left pane of the Display window in the Control panel to display the screen resolution settings (Figure 4–44).

Q&A

What is the screen resolution?

The screen resolution specifies how many pixels displays on the screen at one time. As you increase the resolution, more content will be displayed on the screen, and all screen elements (windows, menus, buttons, and so on) will appear smaller.

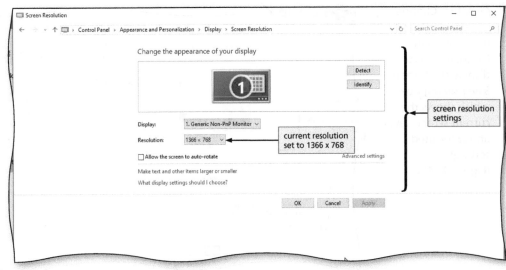

Figure 4–44

To Change the Screen Saver

Another element of a desktop theme that you can modify is the screen saver. A **screen saver** is a moving picture or pattern that is displayed on the monitor when you have not interacted with the computer for a specified period of time. Originally, screen savers were designed to prevent the problem of **ghosting** (where a dim version of an image would permanently be etched on the monitor if the same image were to be displayed for a long time) by continually changing the image on the monitor. Although ghosting is less of a problem with today's monitors, people still use screen savers. Screen savers can be animations, designs, and other entertaining or fascinating activities that are displayed on the screen after a period of time has passed without any computer activity. You can determine how long this interval should be. Screen savers stop executing when you press a key on the keyboard, move the mouse, or touch the screen. Windows 10 provides a variety of screen savers from which you can choose. *Why? Your computer currently has no screen saver configured, and you want to select and enable one.* The following steps change the screen saver.

• Click the 'Appearance and Personalization' button in the address bar of the Screen resolution window to return to the 'Appearance and Personalization' window (Figure 4–45).

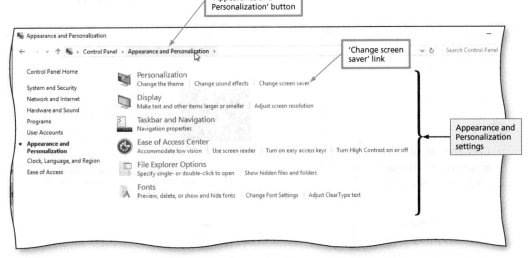

Figure 4–45

②

- Click the 'Change screen saver' link (shown in Figure 4–45) to display the Screen Saver dialog box, which shows the current screen saver and associated settings (Figure 4–46).

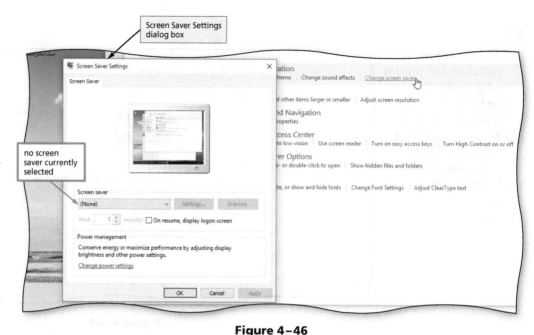

Figure 4–46

③

- Make a note of the screen saver (if any) that currently is selected.

- Click the Screen saver button to view a list of available screen savers (Figure 4–47).

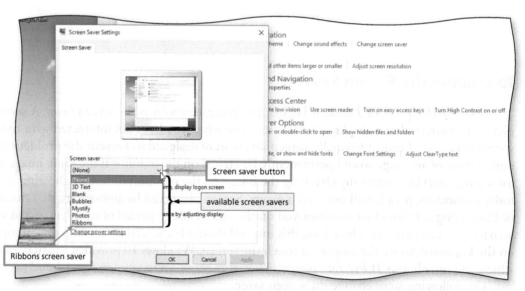

Figure 4–47

④

- Click Ribbons in the list of available screen savers to select it (Figure 4–48).

⑤

- Click the OK button to apply the changes to the screen saver settings.

- If desired, repeat Steps 2 through 5 to set the screen saver back to the original setting from Step 3.

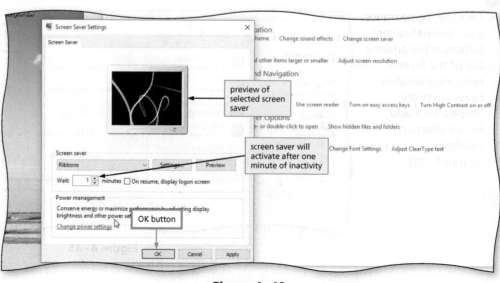

Figure 4–48

To Display Task View and Add a Desktop

Task View allows you to see thumbnail images of all windows and apps you currently have open or running. Viewing thumbnail images of all open windows and apps makes it easy for you to switch between apps if you have multiple windows open at one time. As mentioned previously, the desktop is a workspace where your open windows and apps are displayed. *Why? If you feel your desktop is becoming cluttered, you can add a desktop that displays some windows, while other open windows remain on your original desktop.* The following steps display Task View and add a desktop.

1
• Click the Task View button on the taskbar to display Task View (Figure 4–49).

Figure 4–49

2
• Click the New desktop button in the lower-right corner of the desktop to add a second desktop (Figure 4–50).

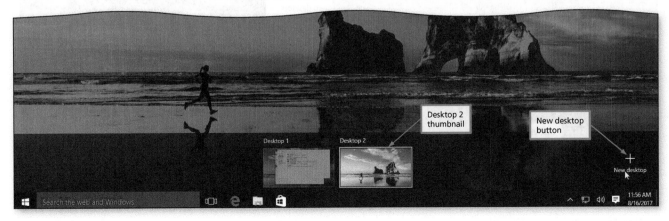

Figure 4–50

3

• Click the Desktop 2 thumbnail (shown in Figure 4–50) to view the second desktop (Figure 4–51).

Desktop 2 is
displayed with no
open windows

Figure 4–51

4

• Click the Task View button to display Task View (Figure 4–52).

Q&A Why are no thumbnail images displayed?

You currently have no apps running or windows open on the second desktop, so no thumbnail images are
displayed.

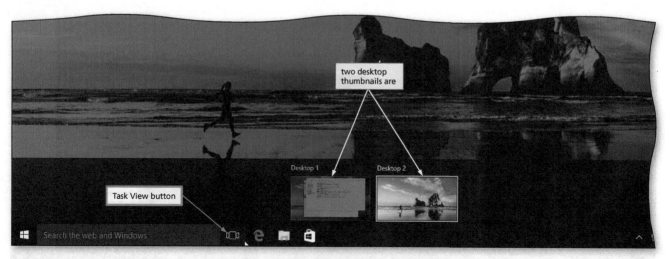

two desktop
thumbnails are

Task View button

Desktop 1   Desktop 2

Figure 4–52

5

- Point to the Desktop 1 thumbnail until the thumbnail images of running apps and open windows are displayed (shown in Figure 4–49).

- Drag the Settings thumbnail to the Desktop 2 thumbnail to move the Settings app to Desktop 2 (Figure 4–53).

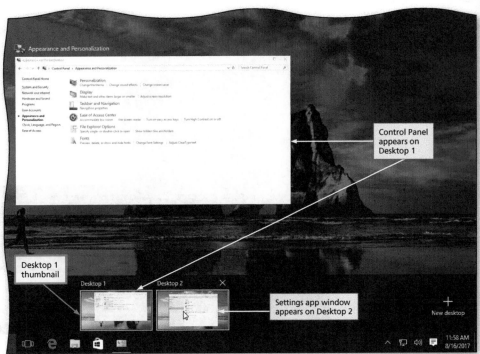

Control Panel appears on Desktop 1

Desktop 1 thumbnail

Settings app window appears on Desktop 2

Figure 4–53

6

- Click the Desktop 2 thumbnail to view the Settings app on Desktop 2 (Figure 4–54).

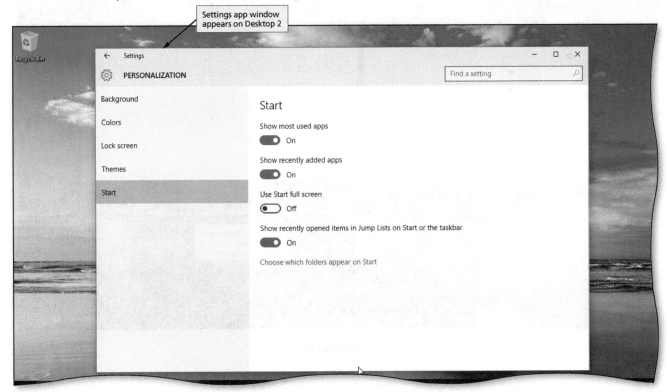

Settings app window appears on Desktop 2

Figure 4–54

7

- Display Task View.

- Point to the Desktop 2 thumbnail to display the Close button (Figure 4–55).

Figure 4–55

8

- Click the Close button to move the Settings app window from Desktop 2 to Desktop 1 and remove Desktop 2 (Figure 4–56).

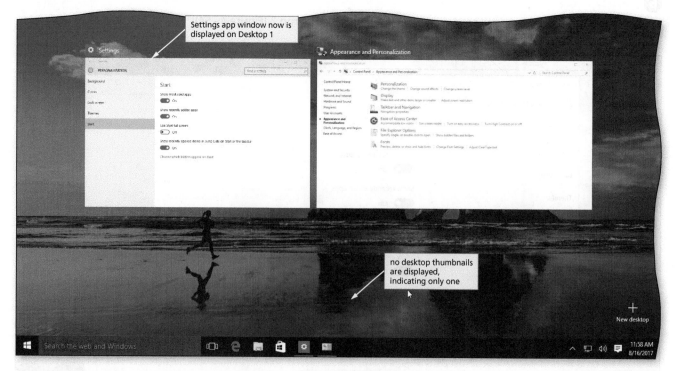

Figure 4–56

9

- Click the Task View button on the taskbar to close Task view.
- Close the Control Panel window.
- Exit the Settings app.

Customizing the Taskbar

Another method of modifying the desktop work environment is to customize the taskbar at the bottom of the desktop. For example, you can move, resize, and hide the taskbar; change the appearance of the taskbar; and change the taskbar properties. The next sections illustrate how to customize the taskbar.

To Unlock the Taskbar

By default, the taskbar is locked into position at the bottom of the desktop. Locking the taskbar prevents the taskbar from inadvertently being moved to another location on the desktop and also locks the size and position of any toolbars displayed on the taskbar. *Why? Prior to moving or resizing the taskbar, you must unlock the taskbar. After moving or resizing the taskbar, you might want to lock it in its new location so that you do not accidentally change its size and position.* The following steps unlock the taskbar.

1

- Right-click an open area of the taskbar to display a shortcut menu (Figure 4–57).

Figure 4–57

2

- Click 'Lock the taskbar' on the shortcut menu to remove the check mark and unlock the taskbar (Figure 4–58).

Figure 4–58

Other Ways

1. Right-click open area of taskbar, click Properties on shortcut menu, click 'Lock the taskbar' (Taskbar and Start Menu Properties dialog box), click OK button

To Move the Taskbar

When the taskbar is unlocked, you can move it to different locations. By default, the taskbar is docked at the bottom edge of the desktop, but it can be dragged to any of the four edges of the desktop. *Why? You feel it is more convenient to access the taskbar at the top of the screen, so you wish to move it there.* The following steps move the taskbar to the top edge of the desktop and then back to the bottom.

● Drag the taskbar to the top of the desktop to position the taskbar at the top of the desktop (Figure 4–59).

Q&A ◄ Why am I unable to drag the taskbar?

If you cannot drag the taskbar, the taskbar is still locked.

Figure 4–59

● Drag the taskbar to the bottom of the desktop to restore its original position (shown in Figure 4–60).

To Enable Auto-Hide

Another way to customize the desktop is to hide the taskbar so that only its top edge is visible at the bottom of the desktop. When the taskbar is hidden, you must point to the bottom of the desktop to display the taskbar (or if the taskbar has been moved to another side of the screen, moving the pointer to that part of the screen will make the taskbar visible). The taskbar will remain on the desktop as long as the pointer hovers on the taskbar. The taskbar does not have to be unlocked to enable Auto-hide. *Why? You want to enable the Auto-hide feature to maximize the amount of available space on the desktop.* The following steps hide and then redisplay the taskbar.

❶

● Right-click an open area on the taskbar to display the shortcut menu (Figure 4–60).

Figure 4–60

2

- Click Properties on the shortcut menu to display the Taskbar and Start Menu Properties dialog box (Figure 4–61).

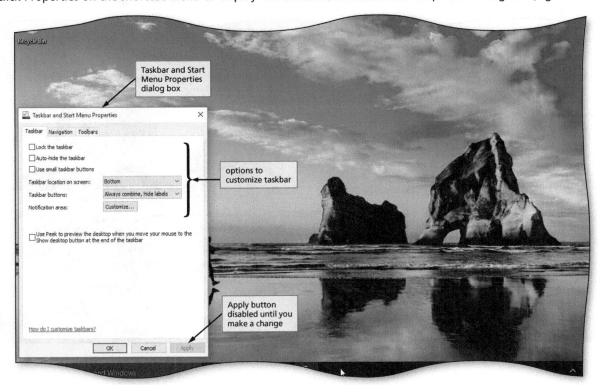

Figure 4–61

3

- Click the 'Auto-hide the taskbar' check box (Taskbar and Start Menu Properties dialog box) to select it (Figure 4–62).

Figure 4–62

● Click the Apply button to apply the Auto-hide feature without closing the dialog box (Figure 4–63).

Figure 4–63

● Point to the bottom of the screen to display the taskbar (Figure 4–64).

Q&A Is another way to display the hidden taskbar available?

In addition to pointing to the bottom of the screen to display the taskbar, you can display the taskbar and the Start menu at any time by pressing the WINDOWS key or pressing CTRL+ESC.

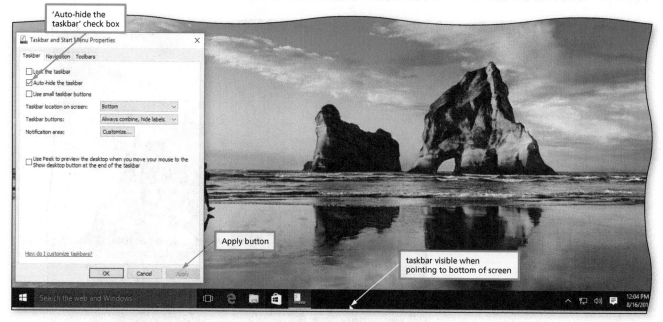

Figure 4–64

● Click the 'Auto-hide the taskbar' check box (Taskbar and Start Menu Properties dialog box) to remove the check mark and deselect the option.

● Click the Apply button to turn off the Auto-hide feature.

To Change Taskbar Buttons

By default, Windows 10 hides button labels and combines buttons when multiple windows are open in the same program. Windows 10 provides options for changing these button settings in the Taskbar and Start Menu Properties dialog box. ***Why?*** *Some people prefer that the taskbar display buttons with descriptive labels and that each open window be assigned its own button on the taskbar.* The following steps change the taskbar button settings.

- Click the Taskbar buttons button (Taskbar and Start menu Properties dialog box) to display a list of taskbar button options (Figure 4–65).

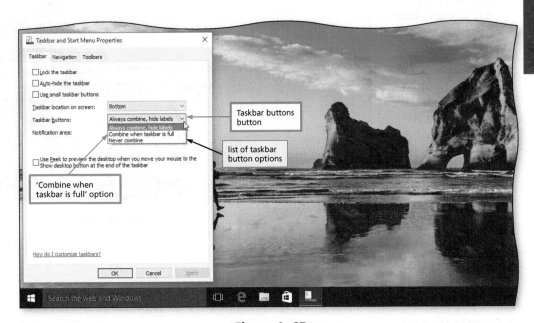

Figure 4–65

- Click 'Combine when taskbar is full' in the list to configure Windows to display a taskbar button for each window and to show labels for each button.

- Click the Apply button to apply the changes to buttons on the taskbar (Figure 4–66).

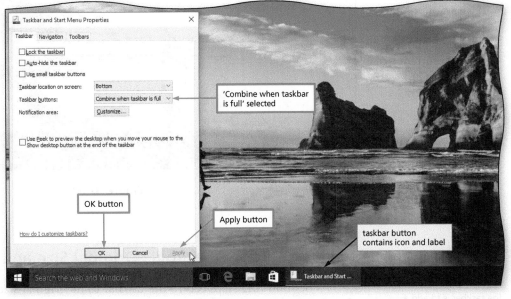

Figure 4–66

- After viewing the changes in the taskbar, click the Taskbar buttons button to display the list of taskbar button options (shown in Figure 4–65).

- Click 'Always combine, hide labels' in the list to cause the buttons to combine and hide the labels.

- Click the OK button (Taskbar and Start Menu Properties dialog box) to close the dialog box and apply the changes to the buttons on the taskbar.

To Resize the Taskbar

Why? *Sometimes, you might have so many items on the taskbar that it becomes difficult to view everything at once. You can resize the taskbar to make it easier to view everything.* The following steps resize the taskbar.

1

- Point to the top edge of the taskbar until a two-headed arrow appears.

- Press and hold the left mouse button to select the taskbar (Figure 4–67).

What if the taskbar is on the left, right, or top edge of the desktop?

If the taskbar is located elsewhere on your desktop, point to the taskbar border closest to the center of the desktop until a two-headed arrow displays.

two-headed arrow is displayed

Figure 4–67

2

- Drag the top edge of the taskbar toward the top of the desktop until the taskbar on the desktop is about twice its current size (Figure 4–68).

taskbar is twice its original size

Figure 4–68

To Return the Taskbar to Its Original Size and Lock the Taskbar

The following steps return the taskbar to its original size.

1 Point to the top edge of the taskbar until a two-headed arrow appears.

2 Press and hold the left mouse button to select the taskbar.

3 Drag the top edge of the taskbar downward until the taskbar is back to its original size.

4 Right-click an open area of the taskbar to display a shortcut menu.

5 Click the 'Lock the taskbar' command to lock the taskbar.

Action Center

The Action Center is a location in Windows where you can view notifications, as well as view and change selected settings on your computer. A **notification** is a message either from the operating system or an installed app that contains relevant information. For example, when Windows installs updates, you may receive a notification that new updates have been installed. The Action Center also provides access to certain settings. For example, you can enable and disable Bluetooth, adjust the brightness, or connect to a network.

BTW
Notifications
Windows and other apps can display notifications in the Action Center. To see more information about a notification, you can click it. You also can clear all notifications by clicking the Clear all link in the Action Center.

To Display the Action Center

Why? *You want to display the Action Center to view the current notifications (if any) and see what settings you can change.* The following step displays the Action Center.

1

- Click the Notifications icon in the notification area on the taskbar to display the Action Center (Figure 4–69).

Q&A Why does my Notification icon look different?

If you have pending notifications, your Notification icon will have a white background. If you have no pending notifications, the icon will have a black background.

2

- Click outside the Action Center to close the Action Center.

Figure 4–69

Changing Folder Options

In this module, you modified the desktop work environment by changing the desktop properties, customizing the taskbar, and viewing Start menu customization options. In addition to these changes, you also can make changes to folders, windows, and the desktop by changing folder options. Folder options allow you to specify how you open and work with icons, windows, folders, and files on the desktop.

To Display the Folder Options Dialog Box

Why? *You first need to display the Folder Options dialog box so that you can view and change settings.* The following steps open the This PC window and then display the Folder Options dialog box.

- Open the File Explorer window.
- Click This PC in the Navigation pane to open the This PC window.
- Click View on the ribbon to display the View tab.
- Click the Options button (View tab | Show/hide group) to display the Folder Options dialog box (Figure 4–70).

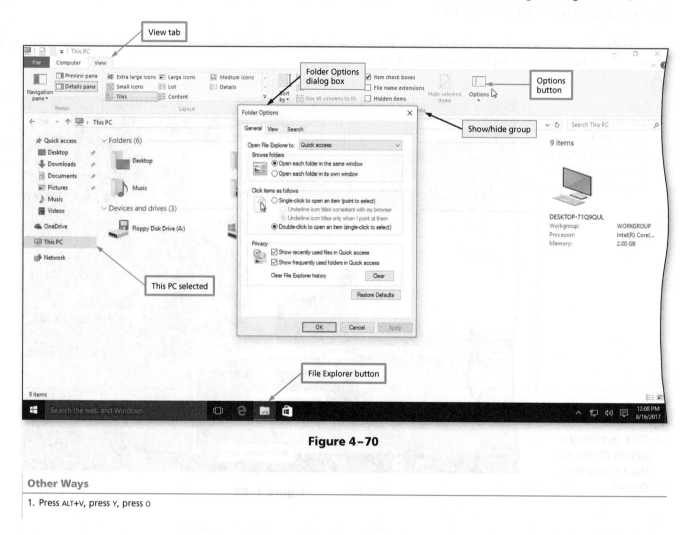

Figure 4–70

Other Ways

1. Press ALT+V, press Y, press O

To Select the 'Open Each Folder in Its Own Window' Option

In previous modules, each time you double-clicked a folder icon in an open window, the new folder opened in the same window where the previously opened folder was displayed. The process of opening a folder in the same window as the previously opened folder is referred to as opening a folder in the same window, and it is the default setting in Windows 10. ***Why?*** *Selecting the 'Open each folder in its own window' option causes each folder to open in its own window, so that you easily can view the contents of each open folder at the same time.* The following step enables the 'Open each folder in its own window' option.

1

- Click the 'Open each folder in its own window' option button in the Browse folders area (Folder Options dialog box) to select it (Figure 4–71).

- Click the OK button to apply the changes and close the Folder Options dialog box.

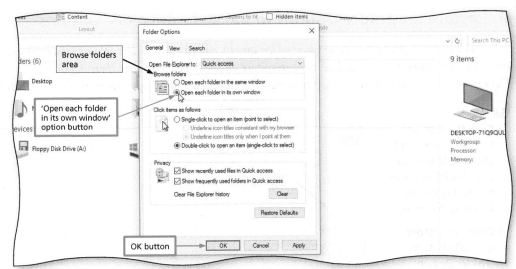

Figure 4–71

To Open a Folder in Its Own Window

Why? You want to view the result of changing the settings in the Folder Options dialog box from the previous set of steps. The following steps open the Local Disk (C:) folder in its own window.

1

- Double-click the 'Local Disk (C:)' icon in the This PC window to display the Local Disk (C:) folder in its own window (Figure 4–72).

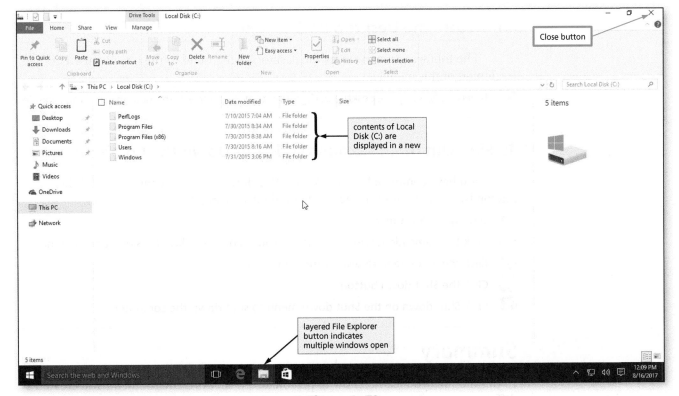

Figure 4–72

2

- Click the Close button in the Local Disk (C:) window to close the window.

To Restore the Folder Options to the Default Folder Options

Why? *After changing one or more folder options, you can restore the default folder options you changed by manually resetting each option you changed, or you can restore all the folder options to their default options by using the Restore Defaults button.* The following step restores the changed folder options to their default folder options.

1

- Click the Options button (View tab | Show/hide group) in the This PC window to display the Folder Options dialog box.

- Click the Restore Defaults button (Folder Options dialog box) to restore the folder defaults (Figure 4–73).

- Click the OK button to close the Folder Options dialog box and then click the Close button to close the This PC window.

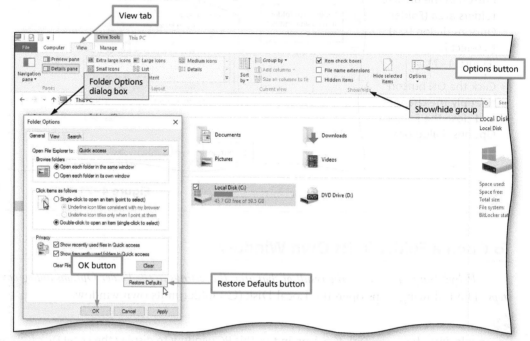

Figure 4–73

To Restore the Desktop Background

The following step restores the desktop background to the one you used at the beginning of this module.

1 If necessary, apply the desktop background that was active at the beginning of this module.

To Sign Out of an Account and Shut Down the Computer

You have completed the work with Windows. The following steps end the session by signing out of the account and then shutting down the computer.

1 Display the Start menu.

2 Click the name identifying your user account and then click the Sign out command.

3 Click the lock screen to display the sign-in screen.

4 Click the Shut down button.

5 Click Shut down on the Shut down menu to shut down the computer.

Summary

In this module, you learned how to personalize your work environment. You created different types of user accounts, including a Microsoft account. You created a picture password, changed the desktop background and accent color, and customized the lock screen. You also worked with the Task View button, managed multiple desktops, customized the taskbar, and displayed the Action Center. Finally, you viewed and adjusted folder options in the Folder Options dialog box.

Apply Your Knowledge

Reinforce the skills and apply the concepts you learned in this module.

Personalizing Windows 10

Instructions: Use Personalization options in the Settings app to set the desktop background, configure Windows to automatically choose an accent color, change the lock screen background, and view additional settings.

Figure 4–74

Perform the following tasks:

1. Run the Settings app and then click the Personalization icon in the Settings window.
2. If necessary, click the Background tab in the left pane and then change the desktop background to a picture of your choosing (do not use the same picture as the one currently displayed). Describe the picture you chose.
3. Click the Colors tab in the left pane.
4. Click to enable the 'Automatically pick an accent color from my background' option to have Windows decide the best background color. What color did Windows choose?
5. Click the Lock screen tab in the left pane. Change the lock screen background to another picture of your choosing. Which one did you select?
6. Click the Themes tab in the left pane and then click the Theme settings link in the right pane. What themes are available on your computer?
7. Click the 'Appearance and Personalization' button in the address bar, and then click the 'Change screen saver' link. What screen savers are available on your computer?
8. Review the available screen savers. Which one do you like most? Why?
9. Change the current screen saver to Mystify and then click the OK button (Screen Saver Settings dialog box).
10. Close the Control Panel window.
11. Exit the Settings app.

Extend Your Knowledge

Extend the skills you learned in this module and experiment with new skills. You will use the search box to complete the assignment.

Creating Custom Themes

Instructions: Use help if necessary to locate pictures, download them, set the desktop background, choose a screen saver, and save the settings as a new theme.

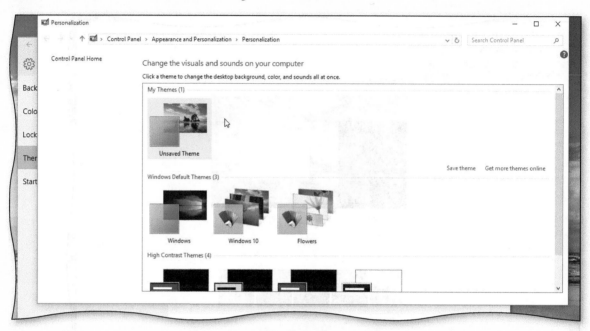

Figure 4–75

Perform the following steps:

1. Using your own pictures or pictures from the Internet that do not have copyright restrictions, locate at least five pictures you would like to use as a desktop background. Download them to a new folder named, Desktop Backgrounds, in the Pictures folder.

2. Using the Settings app and the Control Panel, perform the following steps:

   a. Configure the desktop background to display the pictures in the Desktop Backgrounds folder. Set the pictures to change every 10 minutes.

   b. Configure Windows to automatically pick an accent color from the background image. What color did you choose?

   c. Enable the setting to show color on Start, taskbar, and Action Center. What happened?

   d. Set the screen saver to Bubbles, and configure Windows to wait 10 minutes before starting the screen saver. Configure Windows to display the logon (sign in) screen on resume.

   e. Save the settings as a new theme and name it EYK 4-1 Theme.

3. While viewing the list of themes, click the link to get more themes online and answer the following questions:

   a. What are the names of three featured themes?

   b. Browse the available themes. Which three themes are your favorites?

   c. How can you download and use these themes?

Expand Your World

Creating and Using a Microsoft Account

Create a solution that uses cloud or web technologies by learning and investigating on your own from general guidance.

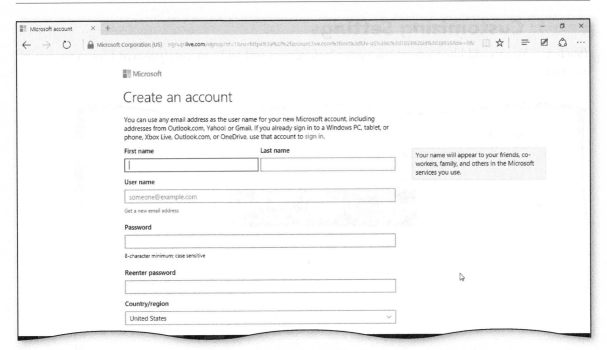

Figure 4–76

1. Click the Microsoft Edge button on the taskbar to run Microsoft Edge.

2. Navigate to the `login.live.com` webpage.

3. Locate and then click the link to sign up for a new Microsoft account. If you are unable to locate this link, look for a link to sign in with a different Microsoft account. Click that link and then click the link to sign up for a new Microsoft account.

4. Complete the requested information on the Create an account webpage and then click the button to create an account.

5. If necessary, create a new user account on the computer using the Microsoft account you just created.

6. Sign in to Windows with the new Microsoft account.

7. Change the desktop background to an image of your choosing.

8. Create and save a document in WordPad and then copy the file to OneDrive.

9. Sign out of the Windows account.

10. Sign in to another computer using the same Microsoft account you have just created (you may need to first add the user account to the computer), and answer the following questions:

    a. What desktop background do you see?

    b. Do you see the WordPad document that you saved to OneDrive?

    c. What happens if you delete the OneDrive document on this computer? Will it still appear on other computers?

    d. What happens to the desktop background on other computers if you change the desktop background on this computer?

In the Labs

Design, create, modify, and/or use files following the guidelines, concepts, and skills presented in this module. Labs 1 and 2, which increase in difficulty, require you to create solutions based on what you learned in the module; Lab 3 requires you to apply your creative thinking and problem-solving skills to design and implement a solution.

Lab 1: **Customizing Settings**

Problem: You would like to customize your lock screen and add a picture password for your user account.

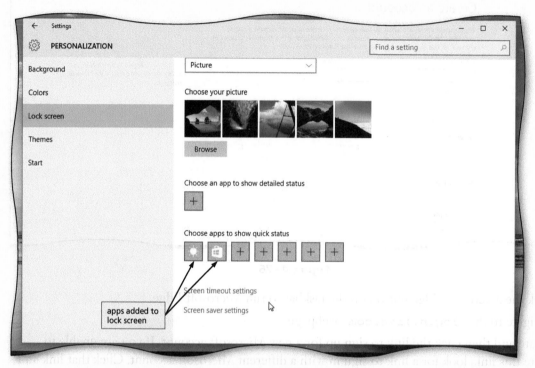

Figure 4–77

Perform the following steps:

1. Copy the img2 picture from the Windows folder to the Pictures folder. You will be using this picture as a picture password later in this exercise.

2. Run the Settings app.

3. Click the Personalization icon and then perform the following tasks:

   a. Click the Lock screen tab in the left pane to display personalization options in the right pane.

   b. If necessary, scroll to display the Lock screen apps area.

   c. Click one of the add buttons (plus sign) in the Choose apps to show quick status area to add a lock screen app.

   d. Click the Weather app to add it to the lock screen.

   e. Click one of the add buttons in the Choose apps to show quick status area to add a lock screen app.

   f. Click the Store app to add it to the lock screen.

   g. Click the Back button to display the categories of settings.

4. Click the Accounts icon in the Settings app window and then perform the following tasks:

    a. Click the Sign-in options tab in the left pane.

    b. Click the Add button in the Picture password area to create a picture password.

    c. After entering your password, click to select the img3 picture that will be used as a picture password.

    d. Use the mouse or touch gestures to add a circle, line, and tap to create a picture password.

Lab 2: Customizing the Taskbar and Desktop

Problem: You want to customize the taskbar and desktop to better facilitate your working habits.

Perform the following steps.

Part 1: Customize the Taskbar

1. Right-click an open area of the taskbar to display a shortcut menu.

2. Pin the WordPad app to the taskbar.

3. If a check mark appears next to the 'Lock the taskbar' command, click 'Lock the taskbar' on the shortcut menu to remove the check mark and unlock the taskbar.

4. Move the taskbar to the left side of the screen.

5. Resize the taskbar so that it is two times its current size, and enable the Auto-hide feature.

Figure 4–78

Continued >

In the Labs *continued*

6. Select the option to never combine taskbar buttons.

7. Lock the taskbar and save the changes.

8. Close all open windows.

Part 2: Customize the Desktop Arrangement

1. Run the Settings app, open the File Explorer window, and then run WordPad.

2. Click the Task View button on the taskbar to display Task view.

3. Add a new desktop.

4. Drag the WordPad window so that it appears on the new desktop.

5. Display the new desktop.

6. Click the Task View button on the taskbar.

7. Delete the desktop you added in Step 3. What happened to the WordPad window?

Lab 3: **Consider This: Your Turn**

Researching Account Types

Problem: You are working in the information technology department for a corporation. Your boss has been wondering if he should allow users to have administrative or standard use account privileges. He wants you to research this using the Internet and create a summary for him to use in making his decision.

Part 1:   Research different user account privileges. Describe the account types and then list some of the advantages and disadvantages of each. Which people would you allow to have an administrative account? Why? Which people would have a standard user account? Why? What risks are involved in giving someone an administrative account?

Part 2:   You made several decisions while searching for this assignment. What decisions did you make? What was the rationale behind these decisions? How did you locate the required information about the different account types?

5 | Advanced Personalization and Customization

Objectives

You will have mastered the material in this module when you can:

- Open the Control Panel and switch views
- View system information and hardware properties
- View and configure the Windows Firewall
- Defragment and optimize a hard drive
- View and adjust hardware and sound settings

- View power plan information
- Change time and region settings
- Display and adjust ease of access settings
- View privacy settings
- Display update and security settings

Introduction

As you have learned, personalizing your work environment can lead to improved productivity. In Module 4, you modified desktop properties by creating a new desktop theme, personalizing the taskbar, and customizing folder options. Other ways, however, exist to customize Windows 10 so that you can get the most from your computer. Technology works best when it supports our lifestyles, providing the tools we need to accomplish the tasks set before us.

The Control Panel window contains categories that allow you to change the properties of an object and, thus, customize the Windows 10 environment (Figure 5–1). In addition, Control Panel provides links to other windows that contain settings, allowing you to further customize your computer. In this module, you will learn how to view and adjust system and security settings, hardware and sound settings, uninstall programs and apps, adjust time and language settings, adjust accessibility and privacy settings, and display and update security settings.

You will be able to complete some of the steps in this module only if you have an administrator account. Recall from Module 4 that a user account with administrative access is capable of viewing and modifying all computer settings.

Normally, user accounts operate in standard user mode, which allows you to use most of the capabilities of the computer. A standard user cannot install software that affects other users or change system settings that affect security. An **administrator account** has full control of the computer and operating system and can change user permissions, install software that affects all users, and change system settings that affect security. When a task requires administrator access, you might be prompted to authorize the task. By default, you are asked for permission only when programs attempt to make a change to the computer. In the Control Panel window, a shield displays next to tasks requiring administrator privileges. Some of the steps in this module require administrative privileges. If you do not have administrative privileges, read the steps instead of performing them.

Figure 5–1

System and Security Settings

You can use the System and Security window to view security and maintenance settings, view and configure the Windows Firewall, view system information, access the device manager, and defragment and optimize your hard drive. Each option provides different opportunities for you to fine-tune your computer. Be aware, however, that some of the advanced system and maintenance options require User Account Control authorization if you are not using an account with administrative privileges. User Account Control requires you to enter an administrator's user name and password before allowing the current user account temporary administrative access.

To Open the Control Panel Window

The following steps open the Control Panel window. **Why?** *To access certain computer settings, you first must open the Control Panel window.*

Ask me anything

1

- Type **control panel** in the search box to display the search results (Figure 5–2).

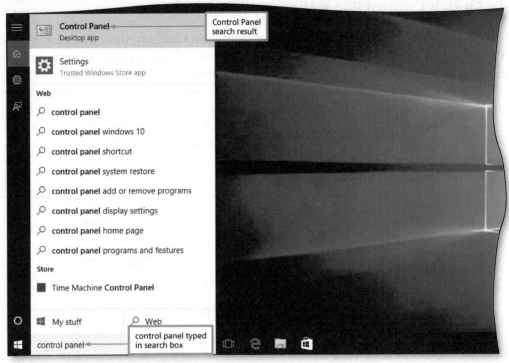

Figure 5–2

2

- Click the Control Panel Desktop app search result to open the Control Panel window. If necessary, maximize the Control Panel window (Figure 5–3).

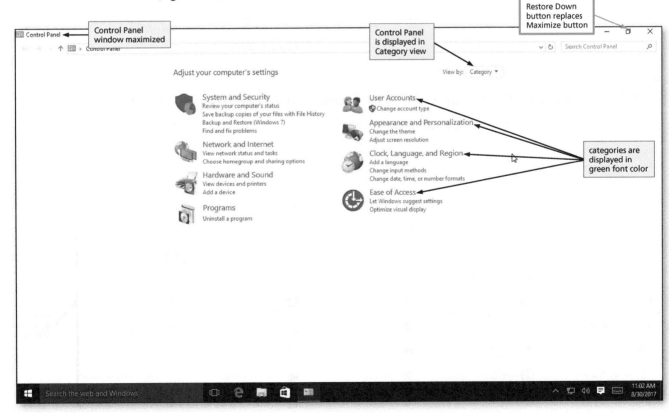

Figure 5–3

To Switch Control Panel Views

By default, the Control Panel window displays in Category view. Category view offers the various Control Panel options organized into eight functional categories. Links to common tasks are provided below each category name. The View by arrow in the Control Panel window allows you to display the items as large or small icons. When changed to icons, all of the individual Control Panel icons display in alphabetical order instead of organized into categories. ***Why?*** *It may be easier to locate the Control Panel setting for which you are searching if the settings are displayed alphabetically. In addition, people who are familiar with previous versions of Windows may find it more familiar to use a different view to locate a particular setting.* The following steps switch to Large icons view and then back to Category view.

1

- Click the View by button in the Control Panel window to display the View by menu (Figure 5–4).

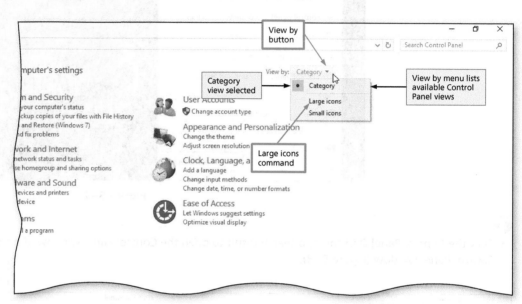

Figure 5–4

2

- Click Large icons in the View by menu to display the Control Panel in Large icons view (Figure 5–5).

Figure 5–5

③

- Click the View by button in the Control Panel window to display the View by menu (shown in Figure 5–4).

- Click Category on the View by menu to return the Control Panel window to Category view (Figure 5–6).

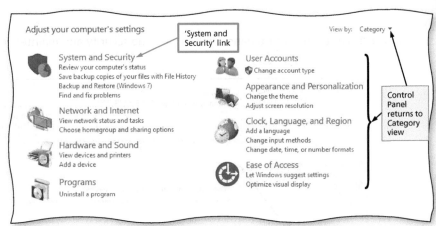

Figure 5–6

To Open the System and Security Window

The following step opens the System and Security window. *Why? You must click the 'System and Security' link to view the system and security settings.*

①

- Click the 'System and Security' link to open the System and Security window (Figure 5–7).

Q&A Why do my links differ from those shown in the figure?

Depending upon the configuration and the devices installed, you might see different links within the System and Security window.

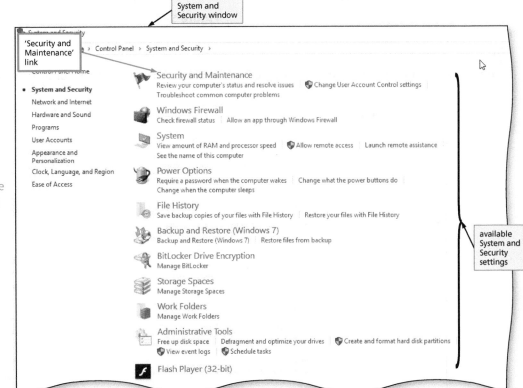

Figure 5–7

To View Security and Maintenance Settings

Why? The Security and Maintenance window allows you to view and monitor your security and maintenance settings, such as the status of your firewall or antivirus program. The following steps display the security and maintenance settings.

• Click the 'Security and Maintenance' link to view the security and maintenance settings (Figure 5–8).

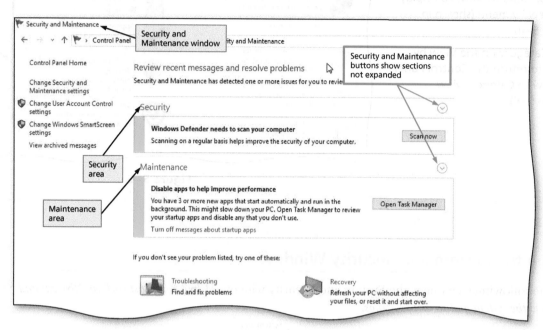

Figure 5–8

2

• If the security area is not expanded, click the Security button to expand the Security area (Figure 5–9).

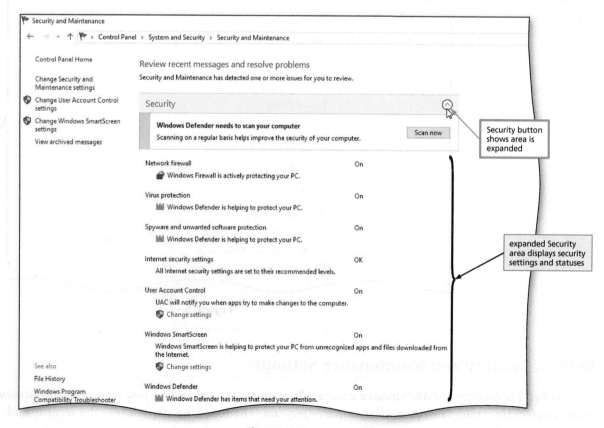

Figure 5–9

- If necessary, scroll to display the Maintenance button. Click the Maintenance button to expand the Maintenance area to view the maintenance settings (Figure 5–10).

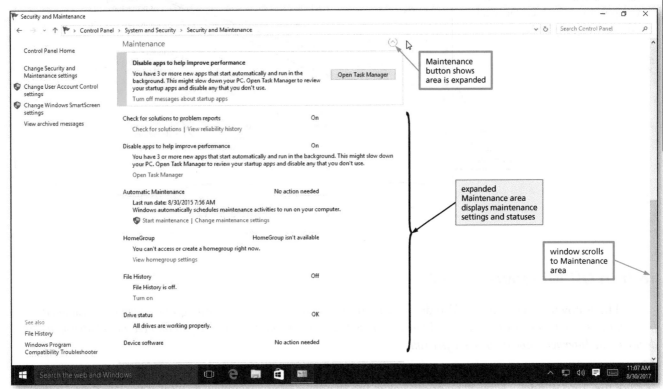

Figure 5–10

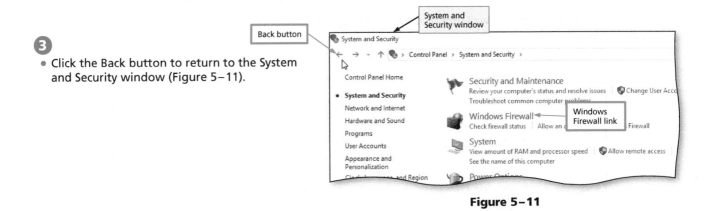

3

- Click the Back button to return to the System and Security window (Figure 5–11).

Figure 5–11

To View Windows Firewall Settings

Windows Firewall is a program that protects your computer from unauthorized users by monitoring and restricting information that travels between your computer and a network or the Internet. Windows Firewall also helps to block malware from infecting your computer. Windows Firewall automatically is turned on by default in Windows 10, and unless you have another program or app that provides a firewall, it is recommended that Windows Firewall remain on. *Why? You want to make sure that Windows Firewall is protecting your computer adequately.* The following step views Windows Firewall settings.

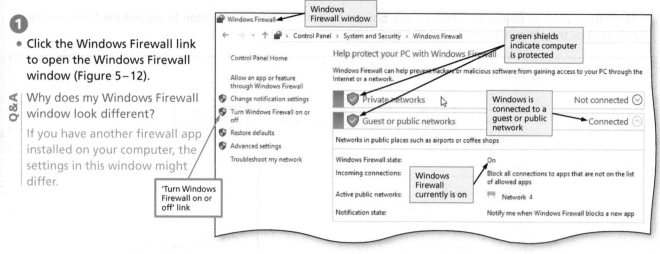

1

- Click the Windows Firewall link to open the Windows Firewall window (Figure 5–12).

Q&A Why does my Windows Firewall window look different?

If you have another firewall app installed on your computer, the settings in this window might differ.

Figure 5–12

To Turn Off Windows Firewall

The following steps turn off Windows Firewall. **Why?** *If you have another program or app that includes a firewall feature, you may need to turn off Windows Firewall. It is not recommended that you connect a computer or mobile device to the Internet without an active firewall.*

- Click the 'Turn Windows Firewall on or off' link in the Windows Firewall window to display the Windows Firewall settings.
- Click the 'Turn off Windows Firewall (not recommended)' option button in the Private network settings area.
- Click the 'Turn off Windows Firewall (not recommended)' option button in the Public network settings area (Figure 5–13).

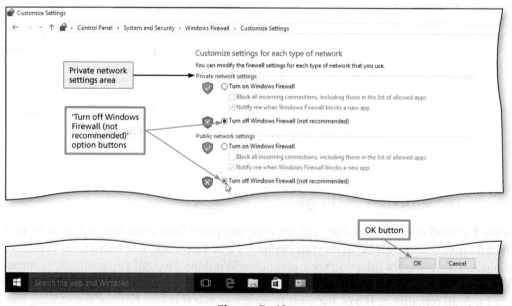

Figure 5–13

2

- Click the OK button (shown in Figure 5–13) to turn off the Windows Firewall and return to the Windows Firewall window (Figure 5–14).

Q&A Why does a Windows Firewall notification display?

As stated previously, it is extremely important to keep a firewall enabled. If Windows detects that no firewall is enabled, a notification will be displayed requesting that you enable Windows Firewall.

Windows Firewall
Control Panel › System and Security › Windows Firewall
Search Control Panel
Control Panel Home
Allow an app or feature through Windows Firewall
Change notification settings
Turn Windows Firewall on or off
Restore defaults
Advanced settings
Troubleshoot my network
Help protect your PC with Windows Firewall
Windows Firewall can help prevent hackers or malicious software from gaining access to your PC through the Internet or a network.
Update your Firewall settings
Windows Firewall is not using the recommended settings to protect your computer.
What are the recommended settings?
Use recommended settings
'Use recommended settings' button
Private networks
Not connected
Guest or public networks
Connected
Networks in public places such as airports or coffee shops
Windows Firewall state:
Off
Incoming connections:
Block all connections to apps that are not on the list of allowed apps
Active public networks:
Network 4
Notification state:
Notify me when Windows Firewall blocks a new app
indications that Windows Firewall is off
See also
Security and Maintenance
Network and Sharing Center
Turn on Windows Firewall
Windows Firewall is turned off. Tap or click to turn it on.

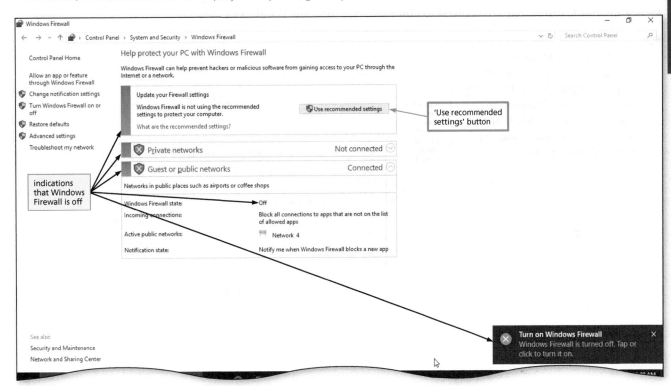

Figure 5–14

To Turn On Windows Firewall

If the Windows Firewall is not enabled and you want to turn it on, you can do so from the Windows Firewall window. ***Why?*** *You always should have a firewall enabled when your computer is connected to the Internet.* The following step turns on Windows Firewall.

1

- Click the 'Use recommended settings' button in the Windows Firewall window (shown in Figure 5–14) to turn on Windows Firewall (Figure 5–15).

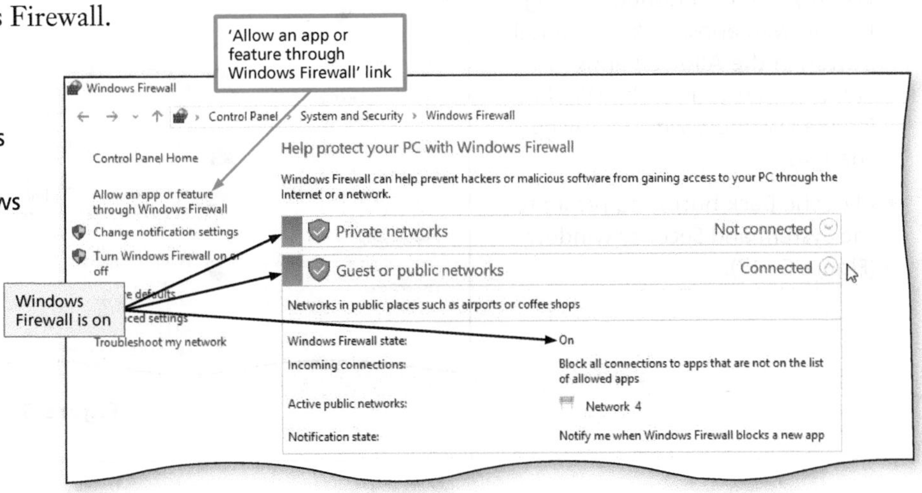

'Allow an app or feature through Windows Firewall' link
Windows Firewall
Control Panel › System and Security › Windows Firewall
Control Panel Home
Allow an app or feature through Windows Firewall
Change notification settings
Turn Windows Firewall on or off
Troubleshoot my network
Windows Firewall is on
Help protect your PC with Windows Firewall
Windows Firewall can help prevent hackers or malicious software from gaining access to your PC through the Internet or a network.
Private networks
Not connected
Guest or public networks
Connected
Networks in public places such as airports or coffee shops
Windows Firewall state:
On
Incoming connections:
Block all connections to apps that are not on the list of allowed apps
Active public networks:
Network 4
Notification state:
Notify me when Windows Firewall blocks a new app

Figure 5–15

To View Allowed Apps and Features through Windows Firewall

The purpose of a firewall is to block unintended communication between your computer and the Internet. Windows Firewall does its best to determine what communication to allow or block, but at times, it is possible that Windows Firewall is blocking communication that you want to allow. When this occurs, you can view and change the apps that Windows Firewall allows to communicate using the Internet. *Why? You have just installed a new app and want to see whether Windows Firewall is allowing it to communicate using the Internet.* The following steps view apps and features that are allowed to communicate through Windows Firewall.

- Click the 'Allow an app or feature through Windows Firewall' link (shown in Figure 5–15) to display a list of apps and features on your computer and whether they are allowed through Windows Firewall (Figure 5–16).

Q&A

How do I allow an app through Windows Firewall?

Click the 'Allow another app' button in the Allowed apps and features list to display a dialog box where you can select the app you want to add. If the app you want to add is not listed, click the Browse button in the Add an app window to locate and select the desired app. When you have selected the app to add, click the Add button in the Add an app window. Next, scroll through the list in the Allowed apps window and select whether the app should have access through Windows Firewall on private and/ or public networks.

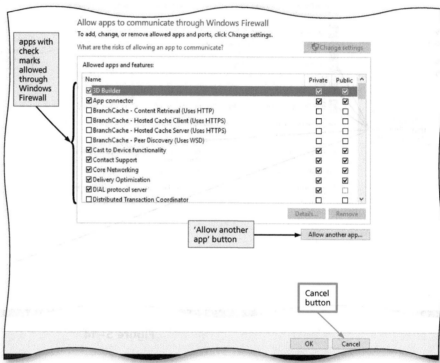

Figure 5–16

- When you have finished viewing the allowed apps, click the Cancel button in the Allowed apps window to return to the Windows Firewall window without saving changes.

- Click the Back button to return to the System and Security window (Figure 5–17).

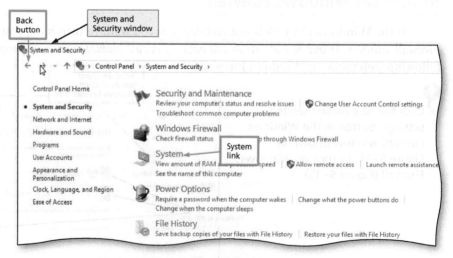

Figure 5–17

To View System Information

The System window displays summary information about your computer. You can access Device Manager, adjust remote access settings, modify system protection settings, change advanced system settings, and update Windows 10 computer or activation information using the System window. *Why? You may need to view information about your computer so that you can determine whether it meets the system requirements for an app you want to install.* The following step opens the System window.

1

- Click the System link (shown in Figure 5–17) to open the System window (Figure 5–18).

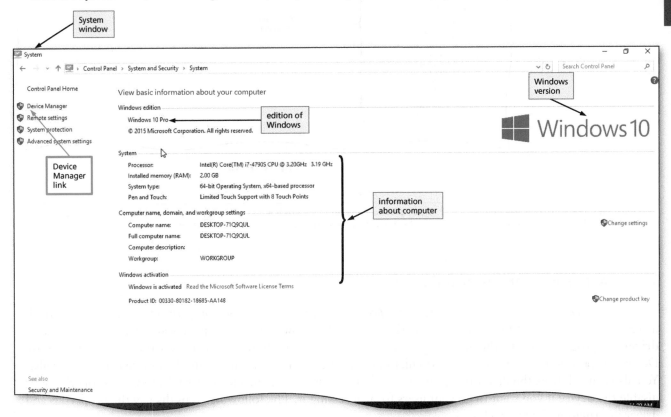

Figure 5–18

Other Ways	
1. Open Control Panel window, change to Large or Small icons, click System link	2. Open This PC window, click System properties button (Computer tab | System group)

To Open Device Manager

Device Manager allows you to display a list of the hardware devices installed on your computer and also allows you to update device drivers, view and modify hardware settings, and troubleshoot problems. *Why? If a device on your computer is not working, you can open Device Manager to see if the device shows up or has any problems.* The following step opens the Device Manager window.

• Click the Device
Manager link (shown
in Figure 5–18) in
the left pane of the
System window to
open the Device
Manager window
(Figure 5–19).

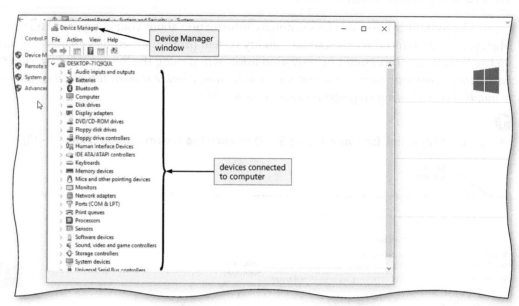

Figure 5–19

Other Ways

1. Open Control Panel, change to Large or
   Small icons, click Device Manager link

2. Type `device manager` in search box,
   click Device Manager search result

3. Right-click Start button, click Device
   Manager

To View the Properties of a Device

Why? *You can use Device Manager to see the properties of the devices installed on your computer.* Normally, device
drivers are downloaded and installed automatically when Windows 10 and its updates are installed. A **device
driver** is a program used by the operating system to control the hardware. You can view the driver details in the
Device Properties dialog box for the particular device. If necessary, you can update the device driver manually.
You also can roll back the driver to a previous working version if the current driver fails to work properly or
disable the device if you want to prevent users from accessing it. The following steps display the properties and
driver information for the keyboard.

• Click the arrow next
to Keyboards to
expand the list of
installed keyboards
(Figure 5–20).

Figure 5–20

2

- Double-click the keyboard entry to display the Keyboard Properties dialog box (Figure 5–21).

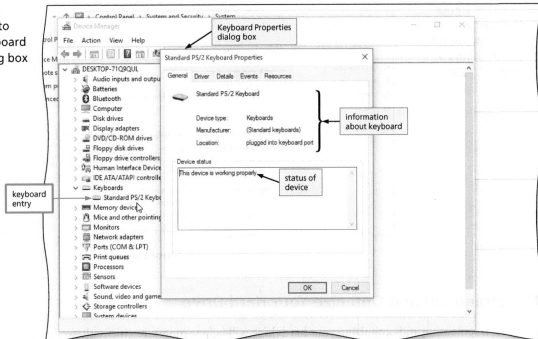

Figure 5–21

3

- Click the Driver tab (Keyboard Properties dialog box) to display the Driver sheet (Figure 5–22).

- After viewing the driver information, click the OK button to close the Keyboard Properties dialog box.

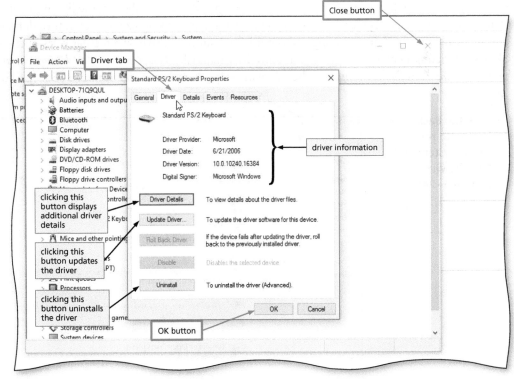

Figure 5–22

4

- Close the Device Manager window and return to the System window (Figure 5–23).

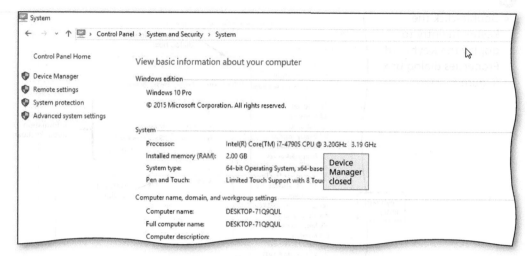

Figure 5–23

To Defragment and Optimize Your Hard Drive

Defragmenting and optimizing your hard drive will help it run more efficiently so that you can access your files more quickly. When you add files on a hard drive, Windows does not always store all the information for the file contiguously. That is, portions of the files may be stored on one location of the hard drive, while the remaining portions are stored elsewhere. As a result, it might take your computer longer to access files that are fragmented in this fashion. Defragmenting and optimizing your hard drive in Windows 10 will move files so that they all are stored contiguously, thus defragmenting your hard drive. While it is recommended you defragment and optimize the hard drive periodically, some experts argue that defragmenting a solid state drive (SSD) will shorten the life of the drive. SSDs are much faster than traditional (magnetic) hard drives, so you might not even recognize the benefits of defragmenting. Windows automatically may be defragmenting and optimizing your hard drive on a regular basis, such as every week, but you always can defragment and optimize your hard drive manually. *Why? You want to defragment and optimize your hard drive so that you can access files more quickly.* The following steps defragment and optimize your hard drive.

1

- Click the Back button to return to the System and Security window (Figure 5–24).

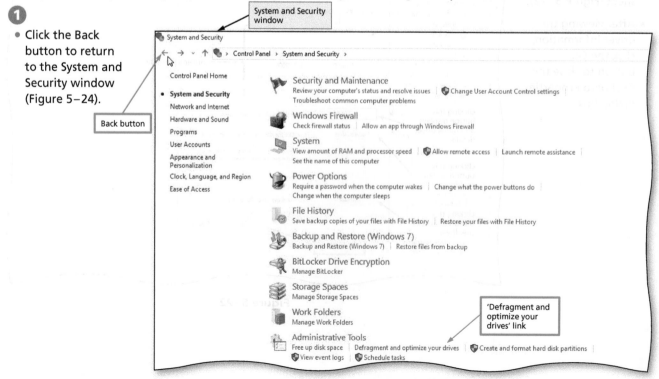

Figure 5–24

②

- Click the 'Defragment and optimize your drives' link to open the Optimize Drives window.

- If necessary, click to select the hard drive you want to optimize and defragment (Figure 5–25).

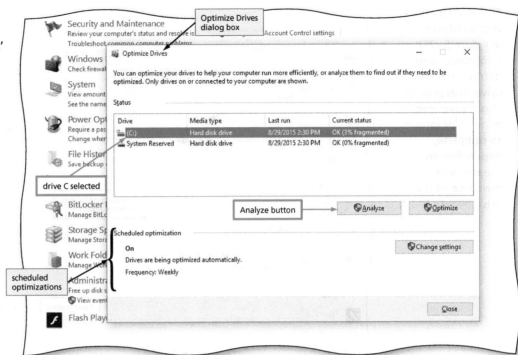

Figure 5–25

③

- Click the Analyze button to analyze the selected drive and determine whether it needs to be defragmented. Depending on the size and condition of the drive, it might take several minutes or longer to analyze. If the User Account Control dialog box is displayed, click the Yes button (Figure 5–26).

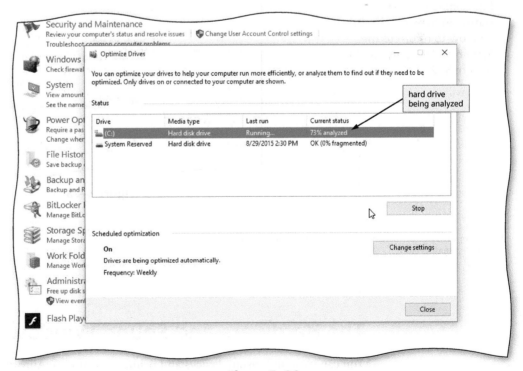

Figure 5–26

4

- Click the Optimize button (shown in Figure 5–25) to optimize and defragment the drive. This process might take several minutes or longer to complete, depending on the size and condition of the drive (Figure 5–27).

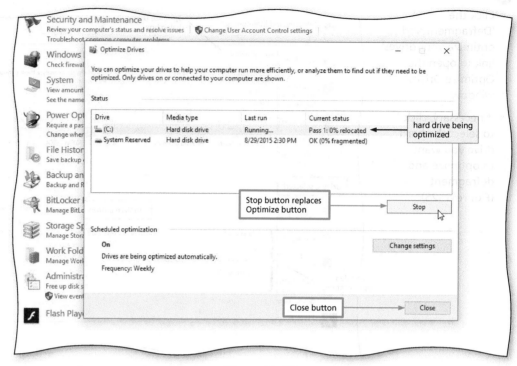

Figure 5–27

5

- When the optimization process has completed, click the Close button in the Optimize Drives window to return to the System and Security window (Figure 5–28).

Q&A

How will I know when the process is complete?

The current status for the drive will display, OK.

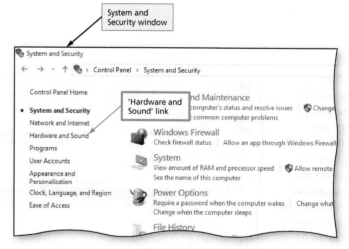

Figure 5–28

Other Ways

1. Type `optimize` in search box, click 'Defragment and Optimize Drives' in search results

The Hardware and Sound Window

You can view and install devices and printers, configure AutoPlay (**AutoPlay** refers to the default action that occurs when you connect a device, such as a USB flash drive, or insert an optical disc), adjust sound settings, configure power options, change display settings, and more, from the Hardware and Sound window.

To View Devices and Printers

When you add a device, such as a printer, scanner, camera, keyboard, mouse, or any other hardware device, Windows 10 usually installs and configures it automatically. If you want to view the devices and printers connected to your computer, you can use the Devices and Printers window to access the appropriate controls. If you connect a device or printer to your computer and it does not work, you can open the Devices and Printers window to see if Windows recognizes it. If Windows does not recognize it, you might need to install the device drivers for the device or printer. Device drivers are available either on a disc that comes with the device or printer or on the manufacturer's website. The following steps view installed devices and printers. *Why? You have connected a device to your computer and want to see if Windows recognizes it.*

1

● Click the 'Hardware and Sound' link (shown in Figure 5–28) in the System and Security Window to display the Hardware and Sound window (Figure 5–29).

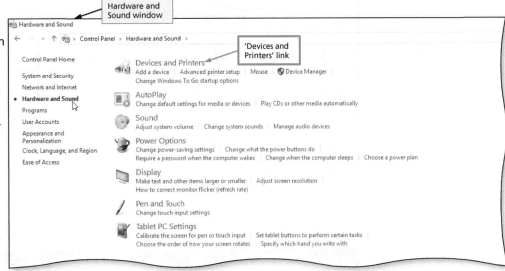

Figure 5–29

2

● Click the 'Devices and Printers' link (shown in Figure 5–28) to open the Devices and Printers window (Figure 5–30).

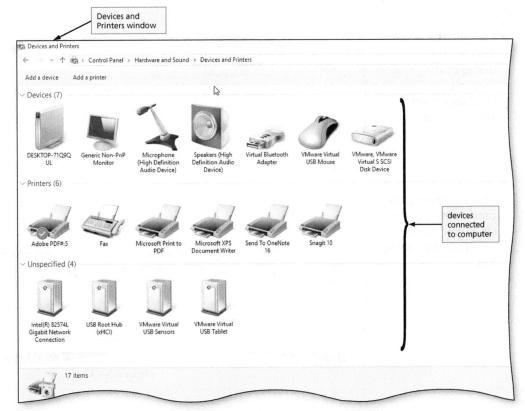

Figure 5–30

3

- Double-click a device in the Devices and Printers window to view the General sheet in the Properties dialog box for that device (Figure 5–31).

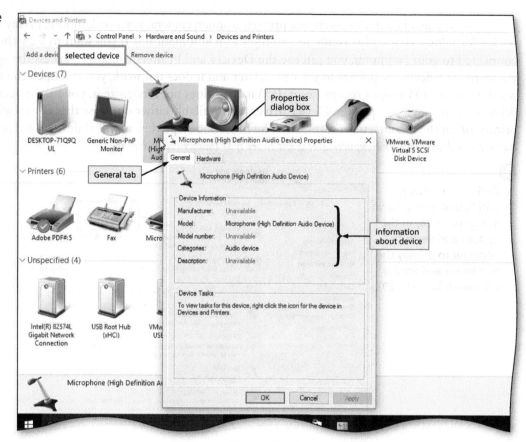

Figure 5–31

4

- Click the Hardware tab (Properties dialog box) to display the Hardware sheet for the device (Figure 5–32).

5

- When you have finished viewing the properties, click the OK button to close the Properties dialog box.

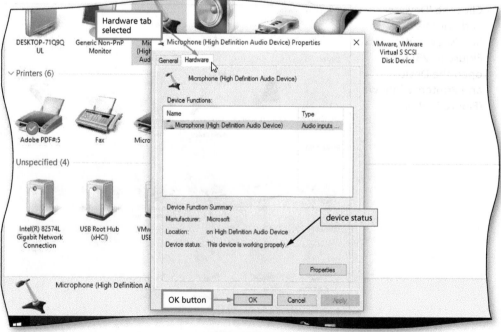

Figure 5–32

To Adjust AutoPlay Settings

Windows 10 allows you to customize the AutoPlay features for your computer. As mentioned previously, AutoPlay refers to the default action that occurs when media and devices are connected to your computer. Once set, the new action will be used the next time you insert the media or device. The following steps configure AutoPlay settings to open content on removable devices automatically when they are connected to the computer. *Why? When you connect a removable device, you typically want to browse the files on the device. Configuring AutoPlay settings will display the removable device contents automatically so that you do not have to perform an extra step to view them.*

1

- Click the Back button to display the Hardware and Sound window (Figure 5–33).

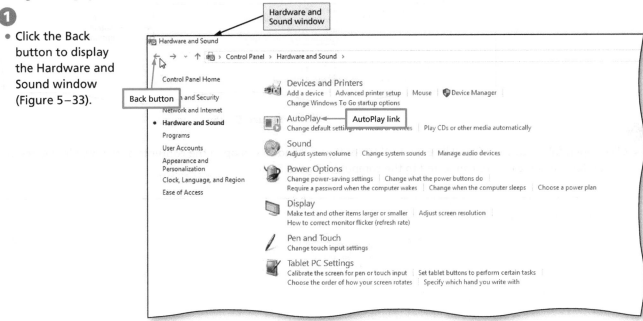

Figure 5–33

2

- Click the AutoPlay link to display the current AutoPlay settings in the AutoPlay window (Figure 5–34).

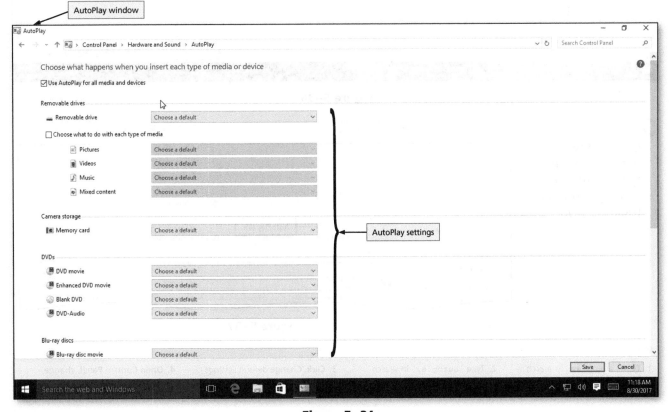

Figure 5–34

3

- Click the Removable drive button to display a list of default options for removable devices (Figure 5–35).

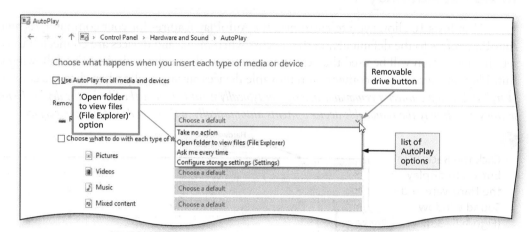

Figure 5–35

4

- Click 'Open folder to view files (File Explorer)' to configure Windows to open the contents of removable devices in File Explorer when they are connected to the computer (Figure 5–36).

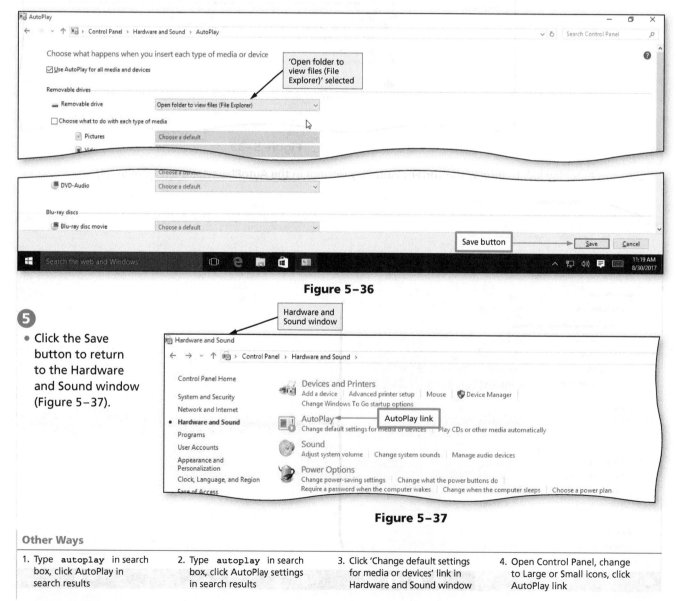

Figure 5–36

5

- Click the Save button to return to the Hardware and Sound window (Figure 5–37).

Figure 5–37

Other Ways

1. Type `autoplay` in search box, click AutoPlay in search results

2. Type `autoplay` in search box, click AutoPlay settings in search results

3. Click 'Change default settings for media or devices' link in Hardware and Sound window

4. Open Control Panel, change to Large or Small icons, click AutoPlay link

To Verify AutoPlay Settings

If you wanted to verify that your AutoPlay settings work properly, you would perform the following steps:

1. Connect or insert a removable device such as a USB flash drive to open File Explorer and display the contents of the removable device.

2. Close the File Explorer window.

To Revert an AutoPlay Setting

The following steps open the AutoPlay window and change the action for removable devices to 'Ask me every time'.

- Click the AutoPlay link (shown in Figure 5–37) to open the AutoPlay window.
- Click the Removable drive button to display a list of default actions (Figure 5–38).

Q&A What if 'Ask me every time' was not the original action set for removable devices?

Click the action that was selected before you changed the action.

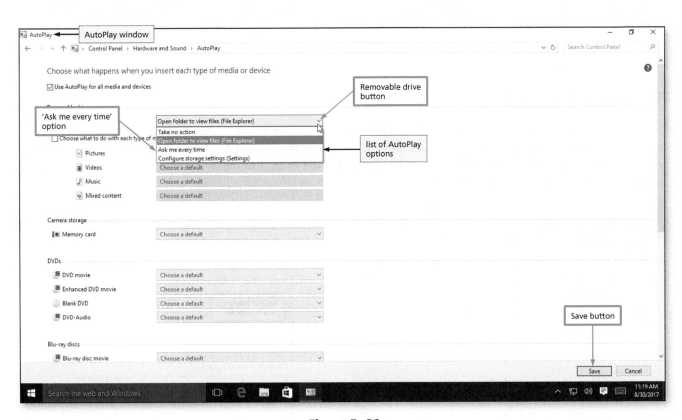

Figure 5–38

- Click 'Ask me every time' to configure Windows to ask you each time what you want to do when you insert or connect a removable device.

- Click the Save button in the AutoPlay window (shown in Figure 5–38) to save the AutoPlay settings and return to the Hardware and Sound window (Figure 5–39).

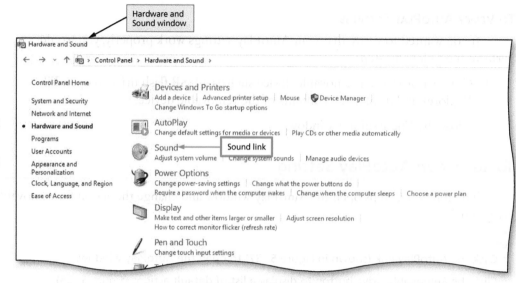

Figure 5–39

Other Ways

1. Type `autoplay` in search box, click AutoPlay in search results	2. Type `autoplay` in search box, click AutoPlay settings in search results	3. Click 'Change default settings for media or devices' link in Hardware and Sound window	4. Open Control Panel, change to Large or Small icons, click AutoPlay link

To View Sound Settings

The sound settings in Windows 10 allow you to adjust speaker volume, change the sounds that play when certain events occur, and manage the devices on your computer that record and play sounds. The following steps view sound settings. *Why? You would like to see the devices that are configured to play audio and see the sounds that play when certain events occur on your computer.*

- Click the Sound link to display the Sound dialog box.

- Click the default playback device (Figure 5–40).

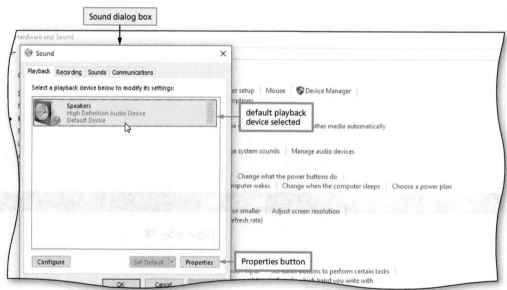

Figure 5–40

2

- Click the Properties button to display the Speakers Properties dialog box (Figure 5–41).

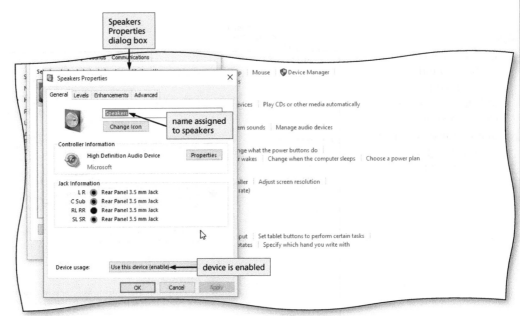

Speakers Properties dialog box

name assigned to speakers

device is enabled

Figure 5–41

3

- Click the Levels tab (Speakers Properties dialog box) to display the Levels sheet, which includes sliders you can drag to adjust the volume for the audio devices on your computer (Figure 5–42).

- Click the Cancel button to close the Speakers Properties dialog box without saving changes.

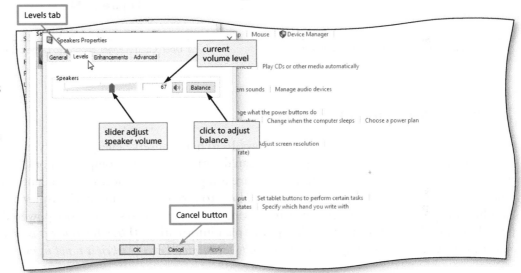

Levels tab

current volume level

slider adjust speaker volume

click to adjust balance

Cancel button

Figure 5–42

4

- Click the Sounds tab (Sound dialog box) to display the Sound sheet.

- Click Asterisk in the Program Events list to display the name of the sound associated with the Asterisk program event (Figure 5–43).

 Experiment

- Click the other program events in the list to view their associated sounds.

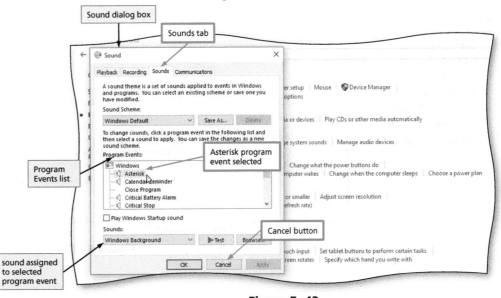

Sound dialog box

Sounds tab

Asterisk program event selected

Program Events list

Cancel button

sound assigned to selected program event

Figure 5–43

5

- Click the Cancel button (Sound dialog box) (shown in Figure 5–43) to close the Sound dialog box without saving changes (Figure 5–44).

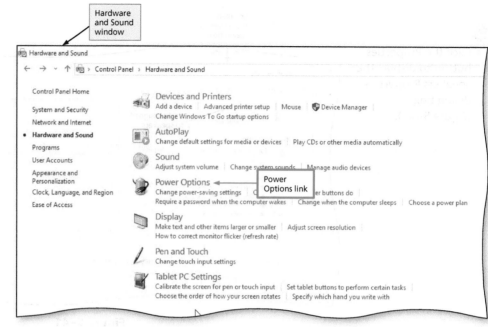

Figure 5–44

Other Ways

1. Type **sound** in search box, click Sound in search results   2. Open Control Panel, change to Large or Small icons, click Sound link

---

To View Power Plan Information

You can adjust power options in Windows 10 to help conserve energy when your computer is not being used. When you customize a power plan, you can determine how the computer should conserve energy when it is plugged in or running on a battery (if you are using a mobile device, such as a laptop or tablet). One way you can conserve energy is by configuring Windows to turn off the computer's display after a set period of time. Another way you can conserve energy is by putting the computer to sleep (a low-powered state) after a specified period of time. The following steps view power plan information. *Why? You think it is important to conserve energy and want to make sure your computer is configured to use minimal energy when it is not in use.*

1

- Click the Power Options link in the Hardware and Sound window to open the Power Options window (Figure 5–45).

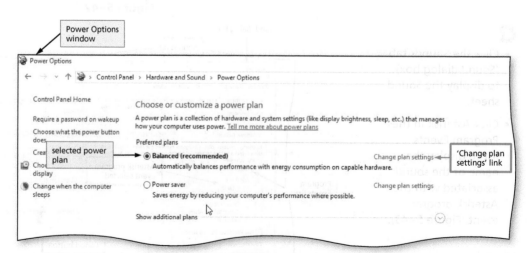

Figure 5–45

2
- Click the 'Change plan settings' link (shown in Figure 5–45) next to the Balanced (recommended) power plan to view the settings for the Balanced power plan in the Edit Plan Settings window (Figure 5–46).

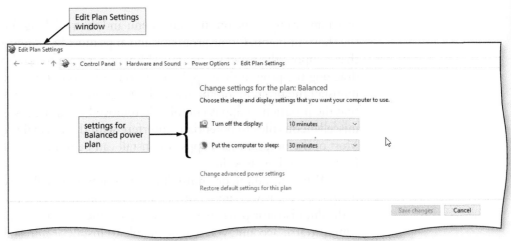

Figure 5–46

3
- Click the 'Turn off the display' button to view a list of options for when the computer should turn off the display (Figure 5–47).

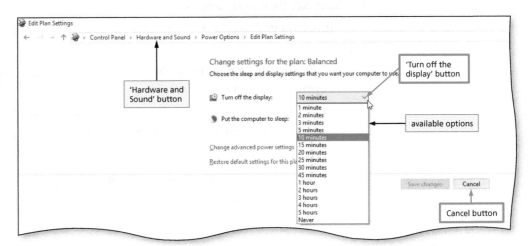

Figure 5–47

4
- Click outside the list to close it.
- Click the Cancel button to return to the Power Options window without saving changes.

Programs and Apps

The Programs window in the Control Panel brings together all of the tools you need when working with the various programs and apps on your computer. From the Programs window, you can uninstall programs and apps, as well as turn a variety of Windows features on and off. View installed updates, run programs made for previous versions of Windows, and view and change default programs.

TO UNINSTALL A PROGRAM OR APP

Some programs and apps include uninstall options as a part of their installation. For example, some programs and apps, when installed, add a folder to the Start menu, which includes an uninstall command that you can use to run the uninstall program. Other programs and apps do not offer an uninstall option or a folder on the Start menu. Instead, a command is available during the installation process to uninstall the software. You also can uninstall many programs and apps by right-clicking the program or app name on the Start menu and then clicking the Uninstall command on the shortcut menu. Other programs and apps must be removed by deleting the files that compose the program or app. Although you can remove programs and apps by dragging the program's or app's folder to the Recycle Bin, it is recommended that you uninstall the program or app using the Programs and Features window. This ensures that the program or app is completely removed from the system without leaving any miscellaneous files to potentially interfere with the normal processes of the computer. Most of the programs and apps you install can be uninstalled from the Programs and Features window, as well.

When installing or uninstalling programs, you will be required to provide the proper User Account Control authorization. If you are not using an account with administrator privileges or do not have the user name and password of an administrator account, you will be unable to install or uninstall a program or app.

TO UNINSTALL PROGRAMS AND APPS

If you wanted to uninstall a program or app, you would perform the following steps.

1. Click the Programs link in the left pane of the System and Security window to open the Programs window.

2. Click the 'Programs and Features' link to display the Programs and Features window, which contains a list of all installed programs and features.

3. If necessary, scroll to and then click the desired program or app to uninstall.

4. Click the Uninstall button to uninstall the selected program or app. If necessary, follow the remaining on-screen instructions.

To View Programs Associated with File Types

When you double-click a file to open it, Windows runs the default program or app associated with the type of file you double-clicked. For example, if you double-click a file that has a .docx file name extension, Windows might open that file using Microsoft Word. If you double-click a file with a .pdf file name extension, Windows might open that file using Adobe Acrobat. The following steps view programs associated with file types. *Why? If you have multiple programs and apps on your computer that are capable of opening the same type of file, you can see which program or app is designated as the default program for that file type. If necessary, you can change the default program associated with that file type.*

1

- Click the 'Hardware and Sound' button on the address bar (shown in Figure 5–47) to return to the Hardware and Sound window.

- Click the Programs link in the left pane to open the Programs window (Figure 5–48).

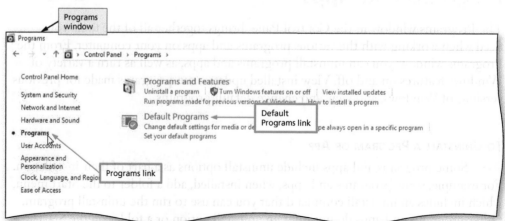

Figure 5–48

- Click the Default Programs link to open the Default Programs window (Figure 5-49).

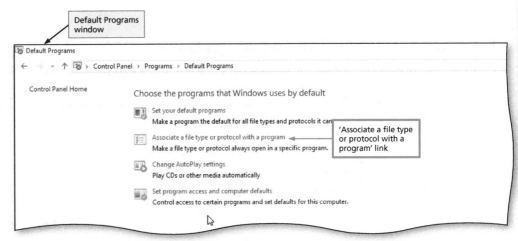

Figure 5-49

- Click the 'Associate a file type or protocol with a program' link to display a list of file types and their current default programs in the Set Associations window (Figure 5-50).

Q&A How can I change a default program?

Select the file name extension for the type of file you want to change, click the Change program... button in the Set Associations window, select the desired program or app in the list, and then click the OK button.

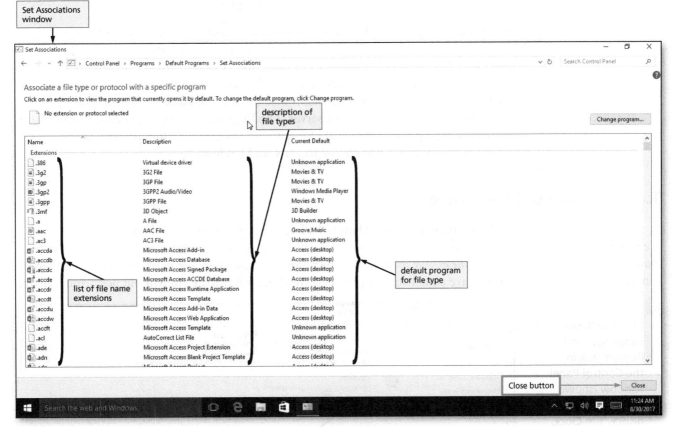

Figure 5-50

4

- Click the Close button to return to the Default Programs window.
- Click the Control Panel button on the address bar to return to the Control Panel (Figure 5–51).

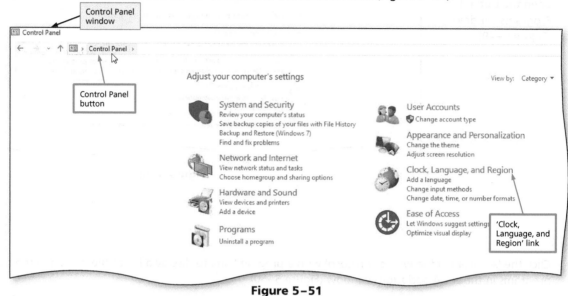

Figure 5–51

Time and Language Settings

The Clock, Language, and Region window in the Control Panel includes the controls for setting the date and time and adjusting the Region and Language options. The Date and Time dialog box is where you can change the Windows display language; change the date, time, and time zone; add additional clocks; and alter Internet time settings. You can use the Internet time settings to synchronize the time and date on the computer with the time and date on an Internet time server. The Region and Language dialog box is where you can change and customize date formats and make other administrative changes related to the language you choose to use with Windows 10.

To Change the Date and Time

Changes to the date and time are made in the Date and Time Settings dialog box. Administrative privileges are required to change the date and time. *Why? You do not think the time on your computer is accurate, so you want to change it so that it displays the same time as your smartphone.* The following steps change the date and time and then cancel the changes. If you do not have administrative privileges, read the following steps without performing them.

1

- Click the 'Clock, Language, and Region' link in the Control Panel window (shown in Figure 5–51) to display the Clock, Language, and Region window (Figure 5–52).

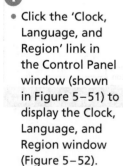
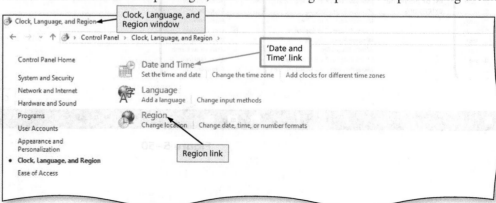

Figure 5–52

2

- Click the 'Date and Time' link to display the Date and Time dialog box (Figure 5–53).

Q&A Do I need to manually adjust the clock for daylight savings time?

No. Windows automatically changes the time for daylight savings time.

Should I change the time or the time zone if I travel?

If you travel to a different time zone, you can use the 'Change time zone' button (Date and Time dialog box) to update the day and time on your computer so that the clock displays the correct time, or you can configure an additional clock to display the time and date of your destination.

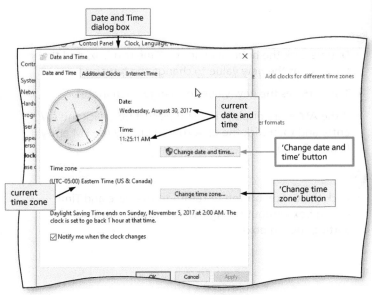

Figure 5–53

3

- Click the 'Change date and time' button (Date and Time dialog box) to display the Date and Time Settings dialog box (Figure 5–54).

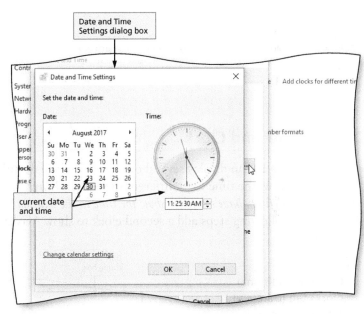

Figure 5–54

4

- Click the right month arrow until the month changes to November. If November already is the current month, you do not need to click the right arrow.

- Click the number 7 in the monthly calendar to select November 7 (Figure 5–55).

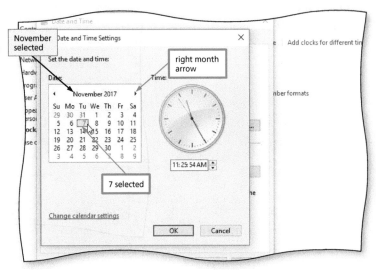

Figure 5–55

5

- Double-click the hour value in the Time text box, and then type 1 as the new value to change the hour.

- Type 45 as the new value to change the minute.

- If the AM entry displays in the time text box, click the AM entry and then click the up arrow to display the PM entry (Figure 5–56).

6

- Click the Cancel button to return to the Date and Time dialog box without saving changes (Date and Time Settings dialog box).

Q&A What if I want to save the date and time changes?

If you want to save the date and time changes, you should click the OK button instead of the Cancel button.

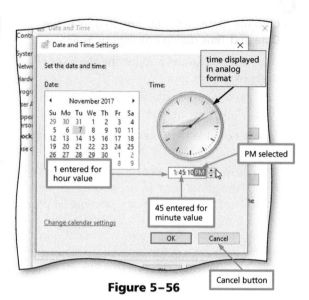

Figure 5–56

Other Ways

1. In notification area, right-click time, click 'Adjust date/time'	2. Type date in search box, click Date and Time search result	3. Type date in search box, click 'Date & time settings' search result	4. Open Control Panel, change to Large or Small icons, click Date and Time link

To Add a Second Clock

Windows 10 can display several clocks besides the default clock in the notification area. Each clock that you add can show the time for a different time zone. *Why? International students, business travelers, and tourists might find it useful to have a clock to show the time in the location they are visiting, as well as the time in their home location.* The following steps add a second clock to show Alaska time, display it in the notification area, and then delete it.

1

- Click the Additional Clocks tab (Date and Time dialog box) to display the Additional Clocks sheet (Figure 5–57).

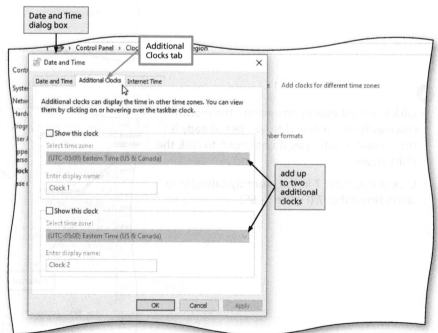

Figure 5–57

- Click the first 'Show this clock' check box to select it.
- Click the 'Select time zone' button to display a list of time zones.
- If necessary, scroll until you see Alaska in the list (Figure 5–58).

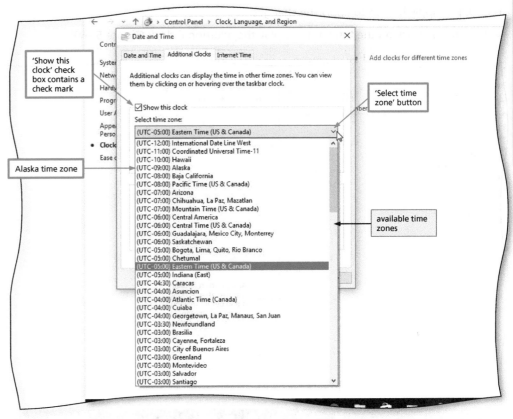

Figure 5–58

3

- Click the Alaska list item to select it. If your time zone already is set for Alaska, select another time zone.
- Type **Alaska** in the 'Enter display name' text box to name the clock (Figure 5–59).

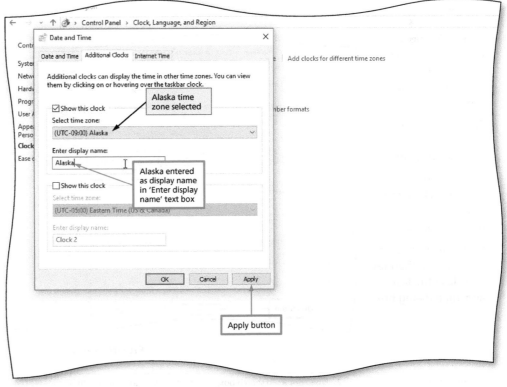

Figure 5–59

4

- Click the Apply button to apply the changes.
- Point to the clock on the taskbar to display the additional clock (Figure 5–60).

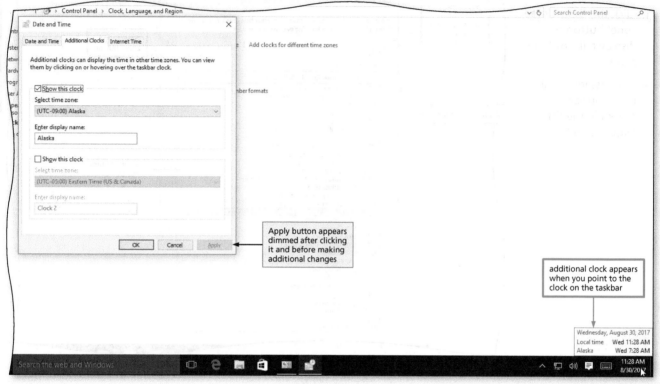

Figure 5–60

5

- Type **Clock 1** in the 'Enter display name' text box (Date and Time dialog box).

- Change the time zone back to the original time zone.

- Click the 'Show this clock' check box to remove the check mark (Figure 5–61).

- Click the OK button to apply the changes and close the Date and Time dialog box.

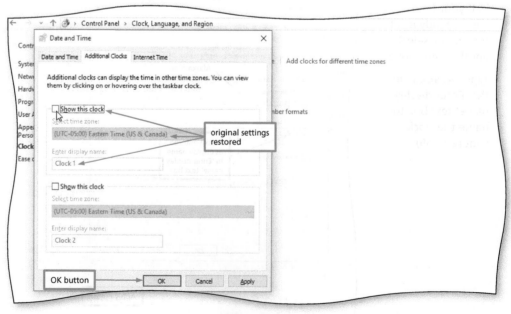

Figure 5–61

Other Ways

1. In notification area, right-click time, click 'Adjust date/time' on shortcut menu, click Additional Clocks

2. Type **date** in search box, click 'Date and Time' search result, click Additional Clocks

3. Type **date** in search box, click 'Date & time settings' search result, click 'Add clocks for different time zones'

4. Open Control Panel window, change to Large or Small icons, click 'Date and Time' link, click Additional Clocks

To View the Date Formats

Windows 10 is designed to work in many regions of the world and in many different languages. Other countries often have different conventions for displaying dates and time. For example, many countries in Europe use the 24-hour clock when displaying time. You can use the Region dialog box to view the formats that Windows 10 uses to display dates. *Why? If you are planning to visit other countries, you can change the date formats so that they will match the formats used by the countries you visit.* The following step displays the Region dialog box.

1

- Click the Region link in the Clock, Language, and Region window (shown in Figure 5–52) to display the Region dialog box (Figure 5–62).

- After viewing the date formats, click the Cancel button to close the dialog box.

Experiment

- Try changing the current format selection and review the various date formats used by other countries.

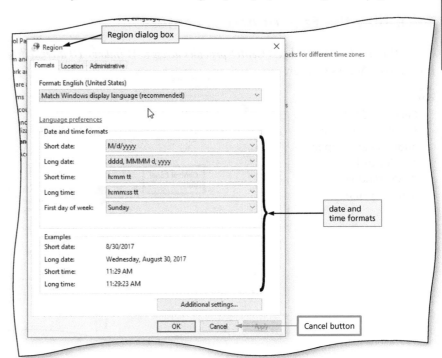

Figure 5–62

Other Ways

1. Type `region` in search box, click Region search result

2. Open Control Panel, change to Large or Small icons, click Region link

Ease of Access Settings

Windows 10 provides specialized customization tools, which are known as **accessibility features**, for people who are mobility, hearing, or vision impaired. All of the accessibility features can be found in the Ease of Access Center. People who have restricted movement and cannot move the mouse (mobility impaired) have the option of using Mouse Keys that allow them to use the numeric keypad to move the pointer, click, double-click, and drag. People who have difficulty hearing (hearing impaired) can enable Sound Sentry, which generates visual warnings when the computer makes a sound and can turn on captions when a program speaks or makes sounds, if captions are available. People who have difficulty seeing the screen (vision impaired) can select a High Contrast theme. High Contrast themes rely on a black or white background and bold colors to create a greater contrast between objects on the screen, which improves an individual's ability to read the text. Windows 10 also offers Narrator, which translates text to speech, and Magnifier, which creates a separate window to display a magnified part of the screen.

These are just a few of the accessibility features that are available in Windows 10. From the Ease of Access Center, you also can access a questionnaire that allows Windows to determine the right accessibility features for you. If you are unsure of where to begin, start with the questionnaire. The following section demonstrates some of the accessibility features.

To Display the Ease of Access Center

Why? *The Ease of Access Center provides access to Windows 10 accessibility settings.* The following steps display the Ease of Access Center.

1
• Click the Control Panel button in the address bar to open the Control Panel window (Figure 5–63).

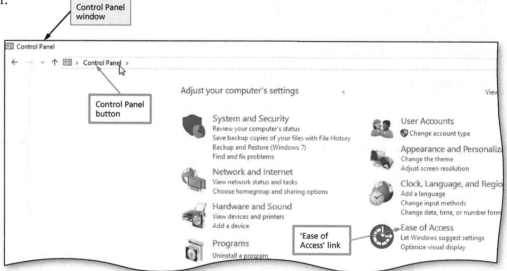

Figure 5–63

2
• Click the 'Ease of Access' link in the Control Panel window to open the Ease of Access window (Figure 5–64).

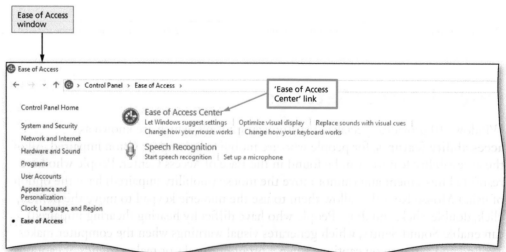

Figure 5–64

③
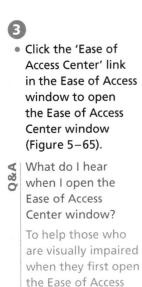

- Click the 'Ease of Access Center' link in the Ease of Access window to open the Ease of Access Center window (Figure 5–65).

Q&A

What do I hear when I open the Ease of Access Center window?

To help those who are visually impaired when they first open the Ease of Access Center window, Windows 10 reads aloud the content on the screen.

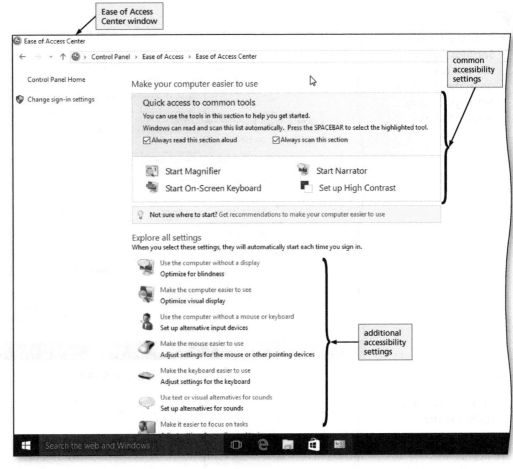

Figure 5–65

To Enable and Configure Narrator

Narrator is an accessibility feature in Windows 10 that reads aloud the content that displays on the screen. While Narrator is reading aloud the screen content, a blue outline surrounds the portion of the screen that currently is being read. *Why? If you are visually impaired and need help knowing what currently is being displayed on the screen, Narrator can read the content to you.* The following steps enable and configure Narrator.

①

- Click the Start Narrator button in the Ease of Access Center window to start Narrator (Figure 5–66).

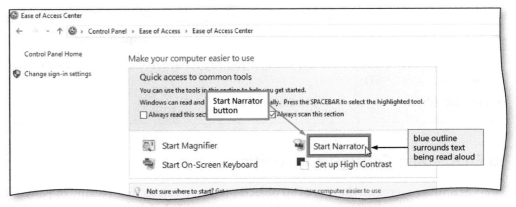

Figure 5–66

2

- Click the Narrator Settings button on the taskbar to open the Narrator Settings window (Figure 5–67).

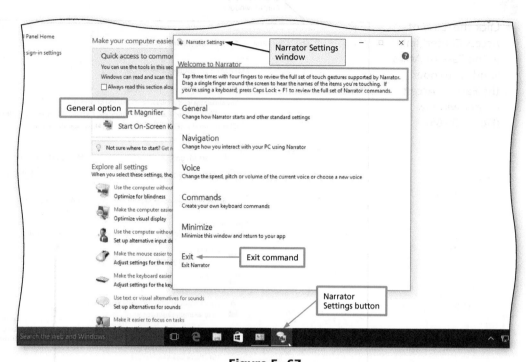

Figure 5–67

3

- Click the General option in the Narrator Settings window to view the Narrator settings (Figure 5–68).

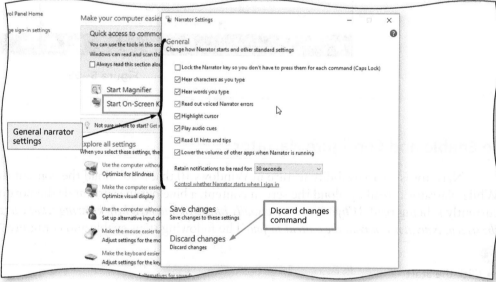

Figure 5–68

4

- Click Discard changes to discard any changes you might have made and return to the Narrator Settings window (shown in Figure 5–67).

- Click Exit (shown in Figure 5–67) to Exit Narrator.

To Enable and Configure Magnifier

Magnifier increases the size of all objects on the screen so that visually impaired individuals can see more easily the content on the screen. When Magnifier is enabled, the entire contents of the desktop cannot fit on the screen at one time; it is necessary to scroll horizontally and vertically to see areas of the desktop that are not displayed currently. **Why?** *Magnifier helps individuals who have poor vision and require larger objects on the screen.* The following steps enable and configure Magnifier.

1

- Click the Start Magnifier button in the Ease of Access Center window to start the Magnifier and increase the size of everything on the screen (Figure 5–69).

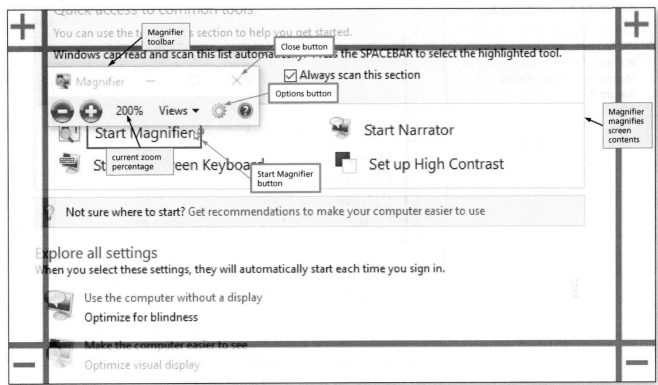

Figure 5–69

2

- Move the pointer around the screen to see different portions of the screen (Figure 5–70).

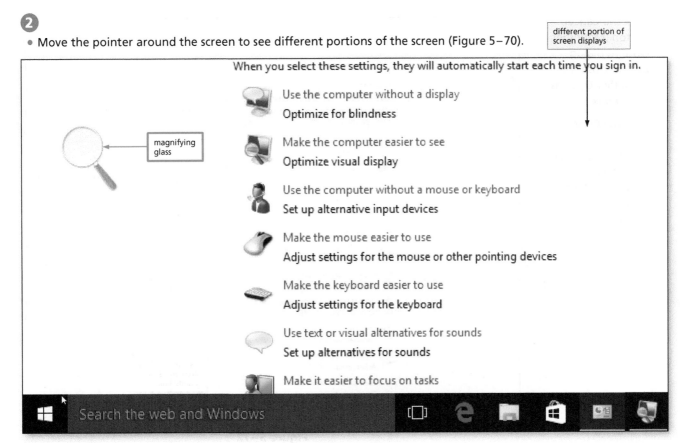

Figure 5–70

3

- Click the magnifying glass (shown in Figure 5-70) to display the Magnifier toolbar.

- Click the Options button on the Magnifier toolbar (shown in Figure 5–69) to display the Magnifier Options dialog box (Figure 5–71).

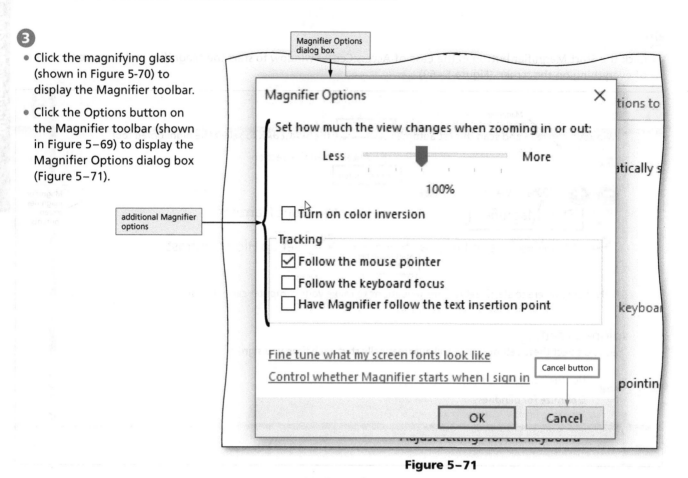

Figure 5–71

4

- Click the Cancel button (Magnifier Options dialog box) to close the Magnifier Options dialog box.

- Click the Close button on the Magnifier toolbar (shown in Figure 5–69) to close Magnifier (Figure 5–72).

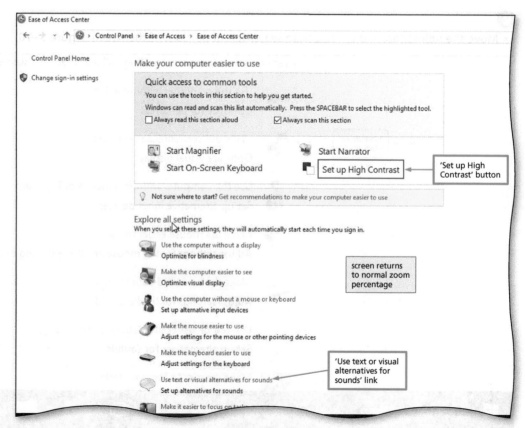

Figure 5–72

To Select and Apply a High Contrast Theme

High contrast themes help individuals who are visually impaired by providing greater contrast between objects on the screen. For example, a high contrast theme might display window backgrounds in a dark color, such as black, and foreground text in a bright color, such as white, yellow, or green. Windows 10 includes four high contrast themes by default: High Contrast #1, High Contrast #2, High Contrast #3, and High Contrast White. The following steps select and apply a high contrast theme. *Why? Using a high contrast theme makes it easier to differentiate between elements in the foreground and background on the screen.*

1

- Click the 'Set up High Contrast' button in the Ease of Access Center window (shown in Figure 5–72) to open the Make the computer easier to see window (Figure 5–73).

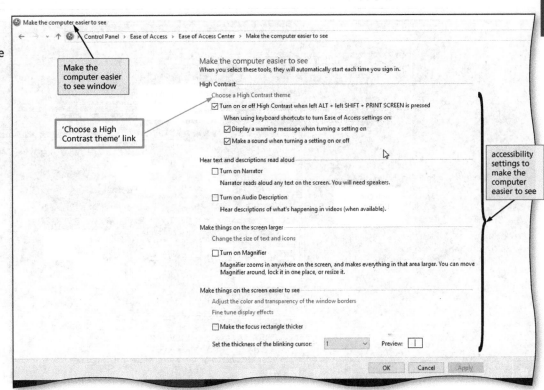

Figure 5–73

2

- Click the 'Choose a High Contrast theme' link to open the Personalization window containing the high contrast themes (Figure 5–74).

- Make note of the theme currently selected so that you can revert back to it at a later time.

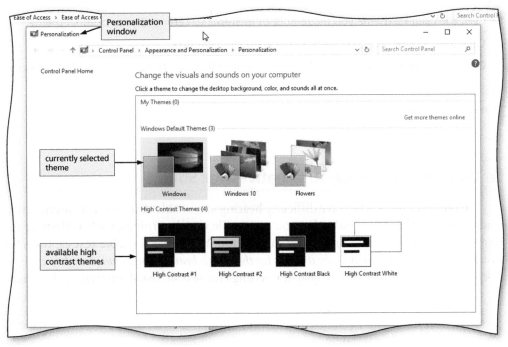

Figure 5–74

3

- Click the 'High Contrast #1' theme to apply the high contrast theme (Figure 5–75).

🔎 **Experiment**

- Click the other high contrast themes to see how they differ from the one you selected originally.

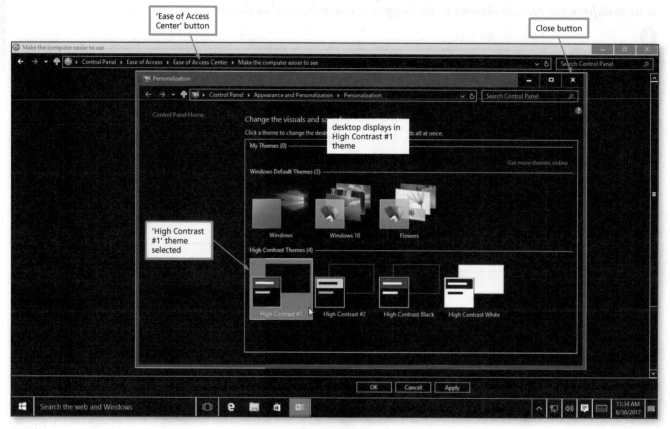

Figure 5 – 75

4

- Click the original theme you made note of in Step 2 to return to your original theme.
- Click the Close button to close the Personalization window.
- Click the 'Ease of Access Center' button on the Address bar to return to the Ease of Access Center.

Other Ways

1. Press LEFT ALT+LEFT SHIFT+PRINT SCREEN, click Yes

To View Text or Visual Alternatives for Sound

Computer users who have difficulty hearing can enable text or visual alternatives for sounds. For example when a sound otherwise would play, you can enable visual warnings, such as flashing the active caption bar, flashing the active window, or flashing the desktop. You also can enable text captions for spoken dialog. *Why? Visual alternatives for sounds make it easier for those with hearing impairments to know when a sound plays on their computer.* The following steps display the settings for text or visual alternatives for sounds.

1

- Click the 'Use text or visual alternatives for sounds' link (shown in Figure 5–72) to open the 'Use text or visual alternatives for sounds' window (Figure 5–76).

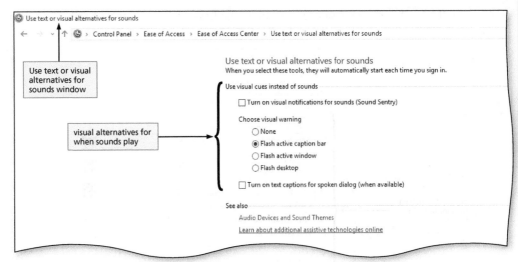

Figure 5–76

2

- Click the Back button to return to the Ease of Access Center (Figure 5–77).

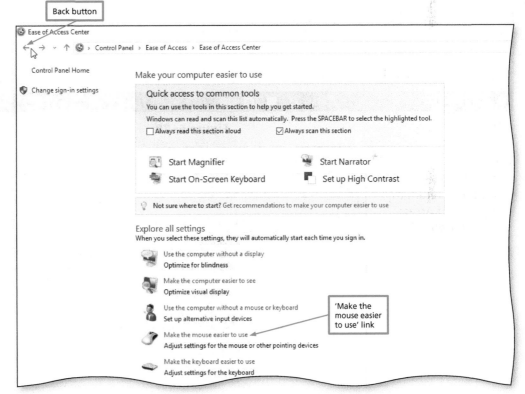

Figure 5–77

To Display Mouse Accessibility Settings

Mouse accessibility settings in the Ease of Access Center allow you to change the appearance of pointers, turn on Mouse Keys (recall that Mouse Keys enables you to move the pointer using keys on the keyboard), and make it easier to manage windows. The following steps display mouse accessibility settings. *Why? You want to know what mouse accessibility settings are available in case any can help you work more efficiently.*

- Click the 'Make the mouse easier to use' link in the Ease of Access Center to display the mouse accessibility settings (Figure 5–78).

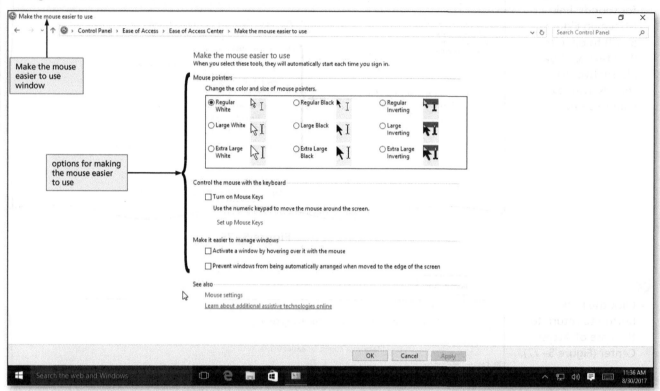

Figure 5–78

2

- Click the Back button to return to the Ease of Access Center (Figure 5–79).

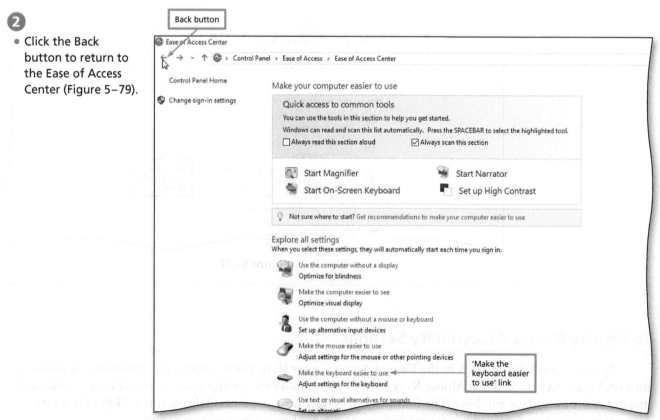

Figure 5–79

To Display Keyboard Accessibility Settings

Keyboard accessibility settings allow you to turn on features, such as Mouse Keys, Sticky Keys, Toggle Keys, and Filter Keys; underline keyboard shortcuts and access keys; and prevent windows from being arranged automatically if you drag them to the edge of the screen. **Sticky Keys** allows you to press and release a key on the keyboard, and Windows will act as if you still are holding down the key. For example, if you are unable to hold multiple keys simultaneously and want to press the ALT+F4 key combination to exit a program, Sticky Keys will allow you to press and release the ALT key and then press and release the F4 key to exit the program. Filter Keys plays a tone when you press a toggle key, such as CAPS LOCK, NUM LOCK, or SCROLL LOCK. Filter Keys ignores keystrokes of the same key that happen in rapid succession. The following steps display keyboard accessibility settings. **Why?** *You would like to see whether keyboard accessibility settings will help you as you work.*

- Click the 'Make the keyboard easier to use' link (shown in Figure 5–79) in the Ease of Access Center window to display the keyboard accessibility settings (Figure 5–80).

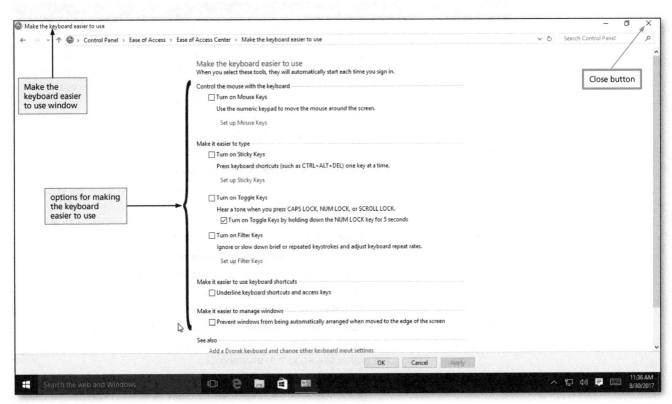

Figure 5–80

2

- Click the Close button to close the window.

Privacy Settings

Windows 10 has a myriad of privacy settings that allow you to control how much information you share, as well as which peripheral devices apps can access on your computer or mobile device. Windows can share information with Microsoft and third-party apps to provide you with a customized experience when using your computer or mobile device. For example, the Weather app can detect your location automatically and display the current weather in your area. Apps may be able to access the camera on your computer or mobile device so that you can take and share pictures and video, or host a video call with someone on the other side of the country. Some individuals are concerned with their privacy and want to limit the amount of information shared without their knowledge. In addition, they might want to control which apps have access to particular peripheral devices on their computer or mobile device. Table 5–1 shows various privacy categories in Windows 10.

Table 5–1 Windows 10 Privacy Settings	
Category	**Description**
General	Contains general privacy settings, including whether to allow Microsoft to collect information across apps for advertising purposes, whether to turn on the SmartScreen Filter, whether Microsoft can monitor how you write, and whether websites can access your language list
Location	Settings control whether Windows can detect your location, keep a history of your locations, and which apps can access your location
Camera	Settings control which apps can use your camera
Microphone	Settings control which apps can use your microphone
Speech, inking, & typing	Settings control whether Microsoft collects information about you to provide more customized results when using Cortana
Account info	Settings control which apps can use your account information, such as your name, picture, and other account information
Contacts	Settings control which apps can access and use your contacts
Calendar	Settings control which apps can access and use your calendar
Messaging	Settings control which apps can read or send messages, such as text messages and MMS messages
Radios	Settings control which apps can use radios, such as Bluetooth
Other devices	Settings control whether apps can share information and synchronize with other devices, such as smartphones
Feedback & diagnostics	Settings control whether (or how frequently) Windows asks for feedback or shares device data with Microsoft
Background apps	Specifies which apps can run in the background, even if you are not using them

To Display Privacy Settings

Why? *You want to view your Windows privacy settings to see what Windows is storing and sending, as well as what features various apps are able to access.* The following steps display privacy settings.

1

- Display the Start menu.

- Click Settings on the Start menu to run the Settings app (Figure 5–81).

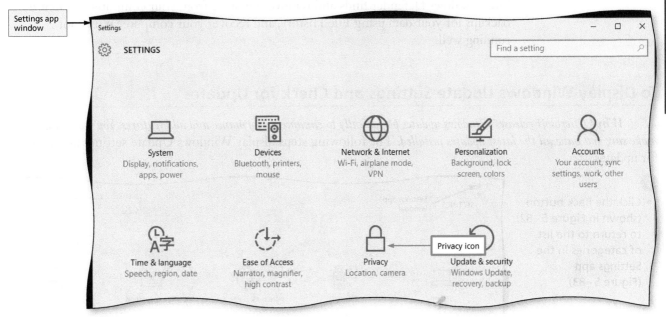

Settings app window

Privacy icon

Figure 5–81

2

- Click the Privacy icon to display the privacy settings (Figure 5–82).

Experiment

- Click the various categories to see the privacy settings for each category.

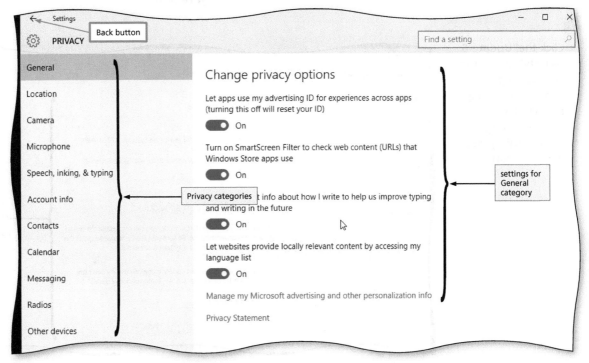

Back button

Privacy categories

settings for General category

Figure 5–82

Update and Security Settings

Update and security settings in Windows 10 allow you to perform functions such as checking for and installing updates to the Windows operating system, configure how Windows Defender finds and removes malware from your computer, configure backups for your data using File History, and recover your computer if it is not running well.

To Display Windows Update Settings and Check for Updates

Why? Microsoft releases Windows updates periodically to enhance performance and add features. You would like to make sure you have all the latest updates installed. The following steps display Windows Update settings and check for updates.

1
- Click the Back button (shown in Figure 5–82) to return to the list of categories in the Settings app (Figure 5–83).

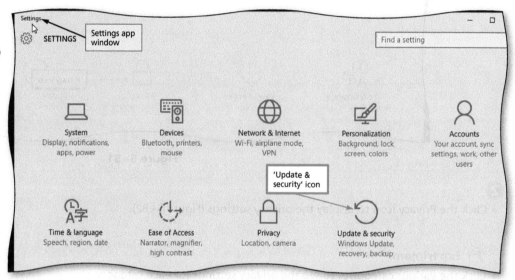

Figure 5–83

2
- Click the 'Update & security' icon in the Settings app window to display the Windows Update settings in the Settings app (Figure 5–84).

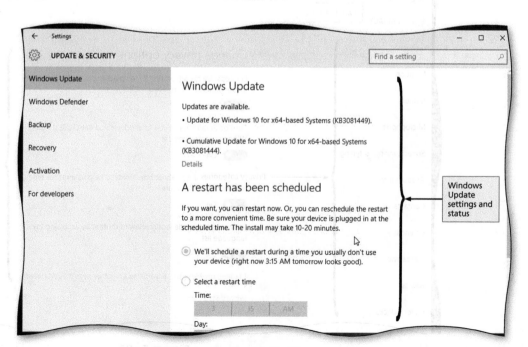

Figure 5–84

To Display Windows Defender Settings

Why? *You want to make sure Windows Defender is enabled and actively protecting your computer.* The following step displays Windows Defender settings.

- Click the Windows Defender tab in the Settings window to display the settings for Windows Defender (Figure 5–85).

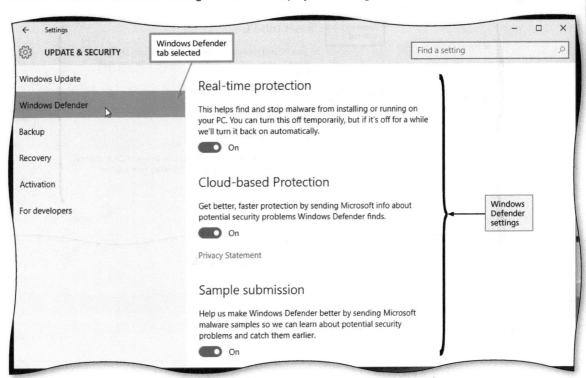

Figure 5–85

To Display Other Update and Security Settings

Why? *You want to view the other update and security settings available in Windows 10.* The following steps display other update and security settings.

- Click the Backup tab to display the backup settings (Figure 5–86).

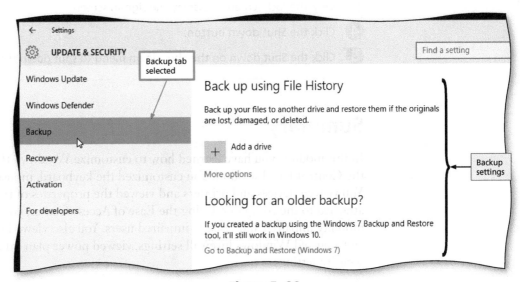

Figure 5–86

- Click the Recovery tab to display the recovery settings (Figure 5–87).

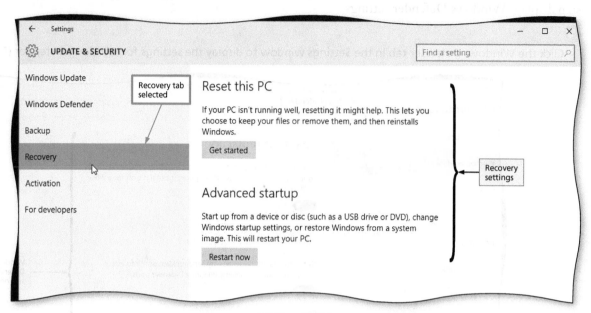

Figure 5–87

- Click the Close button to exit the Settings app.

To Sign Out of Your Account and Shut Down the Computer

After completing your work with Windows, you should follow these steps to end your session by signing out of your account and then shutting down the computer.

1 Display the Start menu.

2 Click the name identifying your user account and then click Sign out.

3 Click the lock screen to display the sign-in screen.

4 Click the Shut down button.

5 Click the Shut down on the Shut down menu to shut down the computer.

Summary

In this module, you have learned how to customize Windows 10 using various links in the Control Panel window. You customized the keyboard, mouse, and date and time. You viewed devices and printers and viewed the properties of the hardware devices attached to the computer. Using the Ease of Access Center, you explored settings for mobility impaired and visually impaired users. You also viewed privacy settings, viewed and adjusted Windows Firewall settings, viewed power plan information, and updated security settings.

Apply Your Knowledge

Reinforce the skills and apply the concepts you learned in this module.

Using System and Security Settings

Instructions: Increase your understanding of Windows 10 by finding answers to the following questions. Submit them in the format requested by your instructor.

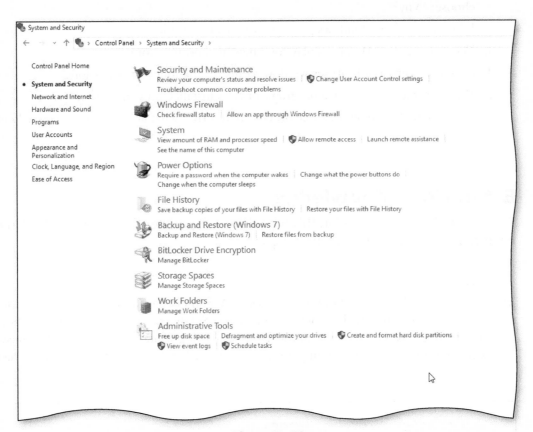

Figure 5–88

Perform the following tasks:

1. Use the links in the System and Security window to answer the following questions:

   a. Is the Windows Firewall turned on?

   b. What is the name of the virus protection installed on your computer?

   c. When was the last time maintenance activities were run on your computer?

   d. What are the names of five apps or features that are allowed through Windows Firewall?

   e. What type of processor does your computer have?

   f. How much memory (RAM) is installed on your computer?

   g. What is your computer name?

   h. What is the current power plan selected for your computer?

   i. With the currently selected power plan, how long is it before Windows turns off the display?

   j. With the currently selected power plan, how long is it before Windows puts the computer to sleep?

Continued >

Apply Your Knowledge *continued*

2. Use the links in the Hardware and Sound window to answer the following questions:

   a. What are the names of five devices that currently are connected to your computer?

   b. What type of keyboard is connected to your computer?

   c. Are there any devices displaying in the Devices and Printers window that you did not expect to appear?

   d. What is the AutoPlay setting for memory cards? If one is not selected, which one would you choose? Why?

   e. What sound does Windows play for a calendar reminder?

   f. What sound does Windows play for a new mail notification?

3. Use the Programs and Features window to answer the following questions:

   a. What are the names of five programs or apps installed on your computer?

   b. If you begin to run out of space on your hard drive, what are two apps you would uninstall? Why?

Extend Your Knowledge

Extend the skills you learned in this module and experiment with new skills. You might need to use Help to complete the assignment.

Troubleshooting Hardware Problems

Instructions: Use the troubleshooting features in Windows 10 to find answers to questions regarding hardware. Display the Control Panel using Small icons view and then click the Troubleshooting link. Use the links in the Troubleshooting window (Figure 5–89) to answer the following questions and then submit your answers in the format requested by your instructor.

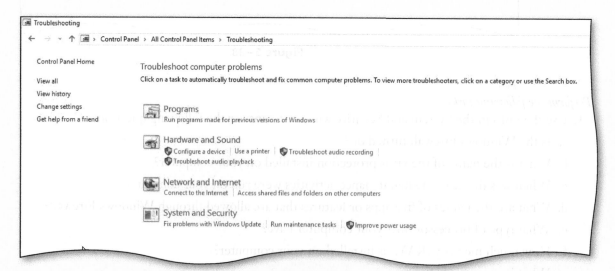

Figure 5–89

Perform the following tasks:

1. What are the steps required to run a program or app that was made for a previous version of Windows? Explain what happens during the troubleshooting process.

2. What steps are required to configure devices that are not working correctly? Explain what happens during the troubleshooting process.

3. What steps should you take if you are having problems recording audio? Explain what happens during the troubleshooting process.

4. What steps are required if you need assistance accessing shared files and folders on other computers? Explain what happens during the troubleshooting process.

5. What steps should you take if you are having problems with Windows Update? Explain what happens during the troubleshooting process.

6. If you continue having problems with Windows after using the troubleshooting features, how can you use Remote Assistance?

7. What is the Steps Recorder? Explain how it might help someone troubleshoot a problem you are experiencing.

Expand Your World

Researching Third Party Apps

Create a solution that uses cloud or web technologies by learning and investigating on your own from general guidance.

Instructions: As you have learned in this module, Windows Firewall (Figure 5–90) helps control whether apps installed on your computer can communicate using the Internet. Other apps are available that can provide the same or similar functionality. You will research various apps and answer questions about your findings.

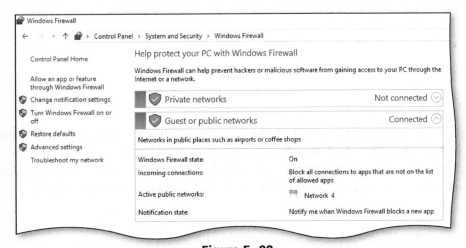

Figure 5–90

Perform the following tasks:

Part 1: Researching Firewall Apps

1. What are the names of at least three other firewall apps that are compatible with Windows 10?

2. Do the three other firewall apps have any features that the Windows Firewall does not? If so, what are they?

3. Does Windows Firewall have any features that the other firewall apps do not? If so, what are they?

4. Of the four firewall apps you have reviewed (Windows Firewall and the three other apps), which one do you prefer? Why?

Continued >

Expand Your World *continued*

Part 2: Researching Antivirus Apps

Windows Defender scans for and removes viruses and other malware from your computer. Research other apps that can scan for and remove viruses and other malware and then answer the following questions:

1. What are the names of at least two other antivirus apps that are compatible with Windows 10?

2. Do the three other antivirus apps have features that the Windows Defender does not? If so, what are they?

3. Does Windows Defender have any features that the other antivirus apps do not? If so, what are they?

4. Of the three antivirus apps you have reviewed (Windows Defender and the two other apps), which one do you prefer? Why?

5. Are the apps you researched free or do they charge a fee? Is an annual subscription fee required that you must pay to receive the latest updates?

Part 3: Researching Accessibility Apps

Windows 10 provides many accessibility features designed to help individuals with various impairments. In addition to the features Windows provides, other companies develop software that can offer additional accessibility features designed to make Windows and its apps more accessible. Research other apps compatible with Windows 10 that provide accessibility features and answer the following questions:

1. What are the names of two apps providing accessibility features?

2. What types of accessibility features do these apps provide?

3. How much do these apps cost?

4. Why might someone use a third-party app instead of the features built into Windows 10?

In the Labs

Design, create, modify, and/or use files following the guidelines, concepts, and skills presented in this module. Labs 1 and 2, which increase in difficulty, require you to create solutions based on what you learned in the module; Lab 3 requires you to apply your creative thinking and problem-solving skills to design and implement a solution.

Lab 1: Developing a Control Panel Guide

Problem: Although most people like to use the Category view when working with Control Panel, your boss favors the Small icons view (Figure 5–91). Your boss asks you to create a Control Panel guide so that other employees can familiarize themselves with the Small icons view and the Control Panel icons. Using WordPad, create a guide with a title and description of the following icons in the Control Panel window: Date and Time, File Explorer Options, Programs and Features, and Windows Firewall.

Perform the following tasks:

1. Open the Control Panel window and change to Small icons view (Figure 5–91).

2. Run WordPad and maximize the Document - WordPad window.

3. Type **The Control Panel Window (Small icons view)** as the title.

4. Type a brief statement about how Small icons view is different from Category view.

5. Type **Date and Time** and then type a brief description of the date and time settings.

6. Type **File Explorer Options** and then type a brief description of the available options for File Explorer.

7. Type **Programs and Features** and then type a brief description of what tasks you can accomplish in the Programs and Features window.

8. Type **Windows Firewall** and then type a brief description of the various Windows Firewall settings.

9. Save the completed document using the file name, Control Panel Guide.

10. Print the completed document.

11. Exit WordPad and then close the Control Panel window.

12. Submit the Control Panel Guide in a format requested by your instructor.

Figure 5–91

Lab 2: Customizing the Computer Using the Ease of Access Center

Problem: You are volunteering at the local senior center, and you have noticed that a number of the residents have difficulty reading the text on the screen and using the keyboard to type text. You decide to change the settings to help them access the computer more easily. You will make the screen easier to read and make it easier to type in WordPad. After seeing how these changes helped some of the seniors to use the computer, you decide to explore additional accessibility options.

Continued >

In the Labs *continued*

Perform the following steps:

1. Open the Ease of Access Center window (Figure 5–92).

2. Click the Start Magnifier button to start the Magnifier and display the Magnifier toolbar.

3. Click the Views button on the Magnifier toolbar. What types of views are listed?

4. Click the Options button on the Magnifier toolbar. What options are available to set?

5. Exit Magnifier.

6. Click the Start On-Screen Keyboard link in the Ease of Access Center. The On-Screen Keyboard allows you to type text in a document window using the mouse.

7. If necessary, drag the On-Screen Keyboard window to position the window at the bottom of the desktop.

8. Run WordPad. Resize and position the WordPad window at the top of the desktop.

9. Using the pointer and On-Screen Keyboard, type the following sentence: **The on-screen keyboard helps individuals type if they are unable to use a traditional keyboard.** and then click the ENTER key on the On-Screen Keyboard two times. *Hint:* To type using the On-Screen Keyboard, click the key on the On-Screen Keyboard corresponding to the character you want to type. Click the SHIFT key on the On-Screen Keyboard to capitalize text. Click the SPACEBAR on the On-Screen Keyboard to insert a blank space.

10. Use the On-Screen Keyboard to type your first and last name and then click the ENTER key.

11. Print the document.

12. Close the On-Screen Keyboard window and then exit WordPad without saving your changes.

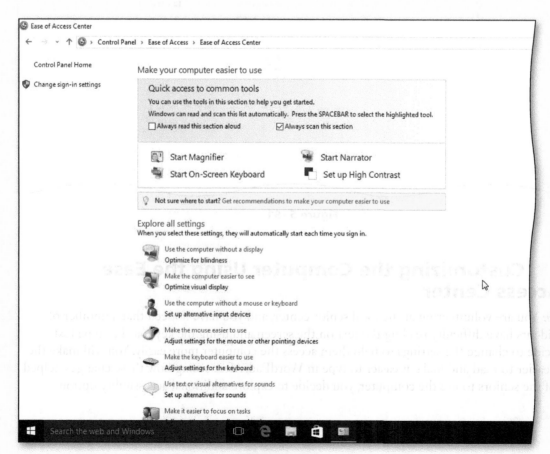

Figure 5–92

13. Open the Personalization window from the Control Panel window, and write down the name of the current theme.

14. Return to the Ease of Access Center and click the 'Get recommendations to make your computer easier to use' link. As you answer the questions in the accessibility questionnaire, select the appropriate options as if you had a visibility and hearing impairment.

15. After you complete the questionnaire, turn on the suggested options.

16. Display the Start menu.

    a. What color is the background color on the Start menu?

    b. Did the size of the commands on the Start menu change? If so, how?

    c. Is each icon on the Start menu fully visible?

17. Open and maximize the Control Panel window.

    a. Are the icons in the Control Panel window easy to see?

18. Close the Control Panel window.

19. Restore the Theme to the original theme you noted in Step 13.

20. Turn off the options you turned on in the Ease of Access Center.

21. Submit the printed WordPad document and the answers to the questions to your instructor.

Lab 3: **Consider This: Your Turn**

Verifying Privacy Settings

Problem: You have just purchased a new computer that comes with Windows 10. You are very concerned about privacy and want to make sure your personal information is not shared without your knowledge. In addition, you want to strictly limit the features on your computer that installed apps can access.

Perform the following tasks:

Part 1: Review the privacy settings on your computer and prepare a list of privacy settings you would configure to guarantee the type of privacy you desire. In addition, prepare a list of other privacy concerns you might have while using your computer.

Part 2: You made several decisions while searching for this assignment. What decisions did you make? What was the rationale behind these decisions? How did you locate the required information about which privacy settings to configure?

6 | Advanced Searching Techniques

Objectives

You will have mastered the material in this module when you can:

- Understand advanced searching techniques
- Find a file by using Boolean operators
- Search for a file by specifying properties
- View and modify the index

- Search for media files using specialized properties
- Save a search and find a file using a saved search
- Refine searches using the search box
- Configure search box settings

Introduction

In addition to the search techniques you learned in previous modules, other methods for searching are available in Windows 10. Searching for files and folders can be an everyday activity. If you want to work with your budget, you need your budget files. If you want to edit some photos, you need to locate your photos. If you want to send an important document to a colleague, you need to know where the document is located.

Windows 10 provides a variety of methods for searching. The easiest method is to use the Search box in the folder where the files you are searching for should be located. You performed this basic type of search in earlier modules. Another way is to use file list headings to organize your files so that you can find items faster. You can use file list headings to organize the contents of folders by filtering or sorting items, after which you can search to find what you want. If you are unable to find your files in one folder, you can use the customize option to change the search location without having to completely re-create the search. Finally, you can search from the search box on the taskbar to locate your programs and files. The search box offers efficient searching without first having to open a folder.

In this module, you will learn how to use these search tools and how indexing decreases search times. You will search for files on the local hard drive by specifying the date, file type, or word or phrase that appears in the file. You also will learn techniques for searching for files using properties (Figure 6–1).

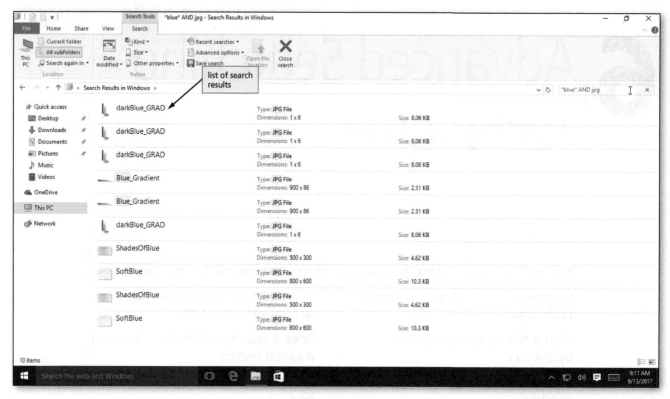

Figure 6–1a

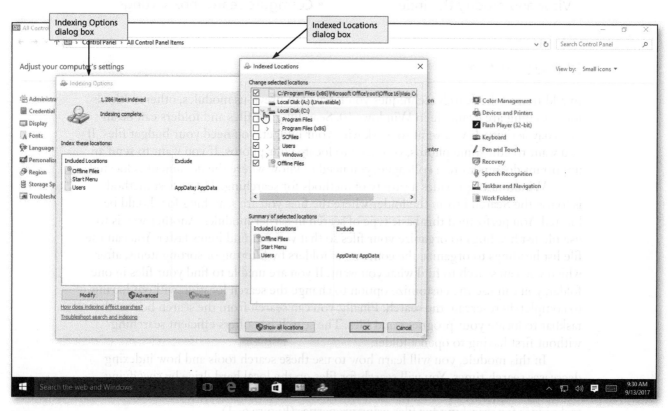

Figure 6–1b

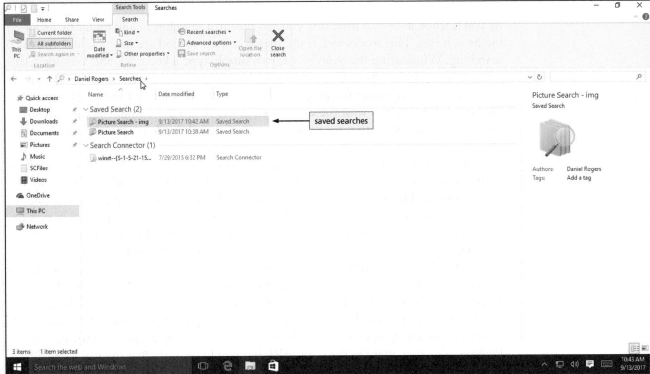

Figure 6–1c

Figure 6–1d

Advanced File Searching

As you learned in earlier modules, you can perform searches in any folder by using the Search box. This works well if the files you want to find are in the folder you are searching. When using the Search box, you simply type a keyword, and Windows 10 searches for matches. Search results can include all or part of a file name, a file type, a tag for a file, or any other file property. For example, if you enter the word, text, into the Search box, all files with the word, text, in the title will be found along with all files of the type text, with a tag value of text, or any other file property with the value of text.

When designing a search, it can be helpful to consider what you know as well as what you do not know. Try to think of keywords or parts of keywords that you can use in your search. The more specific the keywords, the more likely that you will locate the files you want. The keywords can be any part of the file name or located in tags or properties. Keywords also do not have to be complete words. Recall that in an earlier module, you used an * (asterisk) as part of your searches. Known as a wildcard, the * takes the place of one or more characters when part of your keyword is unknown. For example, searching for *rd would result in matches for all words that end in rd, such as word, board, and herd, whereas *.bmp would match all files that have a file name extension of .bmp. If you know that a file you want to find begins with the letter, h, and ends with the letter, m, you can use the wildcard to create the search keyword, h*m. Perhaps you know that the file is an MP3, but you know only that the name has the word, hey, as part of it. You are unsure if it begins with hey, has hey in the middle, or ends with hey. You would use *hey*.mp3 to find all MP3 files with the word, hey, in the file name.

You also can design a **Boolean search**, which is a type of search that uses Boolean operators. A **Boolean operator** is used to expand or narrow a search. Table 6–1 lists the Boolean operators with examples and explanations. If you know that a photo you want to find was taken on vacation and you added the tag, our vacation, to your photos, as well as saved them as JPEG files, you could structure your search as follows: *.jpg AND tag: our vacation. Be aware that the Boolean operators AND, NOT, and OR must be typed in all uppercase letters. If you type them in lowercase, Windows 10 will not treat the word as a Boolean operator. Also, you can use only one Boolean operator in a search at a time.

BTW

Search Box

Some would argue that the search box on the taskbar is the handiest tool in Windows 10. If an icon for a program or app does not appear on the Start menu, many people use the search box on the taskbar to locate the program or app icon and then click the icon to run the program or app.

BTW

Years

When you type numbers in the Search box, Windows 10 searches for files that match the number. If you type a four-digit number, such as 2017, the search results will include files that have any of their date properties matching the year 2017. This is convenient if the only fact you can recall about a file you want to find is that it was created in a particular year.

Table 6–1 Advanced Search Operators

Operator	Example	Search Results
AND '+' (plus)	text AND type: TXT	Finds all files with text as part of a property with a file type of TXT
OR '–' (hyphen)	text OR WordPad	Finds all files with either text or WordPad as part of a property (name, tag, file type, etc.)
NOT	June NOT bug	Finds all files with June as part of a property but they will not have bug as part of any property
<	date: < 11/11/2017	Finds all files with a date property value of before 11/11/2017
>	size: > 20 MB	Finds all files with a size property value of greater than 20 MB
" "	"Sunny day"	Finds all files with the exact phrase "Sunny day" as part of a property
( )	(Sunny day)	Finds all files with both Sunny and day as part of a property; the order of the keywords does not matter

To Search Using Boolean Operators

Why? *You want to locate files meeting two criteria.* The following steps use the Boolean operator, AND, to find all files that have the keywords, blue and jpg.

1

- Open the This PC window.

- If necessary, maximize the This PC window.

- Display the contents of the hard drive.

- Display the contents of the Windows folder (Figure 6–2).

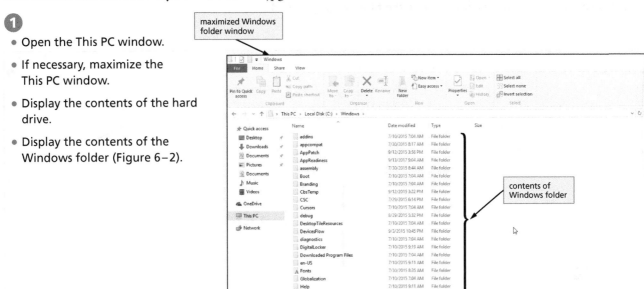

Figure 6–2

2

- Type ***blue* AND jpg** into the Search box to specify what you want to find (Figure 6–3).

Q&A Why do my results differ from the figure?

Depending upon your computer's contents, you might have different files appear or none at all.

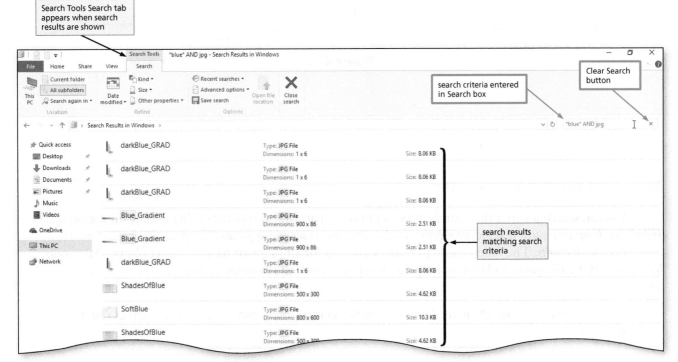

Figure 6–3

- After viewing the results, click the Clear Search button (shown in Figure 6–3) in the Search box to end the search and display the contents of the Windows folder.

- Click an open area of the window to close the filter list (Figure 6–4).

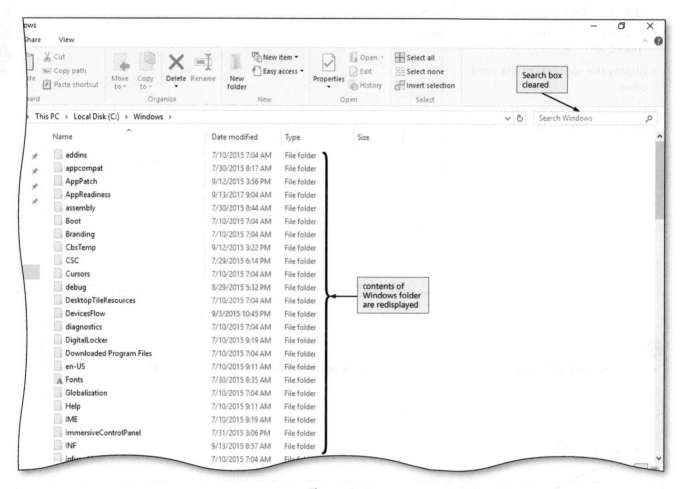

Figure 6–4

To Search for an Exact Phrase

You can search for files that match an exact phrase as part of its properties using double quotation marks. **Why?** *You know two words that appear together in the file name, so searching for an exact phrase will help limit the number of search results.* The following steps begin searching for all files that have the exact phrase, Microsoft Windows, in the file name and then modify the search to reduce the number of results.

- Type **"Microsoft Windows"** in the Search box as the search criteria and to begin searching for results (Figure 6–5).

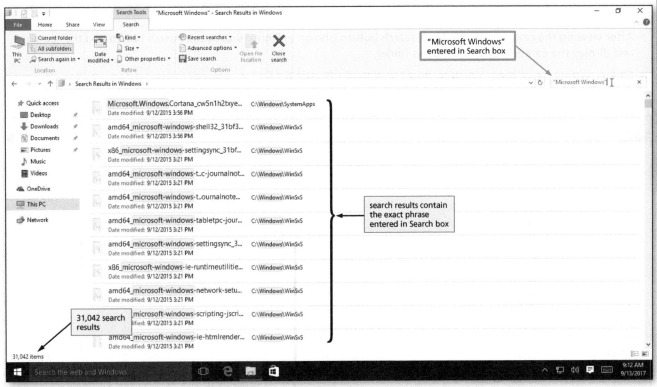

Figure 6–5

2

- Type **NOT x86** in the Search box following "Microsoft Windows" to narrow your search and reduce the number of search results and then press the ENTER key (Figure 6–6).

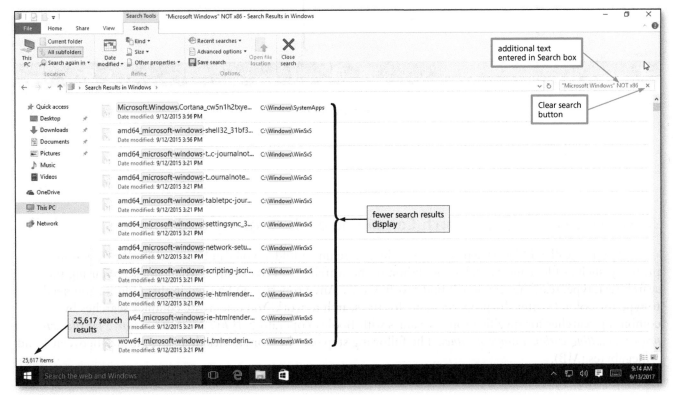

Figure 6–6

3

- After viewing the results, click the Clear search button (shown in Figure 6-6) in the Search box to end the search and display the contents of the Windows folder.

- Click an open area of the window to close the filter list (Figure 6–7).

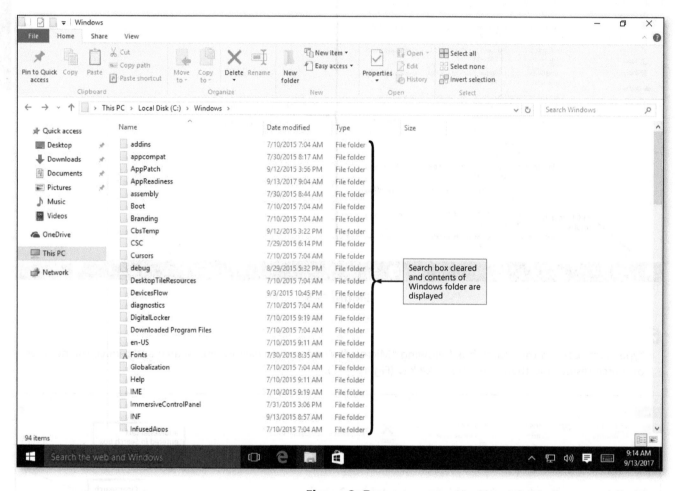

Figure 6–7

To Structure a Complex Search Combining a File Property and a Range

As you recall, all files have properties. When searching a folder, you can be more specific by adding a property, such as file name, type, tag, or author, to the search text. For example, when you search using the search text, type: text, the search will find text files only. Any property can be used in this fashion. You need to type the colon (:) after the property name for the search to work. You can create complex searches by combining searches for specific property values with Boolean operators. *Why? You want to search for files with properties falling within a range of values.* The following step searches for all files that range in size between 1 and 5 megabytes (MB).

1

- Type `size:>1MB AND <5MB` in the Search box to specify that you want to see all files that are between 1 and 5 MB in size (Figure 6–8).

Q&A Can I specify size in kilobytes (KB) or gigabytes (GB)?

Yes. When working with the Search box to search using file size as the criteria, you can specify kilobytes (KB), megabytes (MB), or gigabytes (GB).

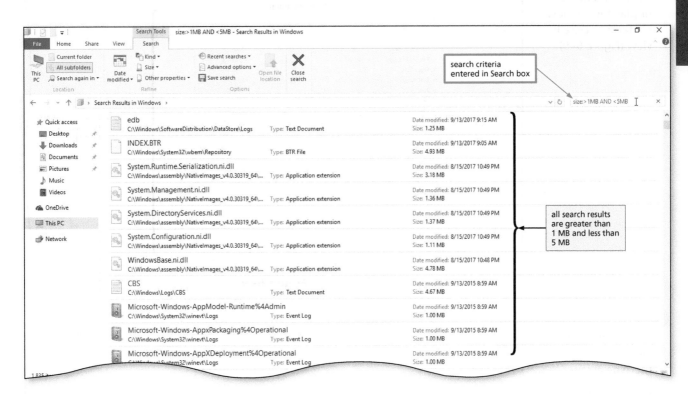

Figure 6–8

To Filter Files Using File List Headings

When using the file list headings, you can sort or filter files according to their headings. **Sorting** files arranges them in increasing or decreasing order, depending upon the file list heading you select. You also can filter files by choosing a date or date range or by choosing a timeframe specified by Windows, such as today, yesterday, or last week. Both options for filtering are based on the existing titles of the files and folders and are available by clicking the file list headings arrow. For example, filtering by the name heading includes options for organizing the files and folders by alphabetical groups (such as A–H), whereas filtering by the type heading includes a list of the file types found in the current folder. These options are most helpful when searching for files about which you already have some information. To sort and filter using file list headings, the contents must be displayed in Details view.

An increasing number of programs are using XML (Extensible Markup Language) files. The following steps filter the Windows folder on the Local Disk (C:) to display only XML files. *Why? You want to see the XML files in the Windows folder on your computer.*

- Click View on the ribbon to display the View tab.

- Click the Details button (View tab | Layout group) to display the window contents in Details view (Figure 6–9).

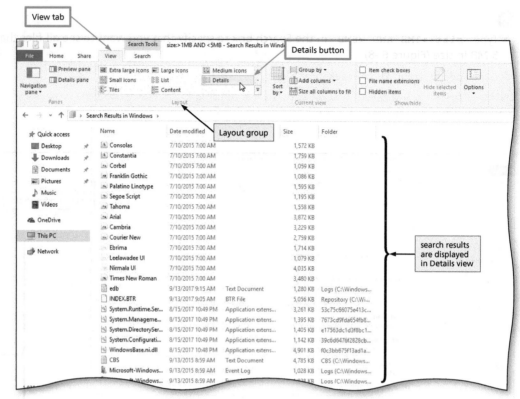

Figure 6–9

- Point to the Type heading to display the Type arrow.

- Click the Type arrow to display the list of filter options for file types (Figure 6–10).

Q&A

Can I change which file list headings are displayed in the window?

Yes. By right-clicking a list heading, you can select which file list headings are displayed. You can add or remove file list headings based on your needs. You also can add or remove file list headings and associated columns by clicking the Add columns button (View tab | Current view group) and clicking the columns you want to add or remove.

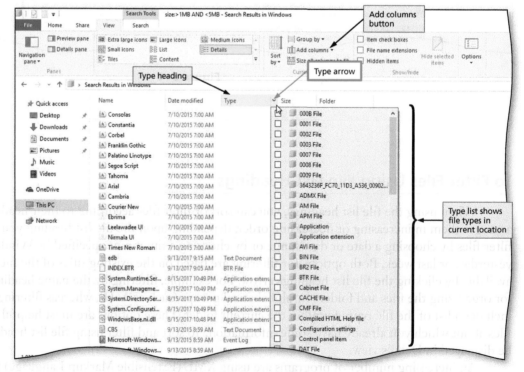

Figure 6–10

3

- Scroll to display the XML Document check box in the Type list.
- Click the XML Document check box to filter the Windows folder for XML files only (Figure 6–11).

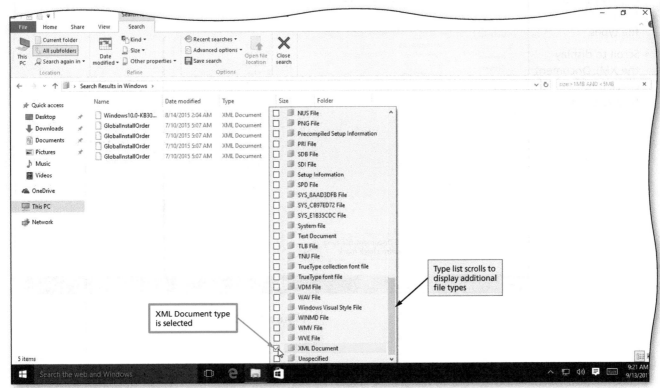

Figure 6–11

4

- Click any open space in the folder window to close the list of filter options (Figure 6–12).

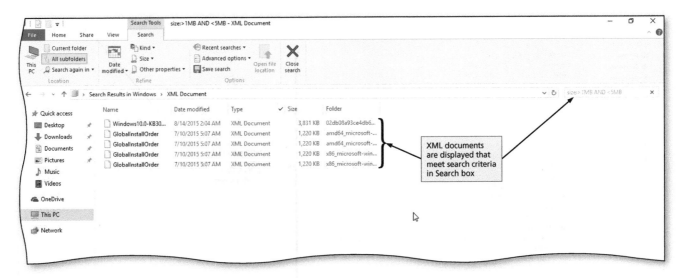

Figure 6–12

5

- After viewing the results, click the Type check mark to display the list of filter options for file types.

- Scroll to display the XML Document check box (Figure 6–13).

Q&A

Why does a check mark appear next to the Type list heading?

The check mark indicates that the window is displaying only certain (and not all) file types.

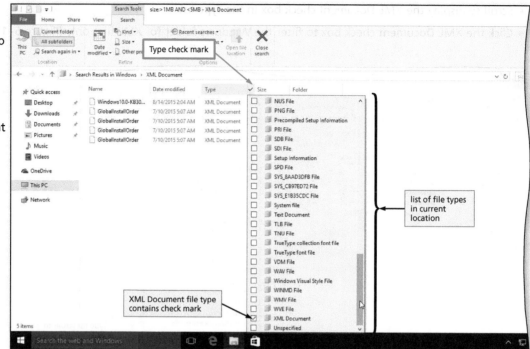

Figure 6–13

6

- Click the XML Document check box to remove the filter.

- Click any open space to close the filter list (Figure 6–14).

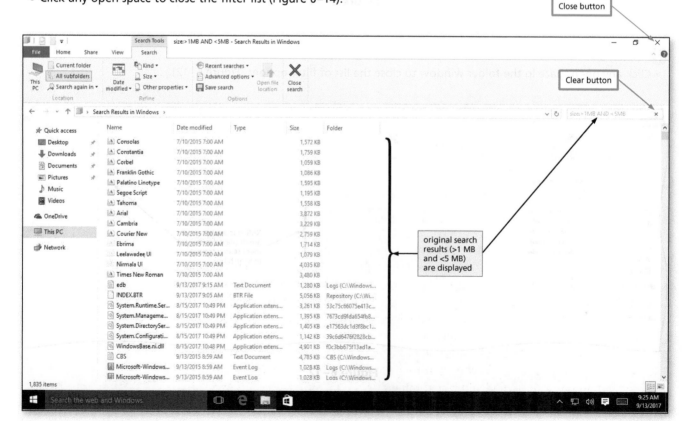

Figure 6–14

7

- Clear the Search box (Figure 6–15).
- Close the Windows folder window.

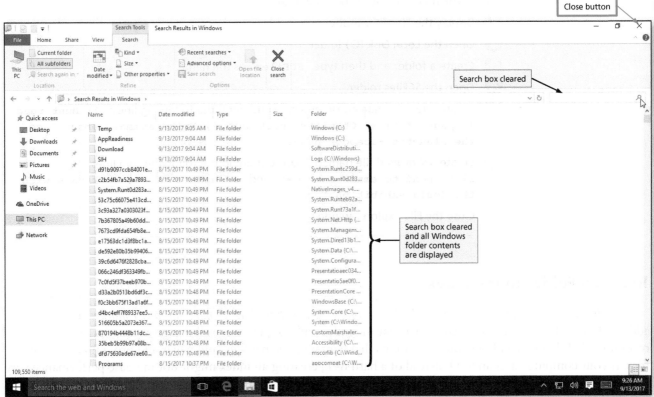

Figure 6–15

Other Ways

1. Click Search box, type `fileextension:xml`   2. Click Search box, type `type:xml`   3. Click Search box, click Search Tools Search tab, click Other properties button (Search Tools Search tab | Refine group), click Type on Other properties menu, type `xml`

Understanding Indexing

Windows 10 uses indexing to increase the speed at which it searches selected folders and files. By default, Windows 10 indexes each user's personal folders, which contain the Documents, Pictures, Music, and Videos folders. Program and system files, such as the C:\Windows folder, are not included as indexed locations. Excluding these folders keeps the index small. In addition, to keep the index at a manageable size, Windows 10 prevents you from indexing network locations, unless specifically designated.

As you have seen while searching the C:\Windows folder, a folder does not have to be indexed to be searchable. If you want to improve performance when searching, however, you might want to add additional folders to the index. It is important to note that the Search folder window relies on the index by default.

To Create a Folder and Files for Indexing

First, you will create a new folder and some files that you will then add to the index. The following steps create a folder named SCFiles and create both a text file and a WordPad file within the new folder.

1 Display the This PC window.

2 Open the Local Disk (C:) folder.

3 Create a folder and then type `SCFiles` as the name.

4 Open the SCFiles folder.

5 Create a text file named Homework containing the following lines: `1) Must read 15 pages from my Chemistry book` and `2) Write summary about Save the Planet's Facebook page.`

6 Create a WordPad file named ToDo containing the following two lines: `1) Respond to email messages` and `2) Update my Facebook page with the Koala exhibit photos.`

7 Close the File Explorer window.

To Add a Folder to the Index

Why? *Adding a folder to the index will allow Windows to search for files in that folder more quickly.* You can add any folders to the index, but remember that the index will not perform well if it grows too large. It is recommended that you add only those locations that contain personal files, and never add program or system files. If your computer uses an SSD instead of a hard disk, creating an index might not increase performance very much. SSDs are very fast and can locate search results in indexed and nonindexed locations very quickly. The following steps add the SCFiles folder to the Search Index by using the Indexing Options dialog box.

- Open the Control Panel window.
- Change the view to Small icons (Figure 6–16).

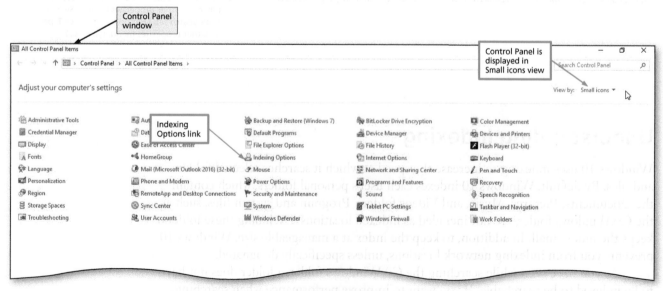

Figure 6–16

2

- Click the Indexing Options link (shown in Figure 6–16) to display the Indexing Options dialog box (Figure 6–17).

Q&A Why is my list of indexed locations different?

Your index might have been modified by the administrator. Also, the number of files you have installed in various indexed locations might be different.

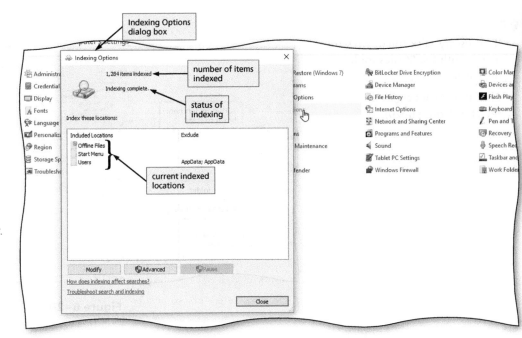

Figure 6–17

3

- Click the Modify button (Indexing Options dialog box) to display the Indexed Locations dialog box (Figure 6–18).

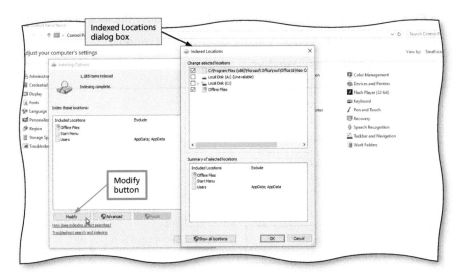

Figure 6–18

4

- Click the Local Disk (C:) arrow to display the list of folders (Figure 6–19).

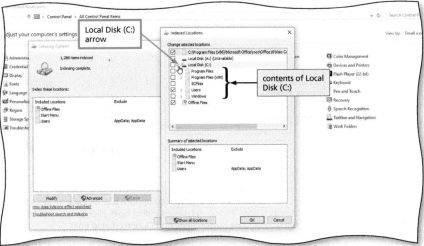

Figure 6–19

⑤

- If necessary, click the down scroll arrow until the SCFiles folder is displayed.

- Click the SCFiles check box to select it (Figure 6–20).

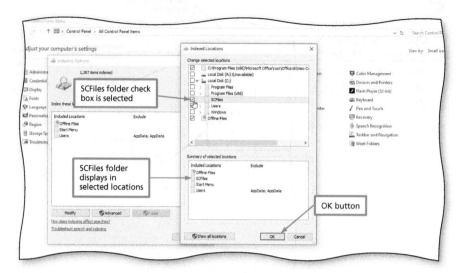

Figure 6–20

⑥

- Click the OK button (Indexed Locations dialog box) (shown in Figure 6–20) to add the SCFiles folder to the Search Index (Figure 6–21).

- Click the Close button (shown in Figure 6–21) to close the Indexing Options dialog box.

- Change the view to Category in the Control Panel window.

- Close the Control Panel window.

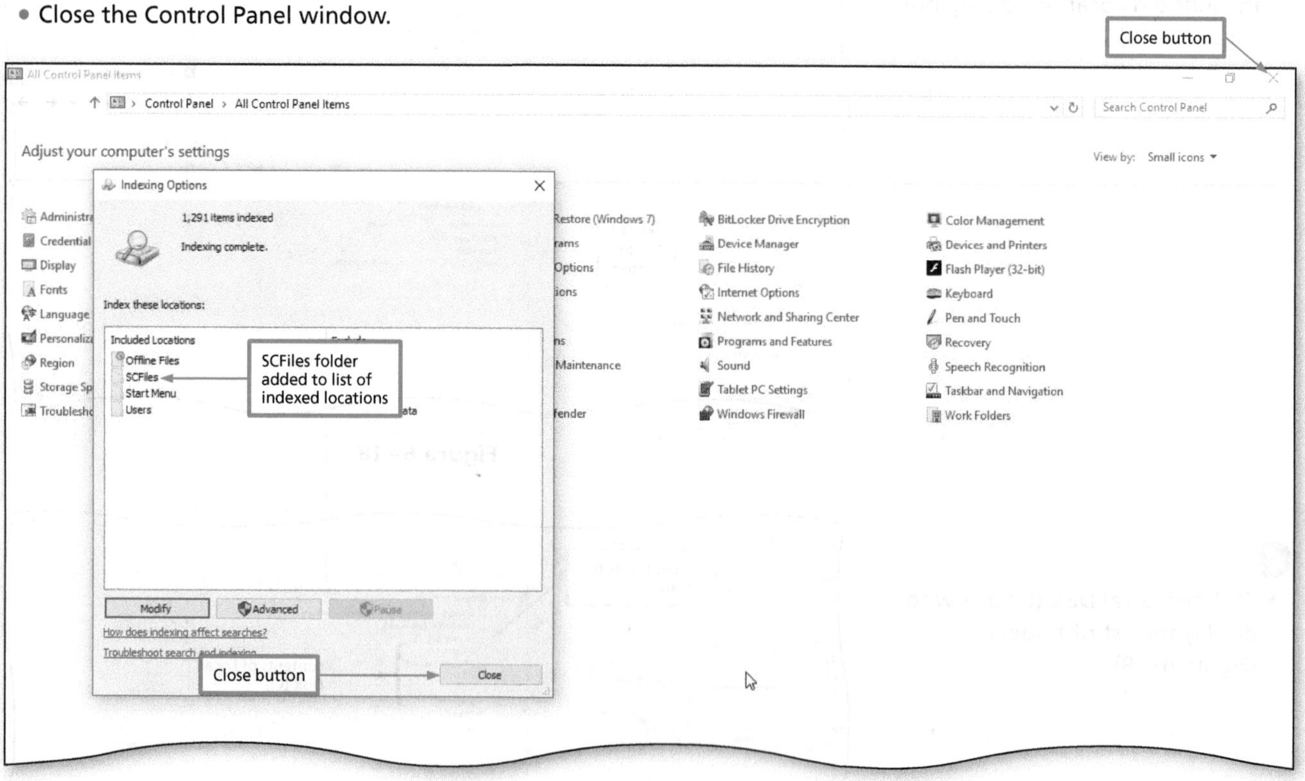

Figure 6–21

Other Ways

1. Click Search box, on Search Tools Search tab, click Advanced options button (Search Tools Search tab | Options group), click 'Change indexed locations' on menu, click Modify button (Indexing Options dialog box), click arrow next to Local Disk (C:), click SCFiles folder, click OK button (Indexed Locations dialog box), click Close button (Indexing Options dialog box)

To Search for a File Using a Word or Phrase in the File

When searching an indexed location, you can search for a file using a word or phrase that appears within the file. *Why? You might not remember the name of the file containing the contents for which you are searching, but you might remember some of the text within the file.* The following steps find all files containing the words, Chemistry and Facebook, and the phrase, Respond to email messages.

- Open the This PC window.

- Display the contents of the Local Disk (C:) drive.

- Open the SCFiles folder.

- If necessary, maximize the SCFiles folder window.

- Type **Chemistry** in the Search box to search for all files containing the word, Chemistry (Figure 6–22).

Q&A Why was the search result not displayed?

When you add a folder to the indexed locations, it might take a while for Windows to index all the file contents. If Windows has not finished indexing the contents of the files in the SCFiles folder, the Homework file might not appear in the search results.

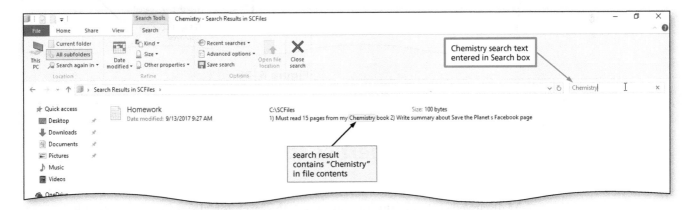

Figure 6–22

- After viewing the results, clear the Search box.

- Type **Respond to email messages** in the Search box to search for all files containing the phrase, Respond to email messages (Figure 6–23).

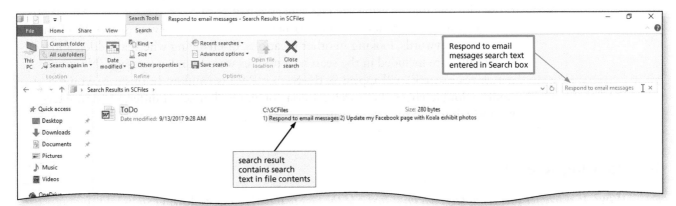

Figure 6–23

- After viewing the results, clear the Search box.

- Type **Facebook** in the Search box to search for all files containing the word, Facebook (Figure 6–24).

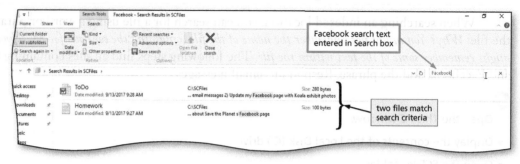

Figure 6–24

- After viewing the results, clear the search results (Figure 6–25).

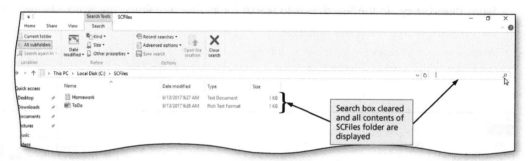

Figure 6–25

Using File Properties to Refine a Search

As discussed earlier in this module, you can search for files using any of the file properties, such as the file's name, author, size, and type. Media files, however, often have additional specialized properties that are searchable. These specialized properties often are assigned values by the file's creators. For example, if you want to find all the photos taken using your Nikon camera, you can enter, camera maker: Nikon, in the Search box to find these pictures. You also can search for a file based on when you last worked with the file or search for files containing specific text. Additionally, if you have edited the properties of a file or folder and added tags, you then will be able to find those files and folders using the tags you assigned.

If your search results are not satisfactory, you can refine your search by changing the search keywords, looking in other locations, or changing whether hidden and system files are included in the search. If no files were found, a message (No items match your search) will appear in the Search Results window. In this case, you might want to double-check the search criteria you entered or select different parameters with which to continue your search.

To Add a Tag to a File

Why? *To search for files using tags, you must first add the tags to the files.* The following steps add the tag, landscape, to the desert picture in the Pictures folder.

1

- Display the Local Disk (C:) window.

- Display the contents of the Windows folder.

- Type **img0.jpg** in the Search box to display all files with img0 in the file name and jpg as the file type (Figure 6–26).

◄ | What if no search results are returned?

Q&A | Type ***.jpg** in the Search box to display other images, and choose one to use for the following steps.

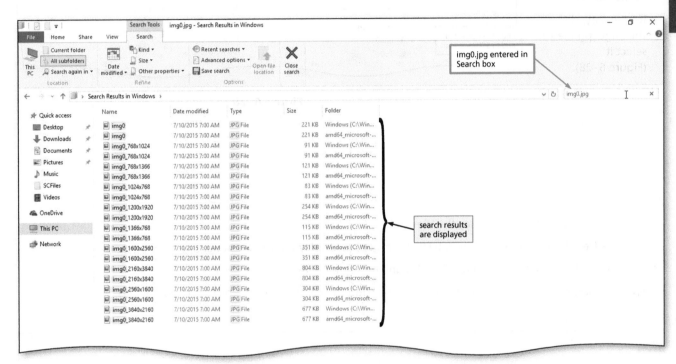

Figure 6–26

2

- Click the first img0 picture to select it.

- Click Home on the ribbon to display the Home tab.

- Click the Copy button (Home tab | Clipboard group) to copy the selected image (Figure 6–27).

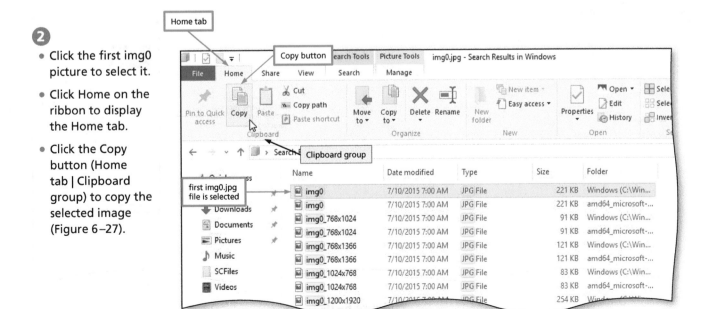

Figure 6–27

- Display the SCFiles folder window.

- Click the Paste button (Home tab | Clipboard group) to paste a copy of the img0.jpg file in the SCFiles folder.

- If necessary, click the img0.jpg file to select it (Figure 6–28).

Q&A Why did I have to copy the file to a different location?

Windows does not allow you to edit the properties for certain files in the Windows folder. By copying the file to a different location, you then can modify its properties.

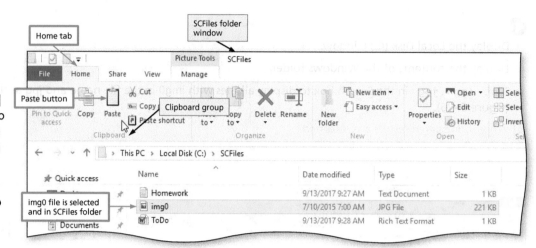

Figure 6–28

- Click View on the ribbon to display the View tab.

- Click the Details pane button (View tab | Panes group) to display the Details pane.

- Click the Add comments label in the Details pane to display a text box.

- Type **desktop background** in the text box to assign the comment to the picture (Figure 6–29).

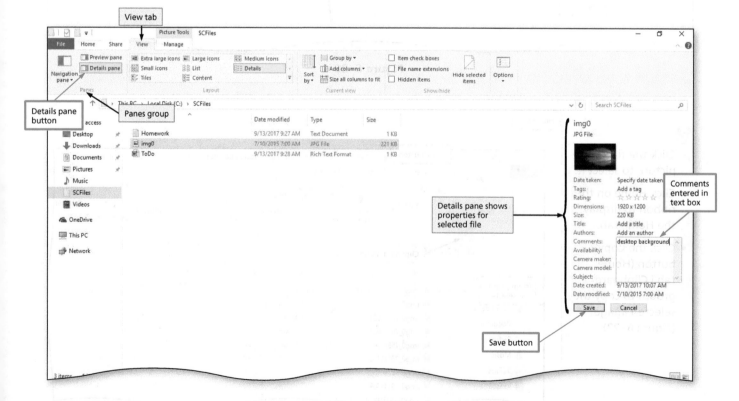

Figure 6–29

5

- Click the Save button in the Details pane (shown in Figure 6–29) to save the change (Figure 6–30).

Figure 6–30

To Search Using the Comments Property

Why? If you have added tags to your files, you can search for files by using the tags property in your search. The following steps find all files in the SCFiles folder with the words, desktop background, in the Comments property.

1

- Type `comments: desktop background` in the Search box to enter the search criteria (Figure 6–31).

Figure 6–31

2

- After viewing the results, clear the Search box (Figure 6–32).

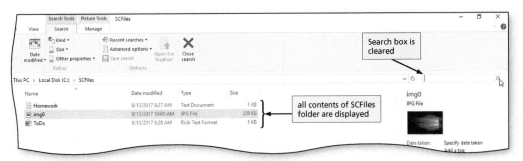

Figure 6–32

To Search Using the Date Property

When searching for a file, Windows 10 allows you to search using date properties. *Why? This can be helpful if you are searching for a file you modified recently, but you do not remember the name of the file or where it is stored.* You can select to find files by using the creation date (using the datecreated: property) or modification date (using the datemodified: property) for a file. The following steps find all files modified since the first of last month.

1

- Type `datemodified:` in the Search box to display a list of date options (Figure 6–33).

Q&A How can I see all the properties available for a file?

Click to select the file for which you want to view properties, click Home on the ribbon to display the Home tab, click the Properties button (Home tab | Open group) to display the Properties dialog box, click the Details tab to display the Details sheet, and then scroll to display all properties. When you have finished, click the OK button (Properties dialog box) to close the dialog box.

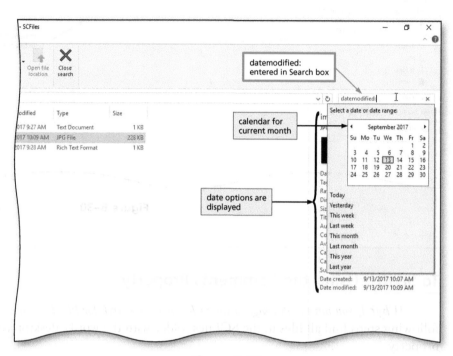

Figure 6–33

2

- Click the left arrow on the calendar to change to the previous month.
- Click 1 to select the 1st day of the previous month and add it to the Search box (Figure 6–34).

Q&A Why are no search results appearing?

The current search is only for files modified on the first day of last month. You will continue modifying the search criteria to search for files modified since the first day of last month.

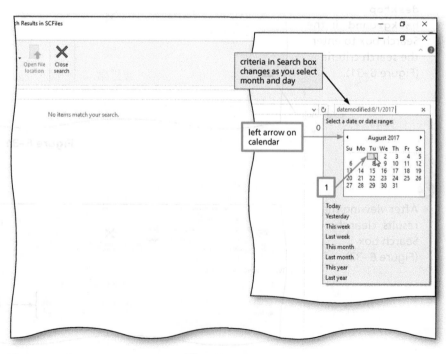

Figure 6–34

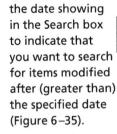

3

- Type **>** before the date showing in the Search box to indicate that you want to search for items modified after (greater than) the specified date (Figure 6–35).

- Clear the Search box.

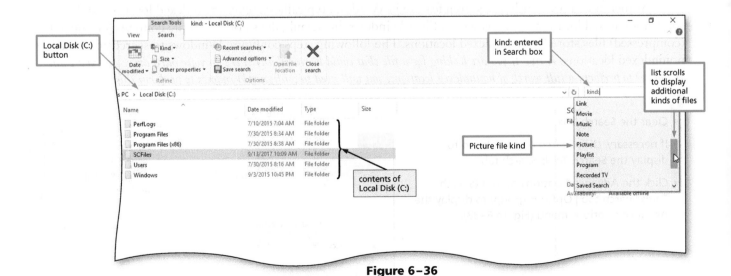

Figure 6–35

Other Ways

1. Click Search box, click Search Tools Search tab, click Date modified (Search Tools Search | Refine group) button, click desired option on Date modified menu

To Search for a File by Kind

Windows 10 allows you to search for specific kinds of files such as documents, games, movies and pictures. *Why? You store many pictures on your computer and want to display all the pictures.* The following steps search for pictures on Local Disk (C:) and display them as search results.

- Click the Local Disk (C:) button on the address bar to display the contents of the hard drive.

- Type **kind:** in the Search box to display a list containing the different kinds of files.

- Scroll to display Picture in the list (Figure 6–36).

Figure 6–36

2

- Click Picture to display a list of pictures stored on the hard drive.
- Scroll to display the search results (Figure 6–37).

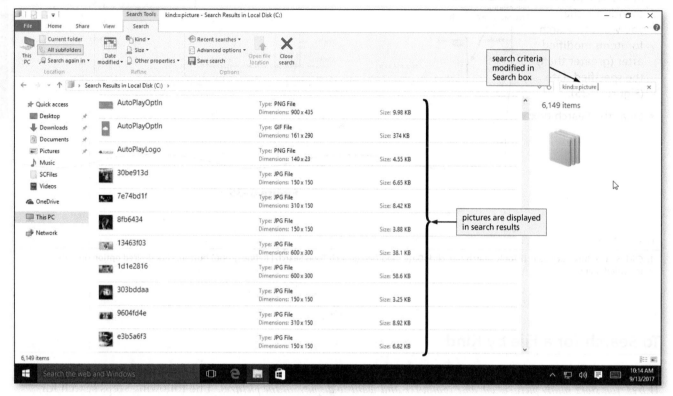

Figure 6–37

Other Ways

1. Click Search box, click Search Tools Search tab, click Kind button, click Picture

To Search Additional Nonindexed Locations

As mentioned previously, the search feature in Windows typically searches the indexed locations and some nonindexed locations (such as system files). Windows, by default, does not search file contents and zipped (compressed) files stored in nonindexed locations. The following steps configure Windows to search additional nonindexed locations. *Why? If you are looking for a file that could be stored anywhere on your hard drive and you want Windows to perform a full search of nonindexed locations, you will need to configure Windows to perform this action.*

- Clear the Search box.

- If necessary, click Search on the ribbon to display the Search Tools Search tab.

- Click the Advanced options button (Search Tools Search tab | Options group) to display the Advanced options menu (Figure 6–38).

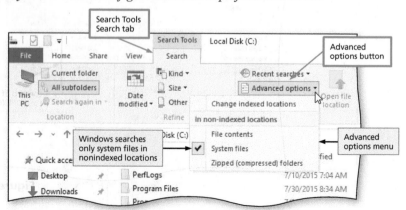

Figure 6–38

- Click File contents on the Advanced options menu to configure Windows to search the file contents in nonindexed locations.

- Click the Advanced options button (Search Tools Search tab | Options group) to display a list of advanced options (Figure 6–39).

- Click 'Zipped (compressed) folders' on the Advanced options menu to configure windows to search zipped (compressed) folders stored in nonindexed locations.

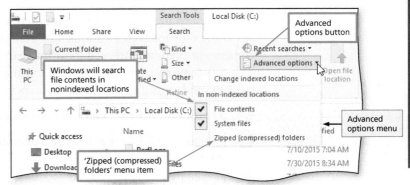

Figure 6–39

- Type **screen** in the Search box to perform a search using the text, screen, in the additional nonindexed locations (Figure 6–40).

Q&A Why does the search take so long to complete?

Windows is searching every file, as well as the contents of each file, which can take several minutes to complete.

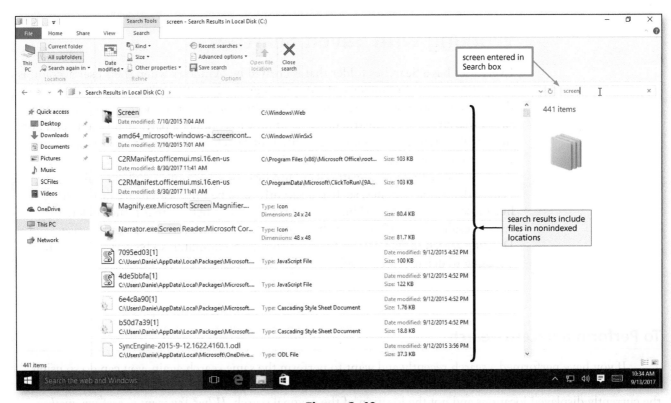

Figure 6–40

- After viewing the search results, clear the Search box.

To Reset the Nonindexed Location Search Settings

Performing searches in nonindexed locations is not always as efficient as searching only indexed locations. For example, if Windows has to search the file contents in every nonindexed location, searches might take at least twice as long. The following steps reset the search settings so that Windows no longer searches file contents and zipped (compressed) folders in nonindexed locations.

1 If necessary, click the Search box to display the Search Tools Search tab.

2 If necessary, click Search Tools Search on the ribbon to display the contents of the Search Tools Search tab.

3 Click the Advanced options button (Search Tools Search tab | Options group) to display a list of advanced search options.

4 Click File contents to remove the check mark and configure Windows not to search file contents in nonindexed locations.

5 Click the Advanced options button (Search Tools Search tab | Options group) to display a list of advanced search options.

6 Click 'Zipped (compressed) folders' on the Advanced options menu to remove its check mark and configure Windows not to search compressed folders in nonindexed locations.

Working with Saved Searches

Every user has a Searches folder that is created by Windows when their user account is created. The Searches folder is the default location for all saved searches. Any searches that you have saved will appear in your Searches folder. It is important to note that a **saved search** is a set of instructions about how to conduct a particular search, and not the actual search results themselves. Different search results might appear each time you execute a saved search.

Be aware that saved searches are not history lists. Some people mistakenly believe that some searches, such as a recently modified file search, are history lists, like those found when working with a browser. They believe that if they delete the search results, they will clear the history on the computer, which is not the case. Deleting search results deletes the files from your computer, so be very careful when choosing to delete search results.

To Perform a Recent Search

If you have performed a search recently and want to perform the same search again, you can do so using the Recent searches list on the Search Tools Search tab. Performing a recent search in this manner will search the currently displayed locations and not the location of the original search. *Why? You want to perform another search for all pictures on your hard drive because you closed the previous search results before having a chance to review them completely.* The following steps use the Recent searches list to perform a recent search.

1

- If necessary, click Search on the ribbon to display the Search Tools Search tab.
- Click the Recent searches button (Search Tools Search tab | Options group) to display a list of recent searches (Figure 6–41).

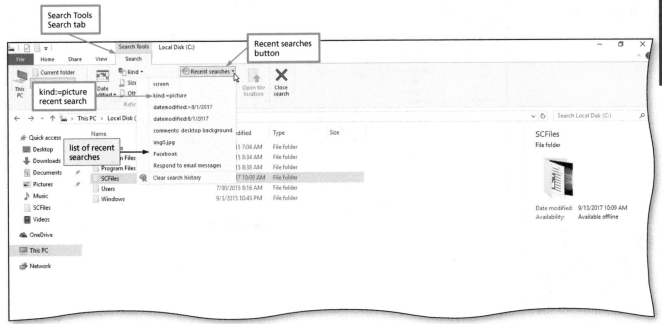

Figure 6–41

2

- Click 'kind:=picture' in the Recent searches list to perform a search for pictures (Figure 6–42).

Q&A What if I perform this same search when the SCFiles folder is displayed?

Because recent searches only search the currently displayed location, performing the search only would display pictures stored in the SCFiles folder.

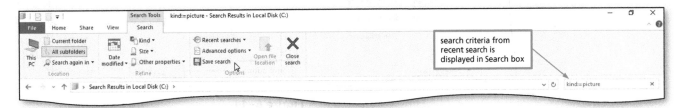

Figure 6–42

To Save a Search

After defining search criteria, you can save a search. By using a saved search, you can perform the same search repeatedly without having to re-create the search each time. The next time you execute a saved search, the search results might differ from the results you received when the search was first performed. *Why? You anticipate performing searches for pictures on a regular basis.* The following steps save the current search as Picture Search.

1

- Click the Save search button (Search Tools Search tab | Options group) to display the Save As dialog box (Figure 6–43).

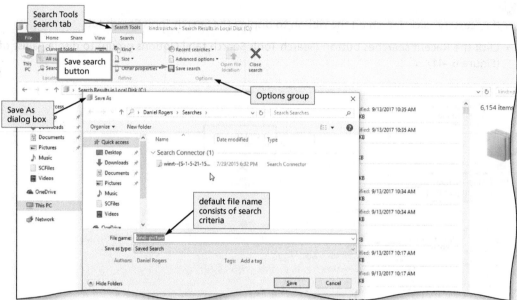

Figure 6–43

2

- Type `Picture Search` in the File name box to enter a file name for the search (Figure 6–44).

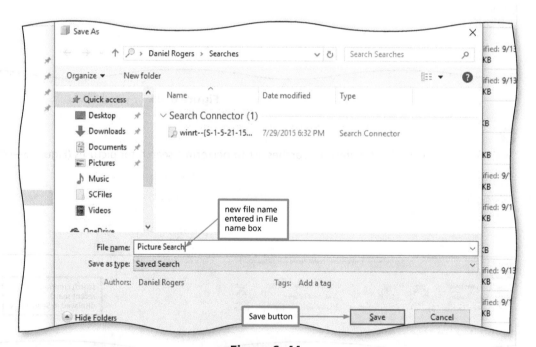

Figure 6–44

3

- Click the Save button (Save As dialog box) to save the search (Figure 6–45).

- Close the Picture Search window.

Q&A Why can I not just continue performing this search from the Recent searches list?

Figure 6–45

The searches that appear in the Recent searches list do not stay there permanently and can be cleared at any time. If you want to ensure that you can perform the same search again in the future without having to reenter the search criteria, you should save the search.

To Open the Searches Folder

Why? *To access saved searches you have created, you first must open the Searches folder.* The Searches folder is located in your user folder, which is created when you create your user account. The following steps open the Searches folder.

- Type **searches** in the search box on the taskbar to display a list of search results (Figure 6–46).

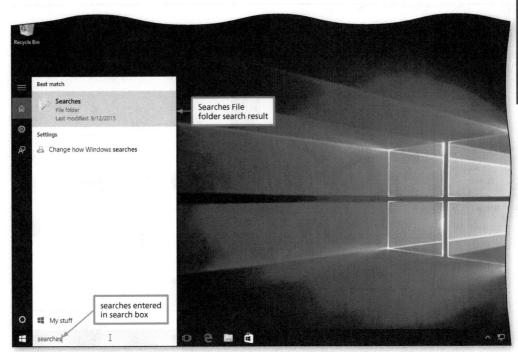

Figure 6–46

- Click the Searches File folder search result to display the Searches folder (Figure 6–47).

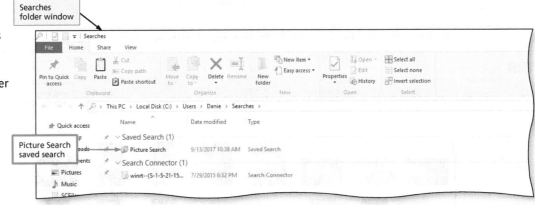

Figure 6–47

Other Ways

1. Open This PC window, display contents of Local Disk (C:), open Users folder, open folder corresponding to your user account, open Searches folder

To Create a Search from a Saved Search

You can use an existing saved search as a starting point for more searches. For example, if you want to search for pictures containing the text, img, in the file name, you can open the saved Picture Search and enter additional search criteria. **Why?** *The Picture Search search results were too extensive, and you want to further limit the search results.* The following steps search for results using the keyword, img, in the saved Picture Search and then save the search using the name, Picture Search - img.

1

- Double-click the Picture Search saved search in the Searches folder window (shown in Figure 6–47).
- Scroll to display the search results (Figure 6–48).

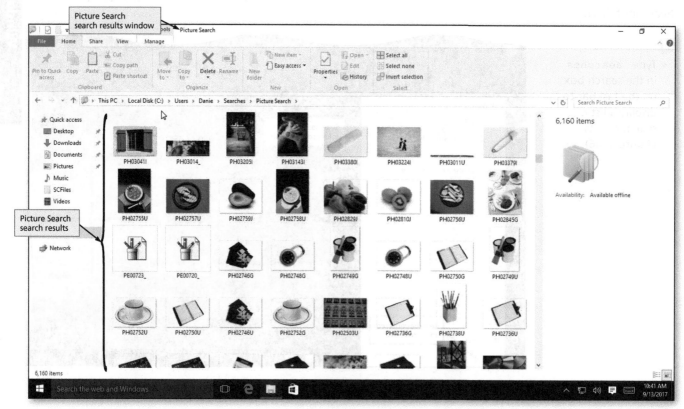

Figure 6–48

2

- Type **img** in the Search box to enter the additional search criteria (Figure 6–49).

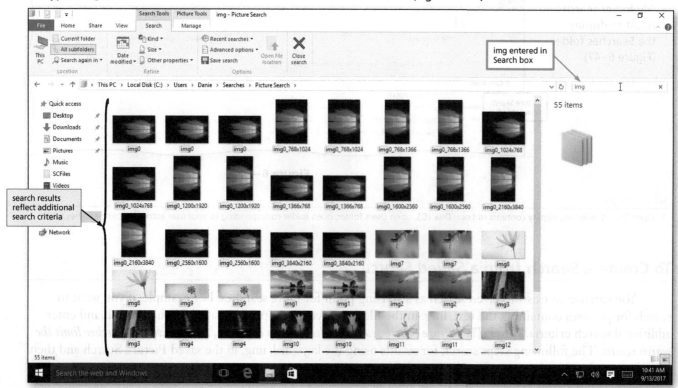

Figure 6–49

3

- If necessary, click Search on the ribbon to display the Search Tools Search tab.

- Click the Save search button (Search Tools Search tab | Options group) to display the Save As dialog box.

- Type **Picture Search - img** in the File name box to enter a file name for the search (Figure 6–50).

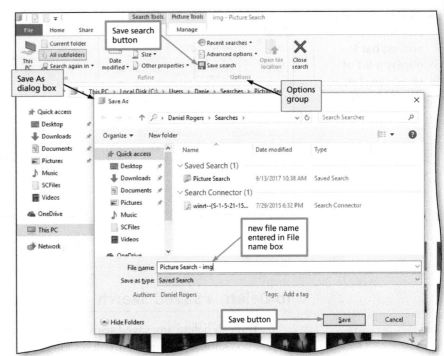

Figure 6–50

4

- Click the Save button (Save As dialog box) to save the search and display the search results (Figure 6–51).

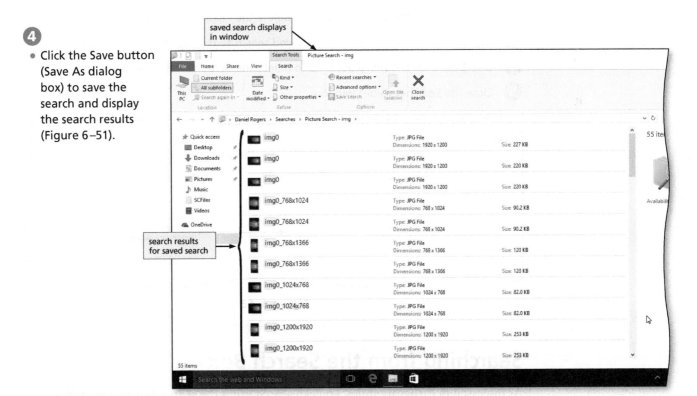

Figure 6–51

5

• Click the Searches button on the address bar to display a list of saved searches (Figure 6–52).

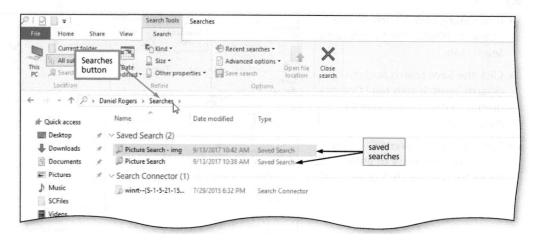

Figure 6–52

To Delete a Saved Search

You can delete any saved search in your Searches folder. Before deleting a saved search, you should be sure that you no longer need it. The following steps delete the saved searches you created in the previous steps.

1 Right-click the Picture Search saved search to display the shortcut menu.

2 Click Delete on the shortcut menu to delete the Picture Search saved search.

3 Right-click the Picture Search - img saved search to display the shortcut menu.

4 Click Delete on the shortcut menu to delete the saved search (Figure 6–53).

5 Close the Searches folder window.

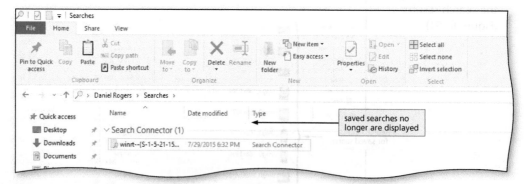

Figure 6–53

Searching from the Search Box

As discussed in earlier modules, you can search using the search box on the taskbar. The search box searches files and folders on the computer, and additionally searches the Internet to find webpages that match your search criteria. The search box also provides a way to configure web searches so that only the most appropriate results display. If you do not want the search box to be displayed on the taskbar, this section also shows how to hide the search box.

To Search My Stuff Using the Search Box

The search box, by default, searches your computer and the web for search results. *Why? If you want the search box to search only your personal files and exclude search results from the web, you can configure the search box to search only your files.* The following steps search My stuff using the search box.

1

- Type **picture** in the search box to display the search results (Figure 6–54).

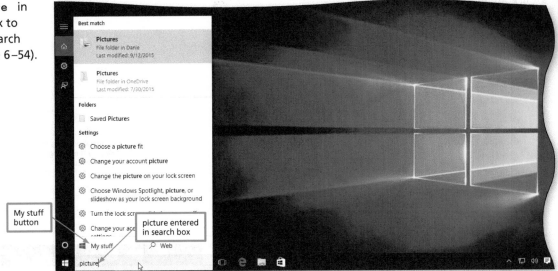

Figure 6–54

2

- Click the My stuff button in the search results to search only this computer for the search criteria (Figure 6–55).

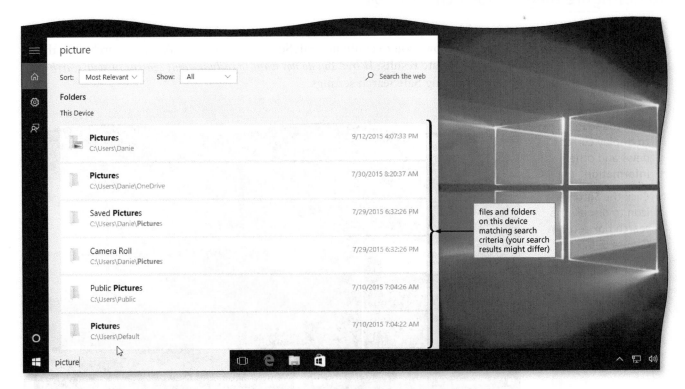

Figure 6–55

- Scroll to display the remaining search results (Figure 6–56).

- Click an empty area on the desktop to close the search results.

Figure 6–56

To Configure Bing SafeSearch Settings

The Internet contains a wealth of information, and some information might not be appropriate for all audiences. For this reason, Windows allows you to configure SafeSearch settings to make sure searches on the Internet provide only the most appropriate results. *Why? You do not want to include adult content in your search results.* The following steps configure Bing SafeSearch settings.

- Click the search box to display current news and other information.

- Click the Settings icon to display the search box settings (Figure 6–57).

Q&A

Why is the Settings icon not visible?

If Cortana is not enabled, you first may have to click the Notebook icon before clicking Settings.

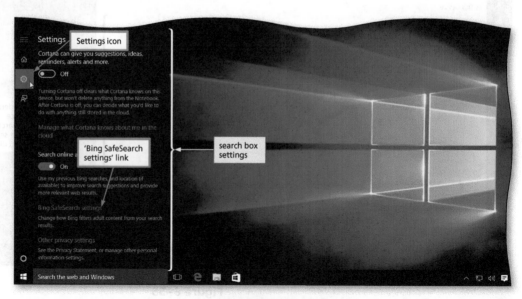

Figure 6–57

2
- Click the 'Bing SafeSearch settings' link to run Microsoft Edge and display your account settings.

- Click the Strict option button in the SafeSearch area to configure Windows to filter out adult text, images, and videos from the search results (Figure 6–58).

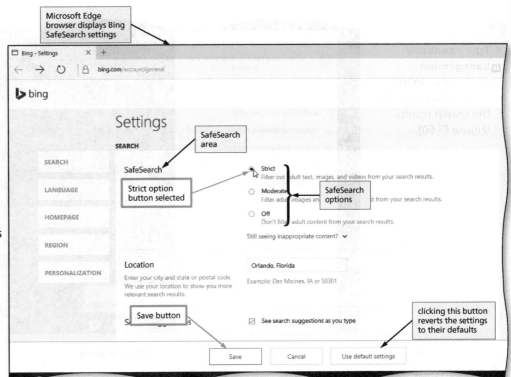

Figure 6–58

3
- Click the Save button to display the Bing webpage (Figure 6–59).

Figure 6–59

4
- Click the Close button to exit Microsoft Edge.

To Search the Web Using the Search Box

In addition to the search box allowing you to exclude information on the web from the search results, you also can choose to display search results only from the web. *Why? You have searched your computer for desktop backgrounds you would like to use, but could not find any that are suitable. You now want to see the desktop backgrounds available on the web.* The following steps search the web using the search box.

1

- Type `desktop background pictures` in the search box to display the search results (Figure 6–60).

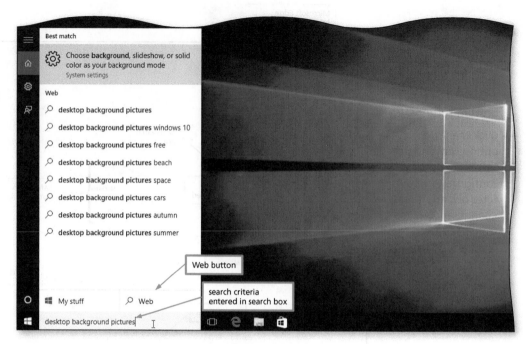

Figure 6–60

2

- Click the Web button in the search results to run Microsoft Edge and display the search results (Figure 6–61).

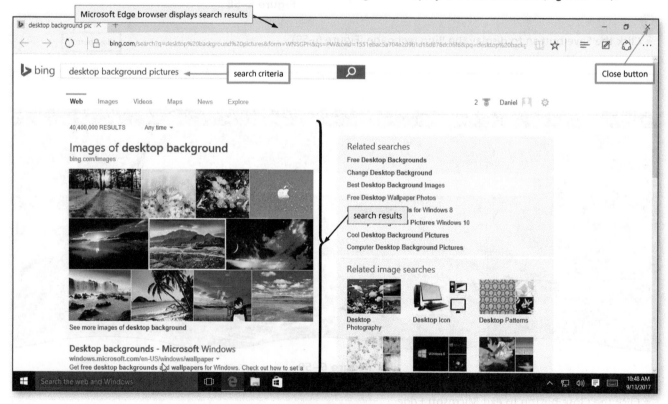

Figure 6–61

3

- Click the Close button to exit Microsoft Edge.

To Configure the Search Box to Exclude Web Results

Why? If you never want to include web results in your search results, you can configure the search box to exclude web results. The following steps configure the search box to exclude web results.

- Click the search box to display current news and other information.
- Click the Settings button to display search box settings (Figure 6–62).

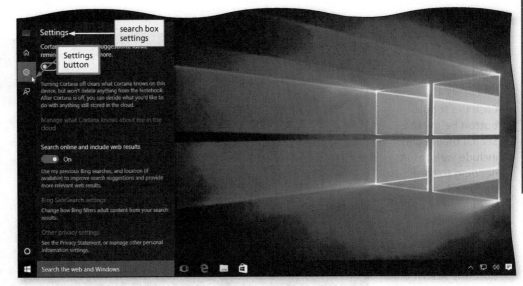

Figure 6–62

- Click the toggle button below the Search online and include web results heading to configure the search box not to include web results (Figure 6–63).

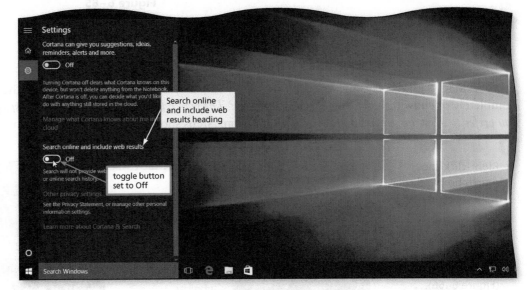

Figure 6–63

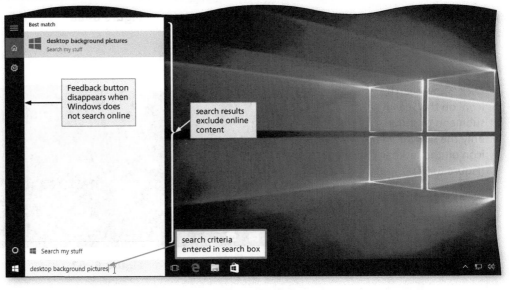

- Type desktop background pictures in the search box to display the search results (Figure 6–64).

Figure 6–64

4

- Click the Settings button in the search box to display search box settings.

- Click the toggle button below the Search online and include web results heading to configure the search box to include web results (Figure 6–65).

- Click an empty area on the desktop to close the search box.

Figure 6–65

To Show the Search Icon on the Taskbar

Windows 10 displays the search box on the taskbar by default, but you also have the option of hiding it completely or showing only the search icon. *Why? The search box takes up a great deal of space on the taskbar, and you prefer to show the search icon instead.* The following steps show the search icon on the taskbar.

1

- Right-click the search box to display a shortcut menu.

- Point to Search on the shortcut menu to display the Search submenu (Figure 6–66).

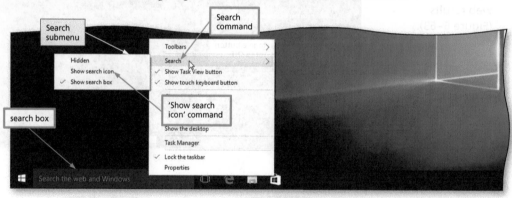

Figure 6–66

2

- Click 'Show search icon' on the Search submenu to show only the search icon on the taskbar (Figure 6–67).

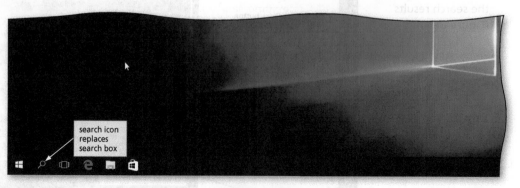

Figure 6–67

3

- Click the search icon on the taskbar to display the search box and search results (Figure 6–68).

- Click an empty area on the desktop to close the search results.

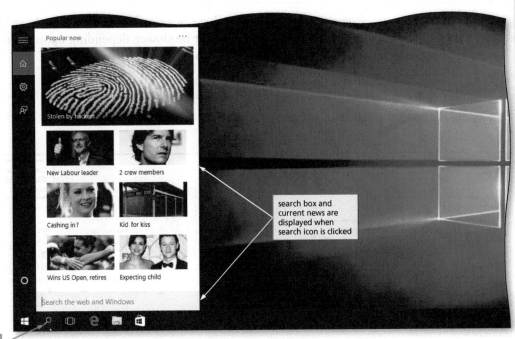

search box and current news are displayed when search icon is clicked

search icon

Figure 6–68

To Show the Search Box on the Taskbar

The following steps show the search box on the taskbar.

1. Right-click an empty area on the taskbar to display a shortcut menu.

2. Point to Search on the shortcut menu to display the Search submenu.

3. Click 'Show search box' on the Search submenu to show the search box.

To Restore SafeSearch Settings

You no longer want to apply a strict filter to search results. The following steps restore the SafeSearch settings.

1. Click the search box to display current news and other information.

2. Click the Settings button to display the search box settings.

3. Click the 'Bing SafeSearch settings' link to run Microsoft Edge and display the SafeSearch settings.

4. Click the Moderate option button in the SafeSearch area to restore the Bing SafeSearch settings.

5. If necessary, scroll to display the Save button at the bottom of the webpage, and then click the Save button to display the Bing home page.

6. Exit Microsoft Edge.

To Remove a Folder from the Index

Why? *When you no longer need a folder to be indexed, you should remove it from the index.* This means that if you search the folder at a later time, the search might be slower, depending upon the size of the folder. The following steps remove the SCFiles folder from the Search Index.

- Open the Control Panel window.
- Change the view to Small icons (Figure 6–69).

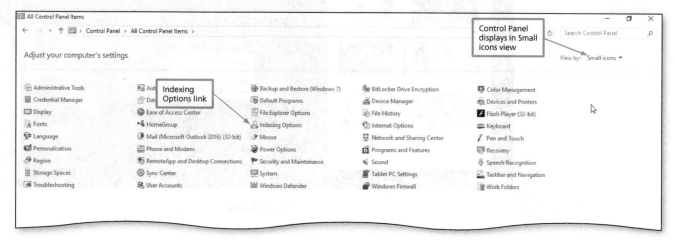

Figure 6–69

- Click the Indexing Options link to display the Indexing Options dialog box.
- Click the Modify button (Indexing Options dialog box) to display the Indexed Locations dialog box (Figure 6–70).

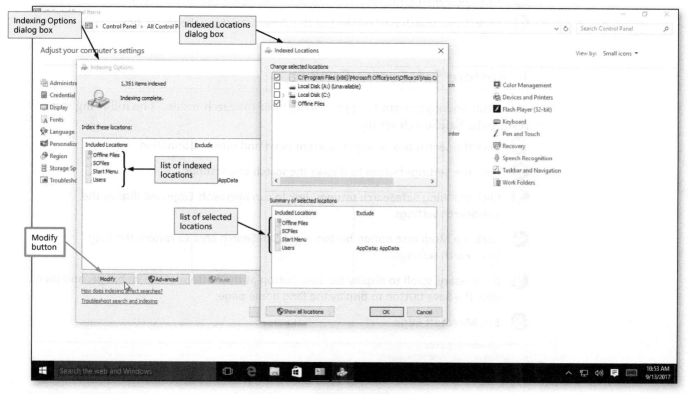

Figure 6–70

3

• Click SCFiles
  in the Summary
  of selected locations
  list to select it
  (Figure 6–71).

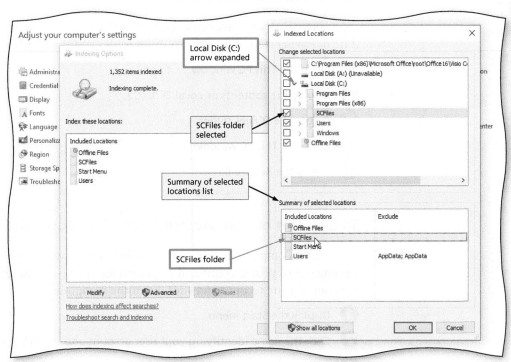

Figure 6–71

4

• Click the SCFiles folder check box
  in the Change selected locations
  list to remove the check mark
  (Figure 6–72).

• Click the OK button (Indexed
  Locations dialog box) to remove
  the SCFiles folder from the Search
  Index and to close the Indexed
  Locations dialog box.

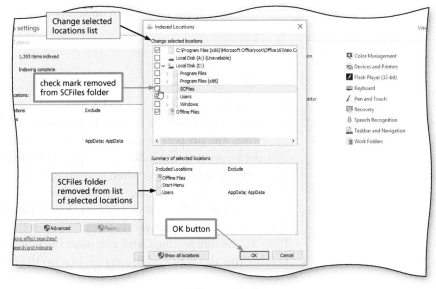

Figure 6–72

5

• Click the Close button (Indexing Options dialog box) to close the Indexing Options dialog box.

• Change the Control Panel view to Category.

• Close the Control Panel window.

Other Ways

1. Click Search box, click Search tab, click Advanced options button (Search Tools Search tab | Options group), click 'Change indexed locations',
   click Modify button (Indexing Options dialog box), click SCFiles in list of indexed locations, click check box next to SCFiles folder, click OK
   button (Indexed Locations dialog box), click Close button (Indexing Options dialog box)

To Delete SCFiles Folder

Now that you have removed the SCFiles folder from the index, you can delete it. The following steps delete the SCFiles folder and the files it contains.

1 Open the This PC window.

2 Display the contents of Local Disk (C:).

3 Delete the SCFiles folder.

4 Close the This PC window.

5 Empty the Recycle Bin.

To Sign Out of Your Account and Shut Down the Computer

After completing your work with Windows, you should end your session by signing out of your account and then turning off the computer. The following steps sign out of your account and shut down the computer.

1 Display the Start menu.

2 Click the name identifying your user account and then click the Sign out command.

3 Click the lock screen to display the sign-in screen.

4 Click the Shut down button.

5 Click Shut down on the Shut down menu to shut down the computer.

Summary

In this module, you have learned how to use advanced search techniques. Using the Search box, you have learned how to search a folder using keywords, Boolean operators, and property data. You filtered files using the file list headings. You added a location to the index and learned the differences between using indexed and nonindexed locations when searching. You have learned how each file type has different properties and that you can search using those properties. Using the advanced search options of the Search box, you found files based on additional properties. You also configured the search box to exclude search results from the web, you configured Bing SafeSearch settings, and you used the search box to search only the web for results. You also replaced the search box on the taskbar with the search icon.

Apply Your Knowledge

Reinforce the skills and apply the concepts you learned in this module.

Exploring Different Search Techniques

Instructions: Open the This PC window and navigate to the Windows folder. Maximize the window if necessary, and then search for images as instructed below.

Perform the following tasks:
1. Open the This PC window and navigate to the Windows folder. If necessary, maximize the window.
2. Search for pictures with the file name, img3 (Figure 6–73).

Figure 6–73

3. Select each search result and copy it to the Pictures folder.
4. Search for pictures containing the word, sand, in the file name.
5. Select each search result and copy it to the Pictures folder.
6. In the Windows folder, search for all files with names that contain the word, gradient, or the word, peacock, using the Boolean OR operator.
7. Select each picture search result and copy it to the Pictures folder.
8. Search for all files with names that contain the keyword, blue, but not the keyword, grad.
9. Select each picture search result and copy it to the Pictures folder.
10. Search for pictures in the .jpg file format that contain the keyword, wmp.
11. Select each search result and copy it to the Pictures folder.
12. Search for pictures that begin with the letters, pe, and have a file size of less than 10 KB.
13. Select each search result and copy it to the Pictures folder.
14. Record the list of the files that you have copied to the Pictures folder in this exercise, and then submit the list to your instructor.
15. Open the Pictures folder.
16. Select all the pictures you copied to the folder in this exercise.
17. Right-click one of the picture icons to display a shortcut menu and then click Delete on the shortcut menu.
18. Click the Yes button (Delete Multiple Items dialog box).
19. Close the Pictures folder.

Extend Your Knowledge

Extend the skills you learned in this module and experiment with new skills. You might need to use Help to complete the assignment.

Using the Search Box to Search for Information

Instructions: Use the search box to find information on the Internet and on your computer.

Perform the following steps:

1. Design a search statement for each of the following topics, and then type the statement into the search box. Expand each search to the Internet; find and print an appropriate webpage for each statement. Create a WordPad document, and record your search text for each example given.

   a. You want to find out journals that are available through the UCF libraries (Figure 6–74).

   b. You want to see current temperature readings for major cities in the United States.

   c. You need information to write a report about the senators that represent your state in the U.S. Senate.

   d. You want to shop for the best prices for a new computer. You already have prices for Dell and Lenovo computers, so you do not want to include those in your search results.

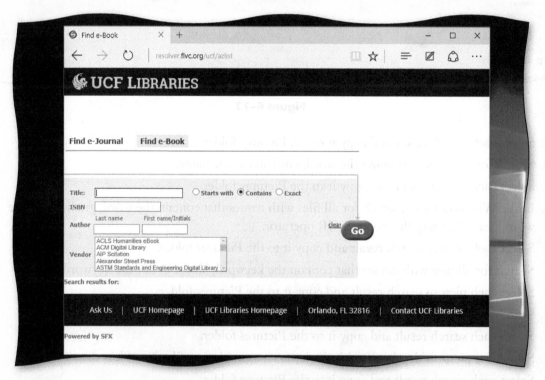

Figure 6–74

2. Design a set of search keywords for each of the following topics, type the keywords you come up with in the search box on the taskbar to test them (expand if necessary), and then write a summary of your results in a WordPad document.

   a. You want to find files you have that contain information about creating an Excel spreadsheet.

   b. You know that you have saved webpages about buying a new motorhome.

   c. You have applied for admission to Kansas State University and have received email messages from the admissions department.

3. Submit your answers and printouts to your instructor.

Expand Your World

Searching the Web

Create a solution that uses cloud or web technologies by learning and investigating on your own from general guidance.

Instructions: If necessary, connect to the Internet. Run Microsoft Edge, and then perform the following searches using search techniques introduced in this module. Type `bing.com` in the address bar and then press the ENTER key to display the Bing search engine (Figure 6–75). Determine the best search criteria to use and then click the link for your preferred search result. Print the webpage for the search result you choose for each item and submit it to your instructor.

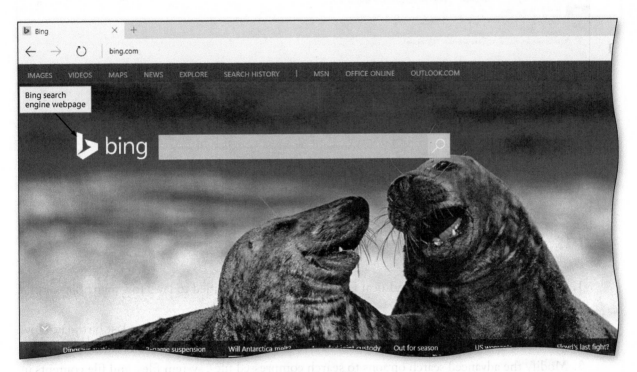

Figure 6–75

Perform the following tasks:

1. Search for a webpage containing information about an undergraduate psychology degree from a university in Texas.
2. Search for a professional photographer in your hometown.
3. Search for top-rated Mexican restaurants in Atlanta, Georgia.
4. Search for travel agents in Seattle, Washington.
5. Search for a dance studio in Hollywood, Florida.
6. Search for a company in Phoenix, Arizona, that builds custom cabinets.
7. Search for a secondhand children's clothing and/or toy store in Missouri.

In the Labs

Design, create, modify, and/or use files following the guidelines, concepts, and skills presented in this module. Labs 1 and 2, which increase in difficulty, require you to create solutions based on what you learned in the module; Lab 3 requires you to apply your creative thinking and problem-solving skills to design and implement a solution.

Lab 1: **Using Windows 10 to Search for Files and Folders**

Problem: In addition to using the Search box to search for files when all you know is their file names, you also can search for files using various file properties (Figure 6–76). Perform searches for files using the guidelines below. Create a WordPad document and type the answers to the questions below.

Figure 6–76

1. Search for files and folders on Local Disk (C:) that were modified today. How many files or folders were found?

2. Search for files and folders on Local Disk (C:) that were modified since your last birthday. How many files or folders were found?

3. Modify the advanced search options to search compressed files, system files, and file contents in nonindexed locations. Search for files and folders on Local Disk (C:) that were modified in the last month. How many files or folders were found? Restore the advanced search options so that compressed files and file contents in nonindexed locations are not searched.

4. Search Local Disk (C:) for .jpg files.

5. List the first five .jpg files found during the search.

6. Scroll to make the first icon visible and then double-click the first icon. Which image is displayed? In which app is the image displayed?

7. Scroll to make the last icon visible and then double-click the last icon. Which image is displayed?

8. Search Local Disk (C:) for music files in the .wav file format using the keyword, WAV.

    a. How many files or folders were found?

    b. Double-click one of the files that was found. What do you hear?

9. Search Local Disk (C:) for video files.

    a. How many files or folders were found?

    b. Double-click one of the videos. What is displayed?

10. Search Local Disk (C:) for all text documents containing the keyword, homework. How many files or folders were found?

11. Search Local Disk (C:) for files with the .gif extension. *Hint:* Type `*.gif` in the Search box.

    a. How many files were found?

    b. What happens when you double-click one of these files?

12. Close the Search Results window.

Lab 2: Searching for Files Based on Content

Problem: You want to test the way Windows 10 can find files based on content. You plan to create four files using WordPad and then practice your search techniques to list files based on content.

1. Create a folder in the Documents folder titled, Lab 2.

2. Create the four documents shown in Figure 6–77 using WordPad and save them in the Lab 2 folder.

3. Search for your classes using the keyword, class. How many results appear?

4. Search for homework assignments using the keyword, Lab 2. How many results appear?

5. Search for your work task list using the keyword, work. How many results appear?

6. Submit your answers to your instructor.

7. Delete the folder and files that you added to the Documents folder.

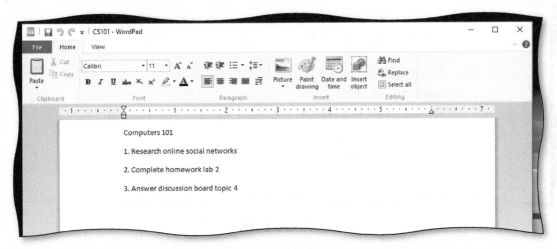

Figure 6–77a

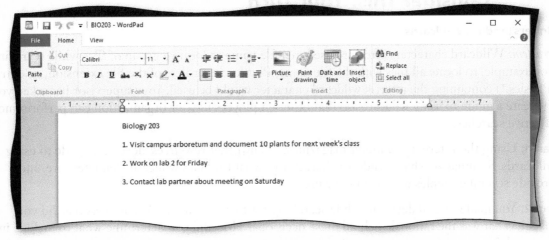

Figure 6–77b

Continued >

In the Labs *continued*

Figure 6–77c

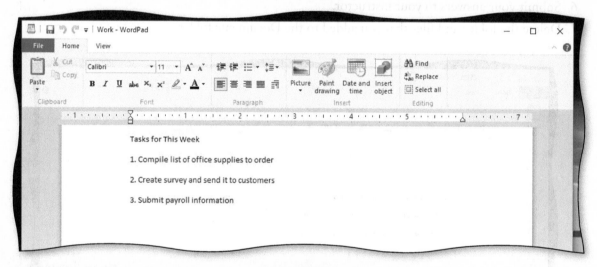

Figure 6–77d

Lab 3: Consider This: Your Turn

Understanding Wildcards

Problem: Wildcard characters often are used in a file name to locate a group of files while searching. For example, to locate all files with the file name, Physics, regardless of the file extension, an entry (Physics.*) containing the asterisk wildcard character would be used. Your supervisor has asked you to create a guide to using wildcards so that other employees in your organization can perform more effective searches.

Part 1: Using the Internet, computer magazines, or any other resources, develop a guide to using wildcards. Summarize what a wildcard character is, what the valid wildcard characters are, and provide several examples to explain their use.

Part 2: You made several decisions while searching for this assignment. What decisions did you make? What was the rationale behind these decisions? How did you determine what to include in this guide?

Index

Note: **Bold** page numbers refer to pages where key terms are defined.

Index

J

jump list
  definition, **WIN 18**
  displaying, WIN 18–19

K

keyboard accessibility settings,
    displaying, WIN 235
keyboard shortcuts
  description, **WIN 6**
  Windows 10, WIN 6

L

live tiles
  definition, **WIN 21**
  moving, WIN 22–23
  resizing, WIN 23–24
  turning off, WIN 21–22
local account
  adding, WIN 148–151
  definition, **WIN 146**
Local Disk (C:) Properties dialog
    box, displaying, WIN 100–101
locking taskbar, WIN 182
lock screen, **WIN 6**

M

Magnifier, enabling and
    configuring, WIN 228–230
maintenance settings, viewing,
    WIN 197–199
maximizing windows, Snap,
    WIN 116
Medium icons view, WIN 67
Microsoft account
  adding, WIN 152–153
  creating, WIN 147
  description, WIN 146–147
  signing into, WIN 153
minimizing windows
  using Shake, WIN 109–110
  using Show Desktop button,
    WIN 117
mouse
  accessibility settings, displaying,
    WIN 233–234
  operations, WIN 5
  Windows 10, WIN 5
moving

documents into folders,
    WIN 68–69
files to Recycle Bin, WIN 83–84
live tiles, WIN 22–23
multiple files into Pictures folder,
    WIN 121
taskbar, WIN 178

N

naming
  documents, WIN 61
  folders in Documents folder,
    WIN 67–68
Narrator, enabling and
    configuring, WIN 227–228
navigating
  within app(s), WIN 14
  using touch/mouse, WIN 3–6
nonindexed location search settings
  additional, WIN 272–273
  resetting, WIN 274
Notebook, search box, WIN 35–37
notification, **WIN 183**
notification area, **WIN 10**

O

OneDrive
  copying backup files to,
    WIN 129–130
  definition, **WIN 129**
  deleting files from, WIN 135
on-screen keyboard, WIN 4
opening
  Control Panel, WIN 194–195
  Device Manager, WIN 203–204
  Documents folder, WIN 59
  document with Wordpad,
    WIN 61–62
  folder in its own window,
    WIN 185
  searches folder, WIN 277
  Security window, WIN 197
  System window, WIN 197
operating system, **WIN 1**

P

paid apps, WIN 28
password
  definition, **WIN 6**
  picture. *See* picture password

pasting, **WIN 119**
PC window
  description, WIN 97
  displaying, folder properties,
    details pane, WIN 104
  displaying, Local Disk (C:)
    Properties dialog box,
    WIN 100–101
  display properties, hard drive,
    details pane, WIN 99–100
  drive contents, viewing, WIN 103
  maximizing, WIN 98
  opening, WIN 98
  previewing, folder properties,
    WIN 103
  switch folders, address bar,
    WIN 101–102
  using shortcut menu, folder
    properties, WIN 104–105
  viewing, folder contents,
    WIN 105
personalization settings
  accent color, WIN 162–164
  adding desktop, WIN 173–176
  control panel, displaying,
    WIN 168–169
  desktop background,
    WIN 158–162
  displaying for Start menu,
    WIN 168
  lock screen appearance,
    WIN 164–165
  screen saver, WIN 171–172
  Task View, displaying,
    WIN 173–176
  theme settings, WIN 166–167
  viewing Display window,
    WIN 170–171
  viewing Screen Resolution
    window, WIN 170–171
Photos app
  definition, **WIN 118**
  viewing pictures, WIN 124–126
picture password, **WIN 6**
  copying pictures, WIN 154
  creating, WIN 154–157
  definition, **WIN 153**
Pictures folder
  closing Search Results window,
    WIN 120
  copying files to, WIN 119–120
  creating folders in, WIN 121
  deleting backing up files,
    WIN 135